TO KILL
ANOTHER

TO KILL ANOTHER

HOMICIDE AND NATURAL LAW

G. J. MCALEER

Transaction Publishers
New Brunswick (U.S.A.) and London (U.K.)

Library of Congress Catalog Number: 2010015556
ISBN: 978-1-4128-1131-6
Printed in the United States of America

Library of Congress Cataloging-in-Publication Data

McAleer, G. J. (Graham James)
    To kill another : homicide and natural law / Graham J. McAleer.
        p. cm.
    Includes index and bibliographical references.
    ISBN 978-1-4128-1131-6
    1. Homicide--Moral and ethical aspects. 2. Justifiable homicide--Philosophy. 3. Natural law. I. Title.

K5171.M34 2010
172'.42--dc22

                                                    2010015556

To my Great Aunt, Sarah Ferns, in thanks for so much love shown.

Contents

Preface

Around 1270 Thomas Aquinas wrote a few pages on homicide. In the 1530s the moral theologian Francisco de Vitoria delivered lectures on Thomas' theory of homicide at Salamanca in Spain. This book defends the claim that together these natural law theorists have developed the best available theory of homicide. In particular, I defend their claim that only public authority has the privilege to intentionally kill. To have rule of law in any meaningful sense there must be protections for the guilty and a prohibition against killing innocents. Over the last fifty years Western law has drifted steadily towards the privatization of homicide. Nuances need to be added, but the basic point is clear enough: public acts of homicide like capital punishment are viewed by many as barbaric, even for heinous crimes,[1] whilst a private act of homicide like the (increasingly routine) starvation of comatose patients is viewed by many as a caring gesture both to patient and wider family. This privatization ongoing in Western law runs counter to the rule of law and does so at the behest of its progenitor, humanitarian ethics.[2]

The dominant mode of contemporary moral culture, humanitarianism aims to relieve human suffering. Basic to this ambition is a valorization of human equality. Humanitarians—whether pop stars, relief agencies, population control and environmental activists, medical ethics boards in hospitals, or social justice advocates—believe that instituting social mechanisms to build a moral sense of equality and deliver an equitable distribution of resources will markedly diminish suffering. An emotional sensibility, humanitarianism is rooted in compassion and benevolence. Indeed, it is a theory about how best to love; a theory that, historically, takes its origin from anti-religious sentiment, elevating man as the measure of the good.[3] A love of God, which might put a value of sorts on human suffering, which assumes a belief that suffering can have meaning, to a humanitarian, is abhorrent. Proper love recognizes that there is nothing noble in suffering, it is just a coarse, stupid failure in the biological order: genuine love works to find human solutions to overcome this failure and diminish suffering wherever it is found. Most fundamentally, humanitarianism is a theory about human vulnerability, and clearly, if Christianity is about anything at all, it is this self-same question.

For this reason, and with great insight, anarchist Max Stirner argues that humanitarianism is a "theological insurrection." No adequate treatment of humanitarianism, and certainly not one approaching this moral phenomenon through the problem of homicide and social order, can ignore the political theology implicit in its claims about ethics and law. I believe the analyses of the next two hundred pages or so justify this claim and I concur with John Paul II: if God is eliminated from law, so is man.[4] John Paul II's famous claim is defensible if it is appreciated that the elimination of God is also the ridding from law of privilege, hierarchy, and moral realism. The argument of this book shows that without such value architectural features the rule of law is impossible. Humanitarian ethics cannot be the basis of law (GS, para. 55 & 57): its equalitarianism weakens the rule of law, includes a dynamism towards totalitarianism,[5] and tyranny is not famous for its careful regard of innocents.[6] This is the (unoriginal) thesis[7] I defend in this commentary on Aquinas' *Summa theologica* II-II, q. 64. My argument expands on what de Lubac put wonderfully commenting on Dostoevsky: "He was present at the 'death of God.' He saw the murderer springing into the saddle for a stupendous career."[8]

Many who have read this far will already be dismayed: "What! Theologians are the best commentators on law? Humanitarianism and equality evils? The state has privilege not possessed by the people? Western law totalitarian?" I can well imagine these, and other, exasperated reactions. Matters are complicated further by the fact that my argument has many parts. In the Introduction, I lay out the principles of my approach to the problem of law and homicide: why Thomas, fused with later Scottish and German moral thought, is so powerful on this matter; why humanitarianism is a prop for totalitarianism; and why even secular thinkers ought to ponder political theology. The Introduction will help readers see what broad argumentative strokes underpin the rather detailed arguments in each of the eight chapters. For now, I want to position the book in relationship to common ideas likely held by readers, explain the essentials of Thomas' position, and sketch some elements of the problem of homicide, at least as these appear in the contemporary West.

Many interested in justice are self-styled progressives to whom the idea that a thinker from the Middle Ages might have the best account of homicide defies belief. Images of torture machines, princely rule, and clerical compulsion immediately spring to their minds, along with the conviction that any thinker of the age was touched by the cruel, arbitrary, and religious tenor of the times. Well-read progressive-minded people see no reason to look further back in history than the Enlightenment—and some would not deign to reach back further than nineteenth century revolutionary literature—when seeking resources for justice. This is not all though: these same readers think that humanitarianism—about which I am a skeptic—is the great fruit of the post-medieval period of social and moral reflection. Like these readers, I think post-medieval thought holds great resources for thinking about justice, but one of the things I will show is that there is a significant continuity between the best in modern thought and Aquinas. This is one of the things I try to show in the book. I also think that humanitarianism has had a "free pass." I am very struck by Jeremy Waldron's claim that though (nearly) everyone supports equality there are few philosophical defenses of the idea, even fewer that are compelling, and (to his mind) only one (Locke's) that can face down the large body of philosophical literature that has rejected the notion down through the ages.[9] Much the same can be said of humanitarianism. Entirely lacking Hume's brilliance, I stand toward humanitarianism as Hume stood towards religion. In Hume's day, religion was thought to be an obvious good in much the same way that people now unreflectingly pride themselves on being humanitarians: people responding to, or at least feeling keenly, the suffering of others, quick to care for those in need, and hopeful that social justice advocacy can make the world a more equal and fairer place. Honestly intellectual humanitarians should welcome my Humean efforts to raise serious-minded questions about what they hold dear. Most basically, I think humanitarianism misunderstands the passions and the depth of the problem of moral contingency. I say more about this just below.

There is also a kind of conservative mindset found in well-read people with a "Great Books" sensibility who tend to eschew theological writers and judge the worthiness of modern writers by the standards of the ancients. In his own time, David Hume was of this cast of mind and this is true today of a goodly number of neo-conservative intellectuals who see next to no reason to apply to Christian reflection in resolving social questions. Not unlike progressives in this regard, nor indeed unlike them in celebrating the benefits of modernity, neo-conservatives tend

to think a dose of paganism is necessary to stiffen the spine of a democratic docility that risks losing its historic gains to harsh forces ready
to test humanitarian civilization. I agree with these thinkers: there is an
autonomous moral order. This is what is meant by natural law, at least
in its bare bones. Conservative secular readers will find large parts of my
book congenial. Nonetheless, law without God collapses into tyranny.

A universally admired secular thinker, and a man who had a noble
soul, is Albert Camus. It is startling that in his last great work on justice,
The Rebel, mercy is nowhere recommended. The elimination or forget-
ting of mercy is a pattern inside humanitarianism. God, it seems, is necessary to remind us of those higher values that soften the cold edge of the
sword of justice that Camus so celebrated: "let me appeal to your pity,
since it is to you in your mercy that I speak, not to a man, who would
simply laugh at me."[10] There is a profound reason for this. Humans are
not adequate to the problem of moral contingency. The pages below
show, I believe, that unless the religious attitude finds a place at law the
humanitarian's avid will to contend with injustice subverts the rule of
law. Only the religious attitude can reconcile the human will to justice
with the brokenness of the world. Thus, I do not think our democratic
societies are as healthy as neo-conservatives think—albeit I agree they
are fragile flowers worth preserving: it is not a simple matter of a bit of
extra spine; rather, within democratic, humanitarian sentiment there is
a constant temptation to subvert precisely what we all hold dear, order
though fair laws.

Neo-conservatives are not much like the third set of readers I imagine
skeptical not of my core thesis but my reasoning. This third set divides
into at least three groups. The most exciting contemporary Christian
reflection is thoroughly anti-modern. It is undeniable that Catholic critics
of modernity, stretching back to de Maistre and up through de Bonald
and Carl Schmitt, make for great reading. I am myself thoroughly impressed by their dialectical prowess and the scope of their philosophical
imagination. These thinkers have counterparts today, albeit significantly
moderated in sensibility, if not logic. Self-styled Augustinian Thomists
are extremely critical of markets and their supporting liberal political
institutions. Thinkers like Tracey Rowland or Bob Kraynak are conservative in a very strong sense: perhaps not militating for a return to "throne
and altar" they nonetheless would not be dismayed if such a return in
the West came to pass. Sharing the same dislike of modernity, a leftist
variety of Christian anti-modernism is Radical Orthodoxy, a primarily
Anglican set of theologians. Strongly averse to markets and the liberal

institutions that sustain their operation, these thinkers also dislike natural law. Advocates of divine positive law, they doubt there exists anything like an autonomous morality and, if such does exist, its vision of, say, property relations, is utterly rejected by biblical authority, the censure of the Prophets, for example. Classical Thomists are the third set of Christian reader. More at peace with liberal institutions perhaps, classical Thomists are able defenders of teleology both in natural philosophy and ethics and see little reason to seek alternative philosophical tools to promote natural law.

In developing my natural law arguments, I rely on many modern thinkers: I find great resources in Camus, Kolnai, Scheler, Schmitt, and Smith. I thus reject the anti-modernism of these varieties of Christian intellectuals. Like them, I accept de Lubac's thesis but I see the problem more narrowly as not so much modernity as the mistaken ethics of humanitarianism, which is a mistaken ethics because it misconstrues both the passions and political theology. In my opinion, these three varieties of Christians do so as well. The most prominent members of the Radical Orthodoxy group have the same political theology as humanitarianism, as far as I can see, and so fatally ignore the moral positivity of privilege and hierarchy. Augustinians and classical Thomists are far more comfortable with privilege and hierarchy but I think both underplay the role of the emotions in any adequate natural law. Humanitarianism is, fundamentally, an emotional sensibility or mood. If, as I think, it is the reigning ethics of our day, then Christian thought must address the question of the passions. In *Ecstatic Morality,* I showed that Thomas' natural law is a theory of love, his ethics is an erotics that shows deference to, and cultivates, the emotions. In *To Kill Another*, I develop this argument further. I draw out this aspect of his natural law by showing continuities between Thomas and Schelerian realist phenomenology, but also the Scots, and especially, Adam Smith. Though the theme is muted in the book, this is why I disagree with Christian critics of the market.[11] These continuities also show why I disagree with strictly teleological interpretations of Thomistic natural law. Like Tom Hibbs, I think Thomas relies heavily in his natural law thinking upon custom and, following Kolnai, I think custom is a matter of moral consensus; that is, shared emotions responding to objective values and disvalues. I thus defend a theory of Thomistic natural law that relies, in part, on moral intuition.

I hope these few comments are enough to either challenge or tantalize skeptical readers to continue with the book. I would now like to briefly state the essentials of Thomas' theory of homicide and say a little about why I think a new commentary on *Summa Theologica* II-II, q. 64 is timely.

Thomas Hobbes has an elegant, if chilling, answer to why all lethal force should be in the hands of the state: on account of a fundamental human propensity to violence, and the ever-present possibility of civil war, the state must possess the totality of violence and be able to bring it to bear decisively.[12] But what is the basis for Aquinas' claim that only public authority can intentionally kill? Aquinas does not agree with Hobbes that natural law can be stripped down to fear: he could never avail himself of the idea that this passion alone generates the public authority to kill. On what moral and political insight does Aquinas rely? I think it inescapable that the argument assumes the moral positivity of privilege and hierarchy (*ille qui secundum gradum sui ordinis vindictam exercet in malos* [ST II-II, q. 108, a. 1, ad 1]).

The Munich School of Phenomenology developed wide-ranging arguments for the moral positivity of privilege and hierarchy. The most famous member of this school is Max Scheler but it also includes Edith Stein (Saint Theresa Benedicta of the Cross), Karol Wojtyla (Pope John Paul II), as well as one of the readers of Wojtyla's second doctoral dissertation, the famous Polish phenomenologist, Roman Ingarden, and, a lesser-known thinker who deserves much more attention, Aurel Kolnai. This school of phenomenology is rigorously realist in contradistinction to Husserl's later idealist phenomenology. The following comment does capture *something* (positive, I might add!) of the phenomenology of Scheler: his work supports, says one commentator, "the ruling elite with metaphysical rhetoric."[13] The truth in this comment is that Scheler and the Munich School advocate for hierarchy and privilege. Aquinas did as well, and so must the Thomist who wants to defend his theory of homicide today. For this reason, the work of the Munich School is a crucial platform for contemporary Thomism.

That Thomas' philosophy of homicide rests upon such a moral basis could not be more dramatic. The traditional theory of homicide, which Aquinas codified, is beset by detractors. Every year, dozens of court cases assess its strength. Indeed, crucial elements of this theory have been rejected, whether permanently or not remains to be seen. But those of us who are happy that the theory, though battered, has yet resisted collapse, have to worry not only about how much longer it can hold out, but also more dramatically, about the basis of the theory. For what law can well stand challenge that assumes privilege and hierarchy? Could

Thomas have based his theory on something more vulnerable to a modern sensibility? Worse, have those most invested in the traditional theory really taken full cognizance of its fragile basis: Have conservatives? Have moral theologians? Has the papal encyclical tradition and Catholic social thought more generally?

At every turn Aquinas' theory is besieged by detractors. These detractors are oftentimes Christians, sometimes popes, but mostly defenders of humanitarian ethics. At first glance, it might seem that Aquinas gave voice to a Western consensus on killing that lasted until about fifty years ago. Back then, a massive war had recently been fought and few doubted the grandeur of the victors' moral purpose. Capital punishment was near universal in all well-ordered republics and monarchies alike. Abortion was a criminal homicide and euthanasia had recently been cited at Nuremberg as an outlaw practice. And few had heard that foxhunting was an immoral killing of an animal. Now, at least in the Western world, not merely is every aspect of this consensus suspect but defenders of the old ways, one might say, are just that: on the defensive. In academic circles, and far beyond in certain quarters, there is moral outrage leveled at anyone who presumes the state can kill or who dares to say that suicide, abortion, and euthanasia are moral wrongs. These changes, I suggest, result from humanitarianism and its acceptance as the ruling ethic for broad swaths of the West. Has the West's moral consensus shifted?

A second glance reveals two different, deeper, realities. First, perhaps there was no consensus. I know of no major philosopher from Descartes on who wrote a treatise on homicide. There may be only four books since Vitoria's time which could be regarded as such: Carl Schmitt's 1932 *Concept of the Political*; Albert Camus' 1960 *The Rebel*; Peter Singer's 1979 *Practical Ethics*; and John Paul II's 1995 *Evangelium Vitae*. *The Rebel*, an ignored book Camus thought his best, shows that as early as the eighteenth century writers were challenging fundamental planks of Thomas' theory of homicide even if not writing formal tracts on the topic. Indeed, Camus shows that since the 1700s perhaps little else was really being thought about but new ways to justify homicide. So, while legal manuals and public consensus remained relatively stable, philosophers and revolutionaries were consistently mounting challenges, sometimes with dramatic results.

Second, despite these intellectual challenges and despite changes in law since the 1950s, perhaps the public consensus on killing even now remains relatively stable.[14] Let us first note some oddities. There is capital punishment in Japan and America and in many other nations besides. Capital punishment was outlawed by vote of conscience amongst Members of Parliament in the United Kingdom in 1965 (until 1957, death had been the mandatory sentence for murder). However, the matter has never been put to a general vote of the people and every poll since has shown that a (sometimes large) majority of the British public wants it reinstituted.[15] Euthanasia has been introduced in a few countries, yet opposition to date remains widespread. Hunting has also come under serious censure from some quarters. A major popular revolt in England against the government ban on foxhunting was finally defused, in Parliament's favor, yet hunting continues in various forms. War goes on as before and with broad consensus. The British strongly supported Prime Minister Thatcher at the time of the Falklands War and after September 11, 2001, no one demurred when the United States violently removed the Taliban government in Afghanistan.

Of course, in early 2003, matters stood otherwise with the war in Iraq to topple Saddam Hussein. Roughly two-thirds of the American public supported the war at the time but the remaining third was quite vociferous in opposition: indeed, in both England and America the media (by and large) made its own opposition clear. The basis for much of the opposition to the 2003 Iraq War helps reveal some current thinking on the logic of homicide. The precise grounds of opposition will be sorted out by historians[16] but one basis was certainly the question of authority: Who has the authority to make war? In the United States, some doubted that the American state had this authority. Much was heard about the need for international authority, that the nation state had no privilege in matters of war,[17] but for some the question was even broader: Does the state have the authority to kill at all?

By Thomistic strictures, contemporary politics is very strange indeed: people claim the private authority to kill the innocent (whether the unborn, newly born, the young, or the aged)[18] and yet deny there is any public authority to kill the guilty.[19] This attitude was typified by Justice Harry Blackmun who famously introduced *Roe's* jurisprudence into American law and also refused to sign any death warrants lest he become part of the "machinery of death." In Aquinas' formulation of homicide, public authority is necessary for licit homicide. When abortion ceased to be a criminal homicide, lauded in the United States as a constitutional right and in Europe paid for by many governments, homicide was permitted on private authority. An abiding inversion of Thomas' basic logic is now seriously proposed. The state has no authority to wage just war or execute guilty people but private authority for homicide does exist, in the case of abortion, and as Peter Singer argues, it ought for euthanasia and infanticide. Thus, an intellectual and cultural shift towards the privatization of homicide is afoot.[20] Strangely, in one sense at least, such a change would be utterly reactionary: it would turn back the clock and return Western jurisprudence to Anglo-Saxon and Ancient Greek notions that homicide is a matter for families to decide both internally and between families. This would, without a doubt, return us to Anglo-Saxon notions of the feud (graphically demonstrated by the Schiavo case in the United States in spring 2005). A guiding question of this book is to ask: Is Aquinas' cancellation of Greek and Anglo-Saxon private homicide a moral, political, and legal good?

It might seem as though the jurisprudence boat on this issue has simply sailed, that privatization has happened, but the evidence is otherwise: Despite widespread legalization, the licitness of abortion is far from settled.[21] Many states the world over now permit this sort of homicide on private authority, others not (Portugal, Chile, Nicaragua, amongst others). Is there public consensus on this matter? In many European countries there is no organized opposition to abortion, though this may be changing.[22] In the United States, of course, it is a politically explosive issue with opinion polls showing that restrictions need to be introduced and there has recently been a spate of increased legislative action to try to bypass the Supreme Court's jurisprudence on this matter.[23] Whatever the politics of the matter, a surprising broader consensus on the issue is discernible. In America the so-called "constitutional right" of abortion is lauded by many as the basis of women's equality[24] yet no one congratulates anyone who has just had an abortion. It is odd that people do not celebrate "the secular sacrament" (Daniel Henninger): supposedly, this sacrament is a fundamental liberty, an advancement of the conditions of women, marriages, children, and families. Why do mothers at supermarkets not turn to the person next in line and show photos of their daughters' abortion "product?" Would not such a photo be a symbol of their daughters' liberty, a symbol of the glory of the Constitution? After all, these same mothers certainly besiege the next in line with photos of their beloved grandchildren. According to the "Pro Child/Pro Family/Pro Choice" fraternity, both photos bespeak the same moral worth. But social practice betrays the theory and an oddity like this is morally significant, I suggest. It shows that broad consensus about the moral value of abortion does not exist, even amongst those who have abortions, those who think they should be legal, and even those who think abortion is a positive moral good. Part of the argument of this book is that moral consensus is an important plank of any adequate moral theory.

*   *   *

It remains to thank those who helped foster this book. Over the last few years, Fr. Joe Koterski, S. J. and Matt Levering have been unstinting in their support of my work, and I sincerely thank them for all their kindness. Michael Henry, editor of the Library of Conservative Thought at Transaction Press, encouraged my interest in Scheler and Kolnai. His work editing the entire manuscript massively improved the clarity and flow of the book's arguments. In recent years, Paul Seaton has been a remarkable discussion partner over drinks on all matter of issues in morals and politics. Thanks are also due to: Dave Zinder, Steve Sherwood, Eric Wilson, John Betz, Steve Miles, Brian Murray, Alex Rosenthal, but especially, Steve Weber. I must thank colleagues in Philosophy and Theology, and Loyola College generally, for a most genial academic home; it is much appreciated. A very special thanks to Peggy Field at Loyola's library for all the books she arranged to loan to me and her remarkable patience with those of us incapable of organizing a decent library search.

Most gratitude, however, goes to my mother and father, my sisters, other family in Scotland and England, and my daughters, Julia, Charlotte, and Beatrice. Lastly, to my wife, Jennifer, whose remarkable legal mind sparked my interest in the underpinnings of law.

Notes

1.   In June 2008, the United States Supreme Court overturned a capital sentence handed down by the state of Louisiana as punishment for a father who raped his eight-year-old daughter. The Court cited "a growing consensus" that capital punishment must be restricted as punishment for acts in which life was taken. Members of the Court dissented in strong terms that any such consensus existed and indeed the 2008 presidential candidates from both the left and right criticized the Court's 5 to 4 decision ("Obama Attacks the Supreme Court Decision Barring Death Penalty for Child Rape," *World Socialist Website*, 26 June, 2008 [wsws.org/articles/2008/jun2008/obama_j26.shtml and last visited July 9, 2008]).

2.   For analyses of humanitarianism, see M. Scheler, *Ressentiment* (Milwaukee, WI: Marquette University Press, 2003) and *Nature of Sympathy* (New York: Transaction, 2007); A. Kolnai, "The Humanitarian versus the Religious Attitude," *The Thomist*, Vol. 7:4 (1944): 429-57; and H. Meier, "On Carl Schmitt's Political Theology" (*pro manuscripto*).

3.   For the intellectual history of humanitarianism, see Max Stirner, *The Ego and Its Own* (Cambridge: Cambridge University Press, 2005), pp. 89-135.

4.   John Paul II, *Address to the United Nations General Assembly* (October 5, 1995), para. 16. Cf. *Fides et Ratio*, para. 90.

5. For this assessment of humanitarianism from within the anarchist tradition, see Max Stirner's *The Ego and Its Own*, pp. 211-19.
6. This logic is fully on display in the well-known work of American jurist Michael S. Moore. Secular and liberal, but a natural law theorist, Moore argues that the state has an authority to kill, what he calls its "law enforcement privilege" (*Placing Blame: A General Theory of Criminal Law* [Oxford: Oxford University Press, 1998], p. 65; hereafter PB). He also claims that liberty trumps innocence when a woman kills her baby on private authority through abortion (PB, 654, 660 & 665; for similar on suicide PB, 763). He also argues that the state can use torture to forestall terrorism. For his example of torturing the child of a known terrorist to extract information on the whereabouts of the father see my third chapter. There I debate his humanitarian argument that torturing the innocent is not an intrinsic evil and so no control on an act of state.
7. This thesis relies on John Paul II's *Evangelium Vitae* and his claims that much of the West is now totalitarian and abortion states are tyrant states (EV, para. 20). Cf. *Fides et Ratio*, para. 89; Benedict XVI, *Regensburg Address* (2006); and the corpus of Kolnai.
8. H. de Lubac, *The Drama of Atheistic Humanism* (London: Sheed & Ward, 1949), p. 171.
9. J. Waldron, *God, Locke, and Equality* (Cambridge: Cambridge University Press, 2002).
10. Augustine, *Confessions* (London: Penguin, 1961), p. 24.
11. On the relationship between Smith, markets, and Catholic social thought please see my essays: "Business and Dignity: An Application of Edmund Burke's Analysis of America," *Festschrift for Fr. James Schall, S. J.* (St. Augustine's Press) (forthcoming); "Vanity and Commerce: How *De malo* Supports Whig Thomism," *Ressourcement Thomism: Sacra Doctrina, the Sacraments and the Moral Life* (Catholic University Press of America, 2010), (forthcoming); "Jack Aubrey Meets Thomas Aquinas: Is It Immoral To Kill for Money?"(*pro manuscripto*); "Business Ethics and Catholic Social Thought," *Nova et Vetera: The English Edition of the International Theological Journal*, Vol. 4, No. 1 (2006), pp. 17-27.
12. Cf. W. Blackstone, *Commentaries on the Laws of England* (Philadelphia: Rees Welsh & Co., 1902), Book 4, c. 1, * 8, & c. 5, * 7 but against Locke's general right of resistance, c. 14, * 181.
13. J. Staude, *Max Scheler: An Intellectual Portrait* (New York: The Free Press, 1967), p. viii.
14. I am more sanguine than Daryl Charles on the idea of an enduring consensus about killing: for a different picture, see his *Retrieving the Natural Law* (Grand Rapids: Eerdmans, 2008).
15. The *Le Monde* poll on the execution of Saddam proved interesting. High majorities supported the execution in the U. S. (82 percent) and the U. K. (69 percent) and even countries with strong rhetoric against both the Iraq war and capital punishment in general registered majorities in favor, e.g., France, Spain, Germany, and Holland (*Jerusalem Post*, January 1, 2007).
16. In the United States, opposition to the Iraq war was not a separate issue from profound hostility to the Bush Presidency on the part of liberals. In conversation, many would acknowledge that their opposition was not principled: A similar war conducted by a president belonging to the Democratic Party would be acceptable.
17. For a very interesting article by a Nobel Peace Prize recipient both on the moral justification for wars of liberation and the peculiar fact that there have been many such national wars in recent decades that elicited no controversy, see José Ramos-Horta, "War and Peace," *Wall Street Journal*, May 13, 2004.

18. H. Hewitt, "Death by Committee: What the Groningen Protocol Says about Our World, and Where It Might Lead Next," *Weekly Standard* (2 December, 2004).

19. Concern with the privatization of homicide is an answer to the question raised by Jody Bottum why pro-life advocates have aligned politically with neoconservative hawks in America (J. Bottum, "The New Fusionism," *First Things* [June/July 2005], pp. 32-6).

20. Peter Singer argues that "traditional ethics" derived from Christianity has collapsed and we are witnessing today "major shifts deep in the bedrock of western ethics" (*RLD*, 1).

21. "Anglo-American law has always treated abortion as a serious crime," at least until 1958, observes Dellapenna, when in the space of fifteen years a practice viewed across centuries as a crime became a vaunted Constitutional right. This transformation has sparked an "intense struggle" that continues to this day. See the monumental work of Joseph W. Dellapenna, *Dispelling the Myths of Abortion History* (Durham, N.C.: Carolina Academic Press, 2006), pp. xii & 10-11.

22. In England, the leading broadsheet newspaper, *The Daily Telegraph*, is especially insistent that the law on abortion must be altered and that some curtailment is necessary. The British Conservative Party for the first time made it an issue in the 2005 General Election and David Steel, the Member of Parliament who first sought an abortion license in Britain, recently argued that the law must become much more restrictive. In a number of European countries, especially Belgium and Italy, a realignment of parties on the right is underway and restrictions on abortion are front and centre in their discussions.

23. Cf. Born Alive Act (2002); Partial Birth Abortion Act (2003); and "Laci's Law" (2003), which make the killing of an unborn child, as part of an attack upon the mother, a separate crime and a homicide. For a recent history of some of these legislative battles and the broader philosophy at stake, see H. Arkes, *Natural Rights and the Right to Choose* (Cambridge: Cambridge University Press, 2002).

24. See comments cited in W. Smith, *Forced Exit* (New York: Random House, 1997), p. 211.

Abbreviations

To cut down on the number of footnotes I have used abbreviations for a number of titles. I list here the ones used throughout. There are others but these concern works that are quoted only in a single section. References to papal encyclicals and other Church documents are by paragraph and not page number. For details of the editions used please see the bibliography. In addition, I make use of the *Wall Street Journal* (WSJ), my *Ecstatic Morality and Sexual Politics* (EM), and Berman's *Law and Revolution* (PR).

Thomas Aquinas
    NE: *Commentary on the Nicomachean Ethics*
    ScG: *Summa contra gentiles*
    Sent.: *Scriptum super libros sententiarum*
    ST: *Summa theologica*

Aurel Kolnai
    HVR: The Humanitarian Versus the Religious Attitude
    I: Intrinsicalism

The following essays are found in Kolnai's *Privilege and Liberty*
    CM: The Meaning of the "Common Man"
    PL: Privilege and Liberty
    TRA: Three Riders of the Apocalypse

The following essays are found in Kolnai's *Ethics, Values and Reality*
    MP2: Morality and Practice II
    FR: Forgiveness

John Paul II
    CA: *Centesimus Annus*
    EV: *Evangelium Vitae*

xxii To Kill Another

VS: *Veritatis Splendor*
TB: *Theology of the Body*

Paul VI
HV: *Humanae Vitae*

Max Scheler
F: *Formalism in Ethics and Non-Formal Ethics of Values*
NS: *Nature of Sympathy*
OA: *Ordo Amoris*
R: *Ressentiment*

Carl Schmitt
CP: *Concept of the Political*
N: *Nomos of the Earth*
PT: *Political Theology*

Peter Singer
AL: *Animal Liberation*
PE: Practical Ethics
RLD: Rethinking Life and Death

Adam Smith
TMS: *Theory of Moral Sentiments*

Francisco de Vitoria
H: *On Homicide*
PW: *Political Writings*

Karol Wojtyla
LR: *Love and Responsibility*
AP: *Acting Person*
PC: *Person and Community*

Church Documents
GS: *Gaudium et Spes*

Introduction

The passions cannot be barren of praise of Him.
—*Edmund Burke*

I hazard a guess that this commentary on Aquinas's question on homicide is the first *extended* commentary written in about 400 years. Treatments of the question, and of Thomas's ideas, are found in theology manuals down through the centuries. I mention some of these in my commentary. However, this book is a commentary in the sense in which de Vitoria's lectures of the 1530s are commentaries, and this you don't find in the theology manuals. Vitoria ranges widely over many topics and considers dozens of arguments made by philosophers since Aquinas. He does not proceed exegetically, carefully weighing Aquinas's words, but he sees himself as a defender of Thomas's basic positions, not only Thomas's commitment to capital punishment or his "extreme" formulation respecting self-defense, but also a signature thesis like intrinsicalism. As discussed in the sixth chapter, Carl Schmitt finds in de Vitoria a Thomist wrestling with, voicing, and developing a change in world consciousness. For him, de Vitoria's originality is less the use of Roman law in a natural law treatise and rather that natural law is given a "planetary consciousness," a new awareness, as de Vitoria wrestles with the implications of the New World. Nothing so grand, I assure you, is happening in my commentary.

Like de Vitoria's commentary, the book is not about explaining what Aquinas says in each article but illustrating and defending Thomas's jurisprudence following his broad themes. Like de Vitoria, I assume readers are well able to read for themselves the Thomas—or Kolnai or others—upon whom I rely. In de Vitoria's hands Thomistic commentary is an open, speculative, combative exercise in theoretical and practical ethics. It is in no way an exhaustive treatment of Thomas's brief text: this is not possible for any single commentary. I imagine there are literally hundreds of philosophical and theological avenues one could take in assessing these few pages of Aquinas. Even the narrow theme I selected—the fate of state privilege in humanitarian ethics—is a far wider topic than the discussions I offer. For example, I do not discuss the role of mercenaries and their standing at law or how their licensing relates to state privilege.[1]

In the standard categories of the academy, this book is a work in applied ethics. I try to show how moral theology can help us understand law. Remarks following centre on three themes: the kind of Thomism used; why humanitarianism is a moral problem, not a solution; and why political theology is an essential ingredient to any adequate treatment of law and homicide. If some of these claims seem odd or aversive—e.g.: Why would anyone be critical of humanitarian sentiment? Isn't social justice self-evidently a good thing?—I must ask for patience until the persuasive reasoning is presented in the body of the book. The foundational claims I want to make about law—really claims about the relationship between emotion and reason, the secular and divine, nature and grace—are not overtly present in the text; that is, the individual topics and discussions have an integrity of their own and raise questions for philosophers, lawyers, and theologians. However, in my own mind, these discrete treatments add up to an indictment of the pervasive ethic that underwrites much of the contemporary West. Ultimately, that indictment is theological. Though I am critical of Carl Schmitt in the book, his claim that basic disputes about law are really disputes between rival theologies does seem right to me.

Standing somewhere between the history and the argument there is, I hope, a clarification of the character of Thomistic ethics. Thomistic studies in the twentieth century revealed the expansiveness of Thomas's thought. Long gone is the image of Thomas as an Aristotelian rationalist metaphysician. It is now a great puzzle how Thomas's fundamental reliance upon, and eclectic blend of, Platonic-Augustinianism, Aristotelianism, and Arabic philosophy; biblical and mystical witness could ever have been overlooked. Twentieth-century reappraisals of Thomas demonstrated his thoroughly theological preoccupations and more, the biblical, doctrinal, and spiritual architecture of his great contributions to philosophy. The Thomas we are familiar with today is a mind of profound speculative reach, seeking philosophical resources far and wide in service of a biblical vision of reality unrelentingly focused on the life of Jesus. It is interesting to wonder whether appreciation of Thomas's moral theory has kept up with this transformation in our understanding of Aquinas's overall project. It is all to the credit of Grisez, Finnis, and

Boyle that they shook up Thomistic ethics. I do not think their understanding of Thomas is correct—as will become evident—but they are right that his ethics contains previously unearthed subtleties. For the most part, this commentary does not rely on a particular interpretation of Thomistic ethics. At times though, it is clear I do have a certain view about Thomas's natural law, a view that some might find peculiar. I read Thomas as something akin to a moral intuitionist. Let me explain.

My arguments draw from three sources: Thomas, the Scottish Enlightenment, and Munich phenomenology. The common thread is sensitivity to the role moral consensus plays in moral and legal adjudication: where an emphasis is put on con*sensus*, the role of a common sensibility. My argument is not exclusively Catholic, therefore. Indeed, against certain trends in contemporary theology, I argue for an autonomous morality.[2] Departing from typical formulations of Catholic ethics, I argue that objective values appealing to sensibility, or intuition, play a far larger role in Thomas's natural law than previously appreciated. Though I love Boethius's writing dearly, he is surely wrong to speak of "the barren thorns of Passion." Burke is closer to the mark. In EM I presented what I called "Ecstatic Thomism," a rigorously object-driven ethics. A traditional understanding of Catholic ethics might run: to get the ethics right, you need an anthropology, and to have a true anthropology, you need a good metaphysics. I think the order of explanation can run both ways. Thomists like Finnis explain moral order by appeal to a set of basic goods which, because they make human life meaningful, may not be gainsaid. Metaphysics and anthropology figure little or not at all in his natural law theory. For other Thomists, Thomas's moral theory is strictly teleological: *all* moral explanation is a matter of understanding the ends to which human nature is ordered. This approach relies heavily on a theory of causality and a metaphysical analysis of nature. I much prefer de Vitoria's more liberal approach. In the space of a couple of pages explaining the prohibition against cannibalism, de Vitoria appeals to the *ius gentium* or moral consensus, the phenomenon of disgust, intrinsicalism, moral hierarchy, civil law, burial practices, authority, and history (PW, 210-12). My preference for de Vitoria's approach is not arbitrary. I find it implausible that ethical life can be boxed neatly inside a one-dimensional ethics. Whether utilitarianism, Kantianism, or some theory of basic goods or ends, appeal to a straitened mode of moral explanation is, I am sure, always going to be inadequate and misshapen. Indeed, I share with Kolnai a certain horror of reductionism and suspect, with him, that the drive towards a monistic simplicity betokens a serious loss of moral wisdom. Thomists should be advocates for a pluralistic moral theory. I tried to show in EM that Thomas himself was such an advocate and I continue that demonstration here.

Thinkers like Grisez are correct: explanations of natural law can pre-scind from a theory of ends and nature. Thinkers of the Grisez School are not ostensibly intuitionists—but is John Austin right: Is every ethical theory other than utilitarianism not, in the last analysis, an intuitional theory?[3] Theirs is a theory about the logic of moral action and not about moral properties out in the world or a moral sense as part of the arma-ture of the soul. My own position begins from a point well made by Tom Hibbs: Aquinas does not deduce secondary precepts of law from the general precepts of natural law. With respect to particular matters, Thomas speaks of custom having the force of law.[4] I think this is true in a very particular sense. In EM, I showed that the general precepts of natural law (famously stated at ST I-II, q. 92, a. 2) express basic intuitions about the good and offer an ontology of inclination and the body and in doing so ably support a general and wide-ranging sexual ethics. As part of that demonstration, I showed that, for Thomas, ethics is a description of value responses, responses to (value) objects and, sometimes at least, value response is on account of an original moral knowledge known through sensuality and thus emotion. This is why I think there is a significant continuity between Aquinas, the Scots—like Smith, Hume, and Reid—and the Munich School. Albeit in different ways, all these thinkers hold that important moral knowledge is lodged in moral consensus or ordinary moral consciousness, that is, custom.

In a 2006 book, Joseph Ratzinger (Benedict XVI) wondered how modern man might still know that "great fundamental structures of val-ues"[5] exist. The *Lord of the Rings* (LotR) shows that these "fundamental structures" of moral insight are not only recoverable but have global ap-peal. LotR is, in its way, a global ethics, a "world ethos" (Hans Küng). Worldwide earnings for the film trilogy stand at around 26 billion (USD). How can such a deeply moral and political film—and it is both of these things—have global success unless its moral and political principles are readily comprehensible and *appealing*? What are those principles? Consider one of the earliest combat film scenes. Aragorn, king-in-wait-ing, fights a captain of the Uruk-hai, a genetically crafted warrior class, after the Uruk-hai have captured Merry and Pippin and mortally wounded Boromir. The captain, a real bruiser, after Aragorn has left his knife in the Uruk-hai's thigh, pulls out the blade and licks his own blood off it with genuine relish. Aragorn, well aware now that defeat also means his body will be outraged, finally manages to victoriously conclude the combat.[6] As Aragorn dispatches the cannibal, the music soars and decency, for a moment at least, wins out. A thought-experiment: imagine a film audience anywhere; but let's pick Malaysia, say, a predominantly Muslim country. The scene described ending, try to imagine someone in the Malaysian audience turning to his neighbor and saying: "Excuse me, I don't understand. I really wanted the Uruk-hai to win that fight. I thought he was the hero. I thought the cannibal seemed so trustworthy, loyal, and kind-hearted." I suggest that such a reaction is inconceivable. Ordinary moral consciousness the world over easily "reads" the moral structure of the scene. The scene expresses a moral consensus. In recent literature, it is Kolnai who dwelt most on the place of moral consensus in ethics.[7] I see Kolnai as the direct heir to de Vitoria's interest in the *ius gentium*[8] and de Vitoria saw, quite clearly I think, that Thomas himself relied on broad sources of moral knowledge.

Innocence is a value object and its specific character roots our horror of seeing innocence defiled. The appeal innocence holds for us accounts for the energy of the prohibition against killing the innocent. This appeal, which is surely a mainstay of the experience of injustice, a felt phenomenon that registers universally, clearly founds our understanding of tyranny and totalitarianism. The same sort of appeal explains why Thomas in his natural law thinking foregrounds the distinction between, and hierarchical ordering of, the pair perfect/imperfect. This pair has a valuational content absent from Descartes's use of infinite/finite, for example. Descartes's quantitative measure makes no appeal akin to Thomas's qualitative measure. The valuation of perfection is not derivable from metaphysics but is a structuring value of reality itself. It is well known that Thomas relies heavily on the Dionysian *bonum diffusivum sui est*. That the good is diffusive and cannot be grasped as otherwise is, I think, a phenomenological fact. Thomas does not, as far as I can see, offer a derivation of this axiom of his moral theory from some metaphysical theory about the relationship between essence and existence. The generosity of being is utterly central to Thomas's conception of reality but it figures in his thought rather like a phenomenological essence, telling us, as I argue in EM, about the lawful character of love.

Scheler thinks that a value, such as charm, is akin to a color or taste quality. "Value-qualities," just like the taste-essence of an apricot, neither are constellations of sensations nor caused by powers or dispositions of things. Rather, argues Scheler (F, 12-15), they are tones, *qualia*, or contents of thoroughly specific kinds, isolatable from every other quality, including any material base or foundation. I agree with this. A value is a clarity: values can be identified, their standing in relation to one another discerned, their relative importance and emphasis registered. Noble people, just acts, and cowardly choices are exemplifications of value qualities, the moral ontological furniture of reality. Rigorously objective, values are structuring agents in that they appeal to human action. The inclinations of natural law, I argued in EM, are portents of values.

Scheler argues that we sense these values as they resonate in our feelings. I think this is sometimes certainly true. For instance, like de Vitoria, Smith, Reid, and Kolnai, I am struck by the profound role disgust plays in moral experience. Scheler and Kolnai both acknowledge continuity between their thought and the Scots'. I speak about this elsewhere.[9] Smith's interest in moral relations centering on sympathetic exchanges registers strongly with Scheler, even though he thinks Smith badly misunderstands sympathy: for Smith, sympathy is mostly projective; a consequence, thinks Scheler, of the legacy of the early modern inability to get clarity about other minds. Commentary on Smith is divided: he is read as a situationist who rejects any vigorous moral ontology but also as a defender of "natural moral evaluation."[10] I think the latter interpretation correct and, more, follow John Austin and read Smith as an intuitionist.[11] Basic to Smith's ethics is his claim that the well-formed attracts and the ill-formed repulses. I cite some of his examples in the text.[12] As I argue elsewhere, Smith's talk of agreeable and disagreeable *objects* before the imagination is, and especially because these objects are fundamentally a matter of comeliness (or not), a reliance on intuition: "Courage, victory, and honour" immediately strike the sympathetic imagination as pleasing and "pain and suffering" as "displeasing" (TMS, 35-6).[13] Smith's talk of objects registering their moral tones in the emotions was well appreciated by Scheler and Kolnai. Kolnai further positioned his ideas of moral consensus alongside the Scot's use of the spectator and Reid's interest in common sense.

In his treatise on law, when talking about the last end, Thomas is making reference to the law of diffusion, and besides a phenomenological essence, this law is, of course, the reality of Christ. If Thomas sources basic norms in moral intuition he nonetheless also sources these norms in the life of Christ. Thomas's natural law is Christological: Christ is both the summation of value and the totality of metaphysics. Indeed, I contend, Thomas is like Bonaventure in thinking that the Cross has metaphysical significance. For this reason, Thomists who insist on the strictly teleological character of Thomas's ethics are right in one important sense: nature matters. Thomas's Christological natural law foregrounds our embodiment. In Christ, love is the love that wounds the lover: it is a love which deposes the propensity of the body's constitutive assertiveness without yet abandoning the body. The body is morally problematic and this is also a problem for moral theory. No adequate account of Thomas's ethics, and, I would argue, no adequate account of law, can be given without attention to his theory of the body and how Christ's embodiment figures valuationally and ontologically. Like Schmitt, I think law is always an articulation of political theology and thus a matter of the meaning of Christ. Later in this introduction I make my first attempt to make this plausible to skeptical readers.

In EM I explored the implications of Thomistic natural law for sexual politics. In the last chapters of that book, I argue that the issues of marriage and fertility, as crucial to social order as the rules of killing, are liable to serious misunderstanding if natural law is excluded from a formative role in national law. Indeed, my point there was to show that John Paul II's claim that most modern Western states are totalitarian is defensible. In this commentary, I seek to defend the claim anew with more attention to the rule of law and God's place at law. Yet how can this possibly be when Western people are so "nice," so humane? How could the ethical sensibility of someone like Bono relate remotely to totalitarianism? Yet I think it is so. Through a variety of issues in law, I show that pressures exist within humanitarianism that drive it on to subvert rule of law. Its appetite for justice, and attendant low tolerance for moral contingency, provokes humanitarianism to diminish protections for the innocent and guilty alike. Why is this dynamic within humanitarianism? I accept Kolnai's definition of totalitarianism: hostility to centers of privilege that curtail unified power. Privileged agents include the nation state, the courts, the military, private schools and hospitals, foundations, and the like; but there are also privileged values, like innocence, toward which deference is required. Elemental to humanitarianism is its equalitarianism: therewith intolerance of both social privilege, which diffuses power amidst social points in a community, and moral hierarchy, which discriminates amongst acts and demands deference from agents.

As a Thomistic commentary of applied ethics, the book is a contribution to Catholic social thought but my primary interest is to identify how humanitarian ethics works as a structural principle in much contemporary law. Following the order of presentation, the legal themes dealt with are: international trade law and constitutionalism; rule of law and capital punishment; criminal procedure; tort law; war and international law;

the necessity defense for homicide and Admiralty law; and criminal and tort negligence. My arguments show why elements of Catholic social thought offer a better jurisprudence than humanitarianism. Supporting the argument briefly stated at the start of the Preface, core themes of the commentary are: (1) Christian love is not the same as humanitarian love. The latter gets what Kolnai calls "moral emphasis" wrong because it rejects hierarchy for equalitarianism. I explain Kolnai's idea in the first chapter and it plays an important role in chapters 3, 7, and 8; (2) the humanitarian also rejects privilege, the social bearer of hierarchy, but privilege is necessary to rightly "read" emphasis. Intentional killing tied exclusively to public authority is a privilege and this is why humanitarianism encourages the privatization of homicide. Private killing collapses into decisionism, wrought by an ethic to resolve suffering that replaces protecting the guilty and innocent as the norm of law. These core themes are taken up through the four modern treatises on homicide, a consideration of which helps Catholic social thought gain clarity about its jurisprudential principles and distinguish its personalism from humanitarianism.

Peter Singer represents humanitarian orthodoxy within Anglo-American academic circles. On humanitarian grounds, he has eloquently proposed the continued privatization of homicide. I examine his ideas in the first, fifth, and eighth chapters. In these chapters, I argue that his equalitarianism must be rejected as totalitarian in inspiration. Singer made a name for himself in *Animal Liberation* by claiming that Christianity fostered, and helps maintain, a tyranny in the West. It seems only fair to wonder about his work and its relationship to tyranny. I assume he thinks a tyrannical philosophy utterly unacceptable. Assuming my arguments do expose the totalitarian temper of his thought, I take that as decisive against his thinking, and presume that he would agree with me. Most basically, I think Singer misconstrues the problem of vulnerability.

John Paul the Great's *Evangelium Vitae* is a contemporary Catholic analysis of homicide, firmly in a theological setting. I think it is underappreciated to what extent his theory of human dignity follows themes in Aquinas and Scheler. Nevertheless, the encyclical contains a significant departure from Aquinas and Scheler on the matter of punishment. So marked a departure, in fact, that I fail to see how the theory of punishment there is compatible with Wojtyla's personalist norm, basic to his thinking in sexual ethics from 1960 on. I defend this thesis in the second chapter where I claim that Catholic thought may have adopted certain ideas from humanitarianism and has not yet found *Catholic* ideas for opposition to capital punishment. More positively, in the third chapter, I rely heavily upon his work on mercy, as well as his analysis of the culture of death, in the fifth chapter. In these chapters I hope the importance of political theology begins to emerge.

Camus is a useful addition to a Thomist seeking to defend Aquinas but also a most thoroughgoing opponent of moral theology. Because Camus is sensitive to moral theology, even whilst rejecting it utterly, his writings are especially troubling to my overall thesis. His critique of mercy requires agile handling. In the third chapter, I show, against Camus, that mercy need not diminish justice: there is a place for mercy at law and this is the moral theological basis of double jeopardy. Addressing his argument against mercy alongside the work of the secular natural law jurist, Michael Moore, the disturbing connection between humanitarianism and dictatorship comes into relief. For this reason, Camus's disprivileging of mercy as a crowning value of law is untenable. The second chapter concerns Camus's justly famous essay on capital punishment and there I show how Aquinas and Scheler blunt his arguments: Camus misconstrues the grounding of punishment in the passions, denying the passions are a privileged site of moral knowledge. However, I do rely heavily on his analysis of Romanticism in the eighth chapter and develop from it a theological argument against humanitarian efforts to purify war.

The sixth and seventh chapters consider the work of Carl Schmitt on war. No one would ever accuse Schmitt of being an advocate for humanitarianism, and it might seem strange to think of him as a Christian personalist, but I think this is true. Duns Scotus' jurisprudence is one of the great targets of de Vitoria's commentary. Said to be "the Hobbes of the twentieth century," Schmitt could just as well be called "the Scotus of the twentieth century." I show why in the sixth chapter discussing his decisionism (also a theme of the third chapter): the idea that acts, not norms, found law. In the seventh, I show why Schmitt, like Camus, can help support Thomism. There, I use his work on Admiralty law to examine the infamous British case of the conjoined twins, "Jodie and Mary." His work on the juristic differences between land and sea show that the English Lord Justices made a "category mistake" in exploring the validity of a necessity defense for homicide.

No one working on the philosophy of law in the Continental tradition can escape the brooding presence of Schmitt. Quite apart from my individual treatments of his work just mentioned, Schmitt influences the book's entire argument about conceptions of law as varieties of political theology. The idea of political theology is not original to

Schmitt, but he gave the ideas of Stirner and Bakunin legs, as it were. His basic claim—that the exception in jurisprudence is analogous to the miracle in theology (PT 36)—I use to show that the progressive logic of humanitarianism tends towards tyranny. It is precisely its will to justice, a theology in which there is no wound, no vulnerability, which drives humanitarianism on to totalitarianism. Humanitarianism is a Christian heresy: it misconstrues the Eucharist, the wound of love. I now state, in compressed form, the political theology that guides the commentary: together, the individual treatments of law in the chapters are the arguments that, I believe, discount humanitarianism and favor law deferential to Catholic political theology. Beyond the negative thesis that humanitarianism destroys rule of law, the commentary's arguments favor acknowledging a reliance of law upon Providence. Natural law jurisprudence, "providential law," one might say, has two aspects: one logical the other contentual. If humanitarianism destroys man, how does God save man *at law*? The logical place of God at law is "the raised position" (Kolnai). Discussed at length in the first chapter, "the raised position" is the idea that the hierarchy of value (thus high and low values) must find a place in concrete social order. In the third chapter, for example, I argue that the doctrine of double jeopardy gives mercy (high value) a place at law. In the sixth chapter, I argue that international law should acknowledge the nation state as an agent of war and in the second, that laws controlling punishment must defer to the desire for felt bodily retribution (low value). In short, good law is a respecter of privileged agents and values.

Regarding the contentual aspect, humanitarian ethics makes diminishing suffering the core test of law. This is a response to vulnerability but the only adequate response to vulnerability is ecstatic vulnerability, to the love that wounds the lover.[14] This law of love is the raised position of the Cross, Resurrection, and Assumption. The core test of law is not suffering but Easter. Rightly concerned with suffering, the humanitarian seeks justice. Justice without ecstatic vulnerability—*My soul chooses hanging*—is perverse justice.[15] In the eighth chapter, I discuss the air strategy NATO used to stop the atrocities of the Serbs in Kosovo. Appealing to a raised position, the privilege of risk-free high-altitude bombing, justice reigned, so NATO thought. As I show in that chapter, perverse justice reigned: the response to suffering was an air strategy that included, as a structural principle, accidental homicide. Desiring justice at no cost of NATO life, rules of engagement shielded airmen from the justice of the warrior, ecstatic vulnerability. Kosovo was the logical summation of humanitarianism: a war to stop suffering and overcome suffering soldiering.

The core error of humanitarianism is the belief that there is a yonder beyond vulnerability. There is not: beyond vulnerability there is only ecstatic vulnerability; the raised position of Easter. There, suffering is assumed into the peace of sacrificial donation: *presently* an always-vulnerable peace, yet a peace always full of the promise of the glory of Peace, wounds scarring as glory. At the limit of law, in this wound (ultimately) scarring over as glory (EM, c. 5), is where God is at law. The rule of law requires that God be a content, an ordering content, of law. "God is love" and alone is equal to law's temptation. Confronted by opacity (first chapter), contingency (third and eighth chapters), necessity (third and seventh chapters), division (seventh chapter), the limits of the body (second and sixth chapters) and of reason (fifth chapter), law's temptation is the absolute perfection of justice. The thirst for justice is apt to turn into the parched throat beseeching Lazarus: justice alone is not equal to the world. Alone equal to the world is the lamb slain before the foundation of the world (Apoc. 13: 8)—love risked as liberty, as donative peace.[16] Where justice presumes to contend with contingency, opacity, necessity, and the like, there it becomes decisionism: not "my weakness is swallowed up in your strength" (Augustine) but law's limitation exposed to the nothingness of the Earth's principalities. A just and prudent fear to contend with the Leviathan—*Will he speak to you soft words?*—is a moderation of the will to justice, the cultivation of a habit of moderation lest a mauled justice find scope throughout law. "Providential law" is the answer to Augustine's question, "To whom shall we cry?" It is an oblation of (not to) the will to justice, the will to justice forsaken for the sovereign cradle of the right hand of the glory of God. Hanging like the good thief with pained confidence we hear, "*This day you shall be with me in Paradise.*" Only through this providential oblation can the virtue of law, the proportionate response of justice, develop. Rule of law demands, therefore, not a will to justice but an asceticism of justice.

Humanitarianism sought to go beyond vulnerability in Kosovo and the criminality of its NATO effort stemmed from a love that rejected the wound of love. This wound is the cost of love's intervention and sometimes the cost of non-intervention. The desire for a yonder beyond love's vulnerability is the error that repeats itself: in some kinds of trade law (first chapter); torture as a response to the terror of horrendous evil (third chapter); the idea of wrongful life tort (fifth chapter); international law as a mediation of conflict (sixth chapter); and the necessity defense for homicide as a justification for surgical procedures (seventh chapter). This desire is even present in some recent Catholic social thought and theology. The odd occluding of the problem of punishment in John Paul II's treatment of capital punishment is a case in point. Odd, because in recent theology it is John Paul II who is most alert to the body, its potential for glory and its very real limitations. In the second chapter, I argue that Catholic thinkers were once alive to the origin of punishment in felt bodily retribution. The precise basis of John Paul II's argument against capital punishment is far from clear. I review a number of possibilities in this chapter. One possibility is that he agreed with de Lubac on the fundamentally graced nature of being human. As I say, this book, as well as a commentary on Aquinas, might also be read as an exegesis of the wonderful sentence of de Lubac's quoted at the start of the Preface. In the fourth chapter, however, I argue that the persuasiveness of de Lubac's analysis of nature and grace suffers from its logical identity with humanitarianism. The idea that grace pervades human nature seems to me to owe a good deal to the fallacious idea that human nature is itself a yonder beyond vulnerability. In the fourth chapter I argue against the politics of this idea and in EM I show why it is a metaphysical impossibility. It is speculative, but perhaps the argument of the fourth chapter reads as an explanation for the occluding of the problem of punishment addressed in the second. Catholicism needs clarity on both topics if Catholic social thought is to engage law well.

I hope these opening remarks orient the reader, clarifying why I think that Thomism is so important to law, that humanitarianism is a false friend to those committed to rule of law, and that the problem of human vulnerability makes political theology an inescapable question for law. Readers oftentimes like to jump around inside a book and this is easy here; the chapters are self-contained. The first chapter, to which I now turn, is essential reading, however: I develop in far more detail both the moral theory assumed throughout and the problem of contingency.

Notes

1. For this discussion, please see my "Jack Aubrey Meets Thomas Aquinas: Is It Immoral to Kill for Money?" (*pro manuscripto*).
2. About these trends, see the introduction to Matt Levering's *Biblical Natural Law* (Oxford: Oxford University Press, 2008).
3. J. Austin, *The Province of Jurisprudence Determined* (Cambridge: Cambridge University Press, 2001), p. 81.
4. Thomas Hibbs, *Aquinas, Ethics, and Philosophy of Religion: Metaphysics and Practice* (Bloomington, IN: Indiana University Press, 2007), pp. 20-22.

5.   J. Ratzinger, *Values in a Time of Upheaval* (San Francisco: Ignatius, 2006), p. 41.

6.   See scene 45 of the *The Fellowship of the Ring* (*The Lord of the Rings: The Motion Picture Trilogy*, Special Extended DVD Edition [New Line Platinum Series, 2002]).

7.   Cf. D. Wiggins, *Needs, Values, Truth* (Oxford: Oxford University Press, 1998).

8.   The *ius gentium*, says Blackstone, is a "great universal law, collected from history and usage" and is both "the law of nature and reason" (W. Blackstone, *Commentaries*, Book 4, c. 5, *67).

9.   "The Conservative Moral Philosophy of Max Scheler and Aurel Kolnai," *Modern Age* (Summer 2006), pp. 217-225. Please also see my introductions to: Max Scheler, *The Nature of Sympathy* (Transaction Publishers, 2007), pp. lv-lxvi and Aurel Kolnai, *Ethics, Value, and Reality* (Transaction Publishers, 2008), pp. ix-xxii.

10. For the former see Griswold's entry in *The Cambridge Companion to Adam Smith* (Cambridge: Cambridge University Press, 2006) and for the latter Haakonssen's *The Science of a Legislator* (Cambridge: Cambridge University Press, 1989).

11. J. Austin, *The Province of Jurisprudence Determined*, pp. 40 & 86. Like Austin, Thomas Reid thinks Hume relies on intuitionism (T. Cuneo, "Reid's Moral Philosophy," *The Cambridge Companion to Thomas Reid* [Cambridge: Cambridge University Press, 2004], p. 245).

12. Smith's brilliant evocation of a murder (TMS, 159) is a dramatic presentation of a comment like Reid's: people "perceive a turpitude in injustice" (T. Cuneo, "Reid's Moral Philosophy," *The Cambridge Companion to Thomas Reid*, p. 247).

13. Please see my, "Business Ethics and Catholic Social Thought," *Nova et Vetera: The English Edition of the International Theological Journal*, Vol. 4, No. 1 (2006), pp. 17-27.

14. For an interesting movie treatment of the idea, see Will Smith's character in *I Am Legend*. Seminal theoretical treatments are: Bonaventure, *The Journey of the Mind to God*, especially the Prologue and seventh chapter; and, as I argue at length in EM, Thomas's natural law theory.

15. On the totalitarian fascination with invulnerability, see C. Lefort, "The Image of the Body and Totalitarianism," *The Political Forms of Modern Society* (Cambridge, MA: The MIT Press, 1986), p. 300.

16. For a treatment of this point, please see my, "'I Am Awaited by Love: And so My Life is Good:' Hope and Children" *Nova et Vetera: The English Edition of the International Theological Journal*, Vol. 6, No. 4 (2008), pp. 829-36.

1

Blood Diamonds and the Limits
of Moral Knowledge

*It is up to the consumer to insist that a diamond is
conflict free.*

—Blood Diamond

Whether It Is Unlawful to Kill Any Living Thing

Some might think the thoughts of moral theologians quite beside the point when the topic at hand is the philosophy of homicide. What has moral theology to do with the philosophy of law? It might seem strange but theologians were the first to systematize a logic of killing. It is a logic, moreover, that has guided Western culture for hundreds of years. Simply read the section on homicide in Blackstone's commentaries on the common law alongside Aquinas' question on killing in the *Summa theologica* (ST II-II, q. 64, aa. 1-8) and my point is obvious.[1] Peter Singer agrees. Drawing up his own battle lines, Singer demands a new logic of killing because our homicide laws are sectarian, relying on "the distinctively Christian idea of the sanctity of all human life" (AL, 198; PE 77 & 125). Another reason the philosophy of law should concern itself with theology is that theology just won't go away.[2] To the horror of many perhaps, theology keeps obtruding into debates about killing, and the popes just won't stay silent either.

Yet theology is not now as clear as it once was that there is a defensible logic to killing. In explaining, defending, and applying Thomas and de Vitoria, I hope to help bring some coherence and conviction to theology on this obviously central issue. This need is very real for those who think a theologically inflected understanding of homicide is important. For whilst it is not too much to say that moral theology put homicide as we

15

know it on the map the medieval synthesis of theology and law is under sustained attack. Thinkers like Singer have had a significant impact on ways of thinking about homicide, at least in certain important circles.[3] These thinkers' outright dismissal of moral theology has the virtue of raising a crucial question: Can natural law ethics withstand, or counter-charge, the revisions to homicide suggested?

Abortion jurisprudence has radically transformed American law, argues Hadley Arkes, a cause and consequence of which is that contemporary law has no answer to the question, "What is man?" Arkes states with concern that "it is no longer taken for granted, as an axiom of the law, that there really are human beings, with a distinct nature as moral agents, which fits them distinctly for law and political life."[4] Because this is denied, humans have no intrinsic dignity and no standing at law save what is granted through legal positivism (NR, 146). And law based on shifting preferences and needs is, as Justice Scalia recently put it, dictatorship.[5] This is a paradoxical consequence of something very deep, however. I suspect the political theorist Chantal Delsol is absolutely correct when she argues that modern thinkers gave up philosophical anthropology[6] as the basis of law out of fear that any positive conception of man can stand as a platform for tyranny. Legal positivism, she argues, relies on a nominalism of shifting definitions understood to give liberty. I think this is probably an accurate description of the deepest motivation behind much contemporary legal thinking but an upshot is that public authority in principle must be eviscerated. Stripped down it might be, but even Aristotle's "political animal" is a positive conception of man: it asserts that the relationship of command-obedience is part and parcel of the meaning of man. Schmitt regards this relationship as basic to the political. Progressive democracy, a quite different thing than the classical liberalism of the Scottish Enlightenment is, as Kolnai points out, an emancipation doctrine. It denies man is a dependent creature (TRA, passim) and therewith rejects the political relationship.[7]

Eliminating the political relationship is the disprivileging of man (CM, passim). Humanitarianism asserts the radical sovereignty of man and its banner is equality, because only if one is equal to others is one free, unlimited. Value hierarchy, the idea that there exist moral claims with intrinsic characters of high and low value, asserts a precedence over human will; intrinsic moral claims ask us, as it were, to bow our heads. The claims of the value hierarchy are set socially in sites of privilege (e.g., the privilege of the British monarch helps secure me, a British subject, my dignity) thus equality sets its face in utter intolerance against privilege. A perfect illustration is Singer's now famous charge of speciesism. I discuss this charge at length in the fifth chapter, and a little immediately below, but note what Singer thinks follows from the charge. The claim is that the traditional law of homicide is partisan. It just is not true, says Singer, and increasingly jurors agree with him, that "all human life is of equal worth."[8] Many individual animals have more characteristics of personhood than do many individual humans. These animals should be the object of our ethical care more than those humans. In particular, "when life is of no benefit to the person living it" (RLD, 193), law should permit intentional killing of the innocent. The traditional jurisprudence of homicide collapses (RLD, 221), thinks Singer, once we realize our laws are parochial—irrationally favoring human animals over persons of other animal species—and once we abandon the belief that there is some significant moral distinction between acts and omissions (RLD, 195-6). I discuss this distinction at length in the eighth chapter, but Singer's point is that the law already accepts killing by dehydration but does so as an omission: judges insisting that there is a fundamental prohibition against the active killing of the innocent. Singer thinks this nicety[9] is philosophically insupportable and the sooner we admit that as a culture we accept the intentional killing of the innocent the sooner justice reigns (RLD, 128-9). Singer wants law to abandon the privilege of public authority killing and to permit both public and private authority to kill the innocent. It is the strangest of conclusions to come to but if Scalia and Delsol are right, then Donoso Cortés, and Nietzsche after him, are right after all: in modernity, dictatorship is inevitable.

Of course, to some, it is patently obvious that Aquinas is a prime example of what Delsol is talking about—a positive conception of man on which hinges tyranny—yet those who want to avoid dictatorship need, I think, to stay close to Aquinas and moral theology. Tyranny can provide public order and yet, as Kolnai points out, Stalin and Hitler may have been impossible in Ancient Rome but condemnation of Nero and Caligula now, and back then, relies on the same moral terms we use against twentieth-century butchers (I, 234, n. 3). There is an enduring moral consensus about public order and Aquinas, I think, identified two of its pillars: only public authority has the privilege to intentionally and directly kill and innocence is a protection against this privilege. *Good* public order cannot be maintained without these two principles.

Contemning privilege, contemporary jurisprudence privatizes homicide, departing explicitly from the first pillar, but implicitly and necessarily from the second also. The point is repeated again and again by

Cicero in the speeches of his murder trials.[10] Whether it is the story line of "Tony B" in the fifth season of the *Sopranos* or Beowulf as a regulator of *wergild* Cicero's point is made.[11] That abandonment of this first principle destroys the innocent is illustrated by Arkes. In a few marvelous pages he sketches how the private authority to kill soon becomes the power to kill those (with sad lives) who ought to, but don't, exercise their right to be killed. Quickly enough, in entirely believable scenarios,[12] one arrives at town worthies killing orphans, for, after all, sad people have a *right* to die (NR, 170-171). There is every reason to think, argues Arkes, that the abortion jurisprudence already in place can be extended to intentional killing of people "who have neither ordered nor consented to their deaths" (NR, 171). Why would we not expect it? Abortion jurisprudence says a woman can kill a child in her womb should the child be inconvenient. Innocence is a "magic wall" (de Maistre) we all still recognize against the lethal power of public authority but it is already no protection against private homicide with its norms of convenience, nor even humanitarian sentiment (see the comments of the English judges in *Bland* [RLD, 65-80]).

In his well-known book, *Animal Liberation*, Singer (AL, 201) quotes at length ST II-II, q. 64, a. 1, but never assesses, Thomas' central premise for why humans can kill animals. Thomas introduces the principle—and it is basic to his defence of capital punishment—that what is more perfect can use the less perfect. Humans can use animals for food and clothing on the basis of this principle. Though never assessed, Thomas' principle is Exhibit A for Singer's accusation of speciesism. Thomas certainly argues here that hierarchy bestows a use and control. For Singer, this is just the assertion of a shocking privilege of the human species to lord it over and exploit other species. Considering Thomas' argument, de Vitoria accepts the use and control consequent to hierarchy and wonders whether there are limits: Can humans use animals for sport, perhaps even when the "kill" is not eaten? To answer this question, de Vitoria develops over many pages a theory of property. Vitoria does not doubt that animals can be used for sport and of more interest to him is when hunting is licit (Singer wants hunting outlawed [PE, 105]). This depends heavily on where the animals are and de Vitoria concludes that property gives hunting privileges (H, 124-5).

The link between privilege, property, and killing is dramatically posed by Proudhon in his thesis that property is an impossibility because homicide. He argues that property inevitably leads to starvation for some and is thus morally impossible.[13] Establishing a principle of the anarchist tradition, Proudhon links privilege and dictatorship, or property and kill-ing, as invariant twins. In recent years, humanitarian organizations have criticized companies for trading in "blood diamonds." I do not doubt that there are factually such things as "blood diamonds."[14] But do such diamonds exist morally? A "blood diamond" is a moral accusation against thoughtless or hardhearted consumers and companies: enamored of the beauty and meaning of diamonds, purchasers—corporate, certainly,[15] and maybe individual consumers—are complicit in the killing of innocents in civil wars in a number of African countries. This is a contemporary variant of Proudhon's thesis. Of course, humanitarians who make this accusation (I assume) do not subscribe to Proudhon's thesis as a prin-ciple true of all property but they share his moral concern that the lure of property is so strong we are willing to "turn a blind eye" to killing. Certainly, this is true of the two film treatments of the issue in recent years, *Lord of War* and *Blood Diamond*. Is this accusation too quick to assume that people, e.g. jewelry merchandisers, really do "turn a blind eye?" What if the conditions of knowledge in diamond trading are such that there is invincible ignorance? I believe there is.

The argument has three stages: after describing aspects of diamond trading, I discuss Aquinas' analysis of action and ignorance, and end arguing that humanitarians fail to ask whether ignorance excuses be-cause humanitarianism struggles to accept the idea of a moral opacity in the world. Arguments made in the third, fifth, seventh, and eighth chapters press the case that humanitarian avidity for the reign of justice invites tyranny. In this first chapter, I make no such claim but the error of the accusation of "blood diamonds" is the same error that prompts the will to justice to lethal acts of "justice." Christianity responds to the opacity of the moral world with a resignation to the mystery of God's providence. However hard to bear for the Christian, it is impossible for the humanitarian. In this and the third chapter I show this resignation is a response to a *moral* phenomenon and not only a matter of revelation. A subtlety emerges here, one easily missed by Christians. The idea of moral opacity or, as Aquinas has it, invincible ignorance, is an aspect of the gradations within moral life. Kolnai placed the problem of moral emphasis front and center in his moral reflection. I think Aquinas did too. Moral emphasis is the idea that moral phenomena make different binding claims upon us. This is another way of speaking about moral hierarchy, and if humanitarians strongly resist hierarchy (consider the role of equality in the utilitarianism of Bentham and Singer, for example), Christians are apt to make confused rankings. Forgiveness, as Kolnai points out, might be a kingly virtue but it hardly evacuates the lower, but far more binding, virtue of justice (FR, 220). That is, a complex relationship exists between the ranking of a value and the strength of its claim upon us. Christians are often shocked by his claim, but I think Kolnai's argument in his essay "Forgiveness" is correct. I show why below. The chapter ends with the argument that unless moral emphasis is respected, constitutionalism founders.

The diamond trade is now an object of close scrutiny: newspaper articles and statements by humanitarian organizations are common; a recent high profile motion picture has an elaborate attendant website advocating regulation of the industry; and law articles speculating how diamond companies might be held liable or prosecuted for human rights violations keep appearing. The industry responded to these sorts of pressures in 2003 with the Kimberley Process. Complying with this process, the "main-street" American jewelry company, Zales, demands its suppliers provide a warranty that runs in part:

> The undersigned hereby guarantees that these diamonds are conflict free, based on personal knowledge and/or written guarantees provided by the supplier of these diamonds.[16]

A "chain of warranties" thus assures company merchandisers that the diamonds they purchase in bulk are untainted. The U.S. State Department estimates that in the late 1990s between 4 and 15 percent of rough diamonds came from conflict areas but celebrates the Kimberly Process with holding that down to "significantly less than 1 percent."[17] As often pointed out, since diamonds amount annually to a sixty-billion-dollar trade, 1 percent still amounts to a $600 million slush fund for weapons.[18]

Others are less sure about the one percent figure. Many bemoan the fact that adherence to the Kimberley Process is voluntary and, at least in Britain, many jewelers acknowledge "they have no real policy on sourcing diamonds."[19] At the height of reflection on the civil war in Sierra Leone, commentators could note, that "not much is known about the mining and trading of Sierra Leone diamonds."[20] As Zales explains in its compliance document, each shipment of rough diamonds is packaged in a tamper-resistant container "soon" after mining. The problem: there are many small mining operations, oftentimes individuals working on their own,[21] and South African officials suspect conflict diamonds are easily laundered before the shipping process even begins.[22] Moreover, at big diamond centers, where stones are often mixed and matched for color, oversight is oftentimes lacking (MK, 6). Indeed, in London, De Beers mixes stones before batching them into no less than 16,000 categories (MK, 7).

Amnesty International wonders whether industry assurances are meaningful. Quite apart from lack of oversight—a survey Amnesty conducted in Britain found only 7 percent of retailers could certify the origin of the diamond jewelry for sale[23]—Amnesty estimated that 2006 saw about $23 million in blood diamonds smuggled directly into the United States.[24] Smuggling is common in African nations, certainly. American drug companies that give away free AIDS drugs to African *governments* color code them so they are easy to identify when they re-emerge on the American market.[25] The experience of American drug companies highlights that even when government officials in certain countries testify to the moral cleanliness of the diamonds some skepticism is appropriate.[26] Others speak of a "smuggling culture in the diamond business."[27] Some claim that a sharp uptick of diamond trading through Israel is a consequence of stricter oversight in Belgium's diamond center, Antwerp.[28] The political and commercial culture of Switzerland makes diamonds imported from transit zones there impossible to trace.[29]

It is likely then that blood diamonds continue to find their way to American markets. Nonetheless, I propose that demands for stricter regulation of the diamond industry are inappropriate. My focus is not the moral obligation that supposedly compels more regulation—though I do doubt such an obligation exists[30]—but whether there exists an ignorance that removes moral culpability. Simply, but accurately enough, no moral problem exists to regulate.

Thomas makes many distinctions respecting action and ignorance. I think these distinctions are overlooked by those seeking to hold diamond traders responsible at law.[31] Wanting to hold corporations responsible for "indirectly funding human rights violations," efforts are made to show corporations knowingly fund war criminals (RR, 1407-8) and so are complicit in violations of the "law of nations" (RR, 1472).[32]

The idea of complicity rests, morally speaking, on knowledge. It is not true that one is only responsible for what is done with knowledge. The Roman idea of the piacular (TMS, 106-7) and its modern variant of strict liability are cases in point and Aquinas' tripartite division of moral disorder into evil, sin and moral wrong (De malo, q. 2, a. 2) explains why. Evil is privation of "due measure in anything." Sin is an evil of narrower scope concerning "acts lacking due order" and disorders of appetite. Such acts done voluntarily are sins and also moral wrongs. A voluntary act—a true human act (*actus humanus*)—engages rational liberty. Only when the core dignity of the person sources an act is the person responsible for moral wrong. However, examples abound where an act causes privation and, assuming the matter is grave, responsibility is inescapable, even if the act has no obvious source in knowledge and will. Negligence is an *actus hominis*, that is, an act done by a human agent, but not the act of the person (*actus humanus*), where the responsibility posited assumes vincible ignorance.[33] In *De malo*, Aquinas defends the idea of responsibility for evil and sin (q. 2, a. 3; q. 3, a. 6) where there is no responsibility for moral wrong because no moral knowledge (q. 2, a. 4). Thomas makes a moral issue of what knowledge we do and do not have.

The idea of complicity requires moral knowledge. Complicity has a peculiar structural feature: another performs the act that causes privation. If I can be held responsible for an act I did not knowingly do, it is surely something else again that I be held responsible for an act I did not knowingly, nor actually myself, do. Indeed, the connective tissue here seems to rely exclusively on knowledge and whether I acquiesce to the act.[34] The moral center of the charge of the "blood diamond" is that my purchase of diamonds makes me a party to, complicit in, the killings fostered by the money traded for the diamonds. Undoubtedly, this is sometimes true.[35] As a customer in a shop or as a merchandiser for a national jewelry chain, I doubt it is ever true. The conditions of knowledge, as sketched above, even absolve negligence (De malo, q. 2, a. 1), I would argue.

The object of the will is an "understood good" (De malo, q. 3, a. 8), and no moral choice can be made if the moral character of the object is not understood. Reviewing Aquinas' analysis of the role of ignorance in action, I now argue that if a Zales merchandiser and *a fortiori*, a customer at Zales, buys a blood diamond that act is "completely involuntary" and so not the purchase of a blood diamond in a moral sense. Keeping in mind the previous description of the diamond trade, consider Thomas' distinction between antecedent and subsequent voluntariness.

Thomas argues that ignorance can remove subsequent but not antecedent voluntariness. Thomas' idea is that if you choose to remain ignorant about the conditions of your acts your thoughtlessness makes your acts voluntary. An example of such "antecedent voluntariness" is willed ignorance: ignorance is "directly voluntary" when one wills to ignore conditions of the act that contribute to its evil. With the Kimberly Process in place, it does not appear true that a Zales merchandiser actively seeks to ignore conditions of buying the diamonds. Nor does the merchandiser seem to give the nod to "indirectly voluntary" ignorance: a case of omitting to seek out knowledge of the conditions of the act one ought to strive to know.[36] With the best will in the world, and due care taken, it remains true in the diamond industry, as the WSJ puts it: "you've got to trust that someone, somewhere, over thousands of miles and months or years of transactions, didn't slip a bad rock in the pile."[37] Nor even can one accuse the merchandiser of "accidentally voluntary" ignorance, as when one wills a choice that generates a concomitant ignorance (Thomas gives the example of drunkenness prohibiting the use of reason). This would only be true if the merchandiser knew, and did not much care, that Zales was resisting practicable reforms to the Kimberly Process. The Kimberly Process is seemingly a reasonable industry standard in which merchandisers and customers can trust.[38]

According to Thomas, even if done in conditions of ignorance, an act is voluntary if those conditions were in some way generated by one of these three varieties of willed ignorance. This is a case of what Aquinas calls "antecedent voluntariness" and contrasting with it is the domain of "subsequent voluntariness." Where the ignorance is invincible, the ignorance "makes a subsequent evil act completely involuntary" (De malo, q. 3, a. 8). I do not doubt that some merchandisers may have suspicions about their suppliers and choose to ignore these qualms. Of course, this may happen sometimes. The point is, however, that Thomas' analysis of ignorance shows that blood diamonds in the moral sense do not simply follow from the fact of blood diamonds. And so it does not follow that even if a merchandiser is buying blood diamonds and passing these on to customers the merchandiser or customer is morally at fault. Granting the transaction follows from, facilitates, and is evil,[39] it is still not a moral wrong. There is no complicity on account of the nature of the ignorance involved. Nor is there negligence, because, for the same reason, the Kimberly Process is a reasonable standard.

Unsurprisingly, humanitarian organizations are at the forefront of wanting to purify the diamond trade. At first blush this humanitarian desire is compelling. Profound reservation is possible, however. At one point, Kolnai casts Thomas as "an Aristotelian naturalist salved with a drop of pantheist mysticism" (MP2, 99). Kolnai objects to Thomas' naturalism because it replaces the good with happiness. For the same reason, Kolnai objects that in humanitarianism the properly moral is reduced to a non-moral value, man (I, 268; HVR, 435). In EM I show that Thomistic ethics is far less an "Aristotelian naturalism" than Kolnai appreciated and far more Christological and intuitive (EM, cc. 4-5). Kolnai also objects to Thomas' naturalism on the grounds that it strictly identifies action and morality (MP2, 98-9): Thomas' famous claim that there are no particular acts that are morally indifferent (De malo, q. 2, a. 5). Kolnai strongly disagrees with Thomas on this point arguing that acts range over moral and non-moral values. Since it is Kolnai's position that institutions and a manifold of social forms and practices stem from, and reinforce, this variety in value, the charge against Thomas is that his moral theory in effect undercuts social and political pluralism. This is a serious charge. However, is not Kolnai's point amply provided for in Thomas' distinctions respecting: acts and omissions; proscriptions and prescriptions; *actus humanus* and *actus hominis*; the virtues; the role of circumstance in shaping the moral object; ignorance; the order of charity; and the roles of the body and anger in justice?

The constituent parts of an action, and the distinctions governing how the parts relate to the norms of action, are many. Thomas and Kolnai agree that human acts are not all equally localizable under a simple rational rubric as suggested by the monistic formulae of utilitarianism or Kantianism. Rather, the moral objects of acts carry a "tone."[40] Kolnai calls this "tone" "moral emphasis" (MP2, 100): objects of the will's choice are laden with values (and claims on virtue)[41] and exhibit "a tone of warning, urging, vetoing, and commanding." The most imperious tones, evident from moral phenomena and traditional moral theory, attach to negative rather than positive precepts. Moral demands intrude upon our daily lives most forcefully as prohibitions, "do not kill," "do not steal," and so on. Negative claims of justice, in other words, make their presence felt; they have strong emphasis (MP2, 105). They impose the strictest duties (De malo, q. 2, a. 1). By contrast, a positive precept like "defend the widow and protect the lowly," certainly does make a claim upon us but less forcefully than "do not kill," and this is evident from our daily practice. These are higher and more admirable values but they also have less emphasis (MP2, 106). To fail in these duties diminishes our moral standing but does not (straightforwardly) make us morally corrupt.[42] Of course, a devotee of humanitarian "social justice" would argue this distinction is unfounded but this species of humanitarianism is precisely what I mean to dispute.

Consider Kolnai's controversial claim that at very best forgiveness is a quasi-obligation (FG, 223; 221). A Christian might argue—whether correctly is another matter—that for the Christian forgiveness is an obligation. Perhaps even a non-Christian might think forgiveness an obligation. Certainly, the contemporary humanitarian wants to replace judgment and condemnation with "understanding," an appreciation for "root causes" that go a long way, maybe all the way, to explaining so-called "immoral acts." The humanitarian impulse displayed here stems from the insight that forgiveness is a very high value indeed; one we should all want to exhibit. However, no matter that it is a high value, forgiveness is also of weak emphasis. By contrast, thinks Kolnai, a somewhat lower value, justice, has strong emphasis.

By way of illustration: imagine one saw the wife of a slain man putting flowers on the grave of her husband's killer. Approaching her we ask, "What are you doing?" We learn the flowers are a token of her forgiveness. On learning this, I think all of us would know we were in the presence of a remarkable person, a remarkable value-realization. Yet, we could well imagine speaking with another woman in the same situation who tells us she will never forgive her husband's killer. We would, I imagine, still be impressed: the woman's sense of justice would register with us. We would not, I think, be nearly as impressed by her as we are with the first woman but nor, in any way whatsoever, would we think her a corrupt moral personality. That is, both values appeal but in a definite hierarchy.

From this phenomenology of moral experience, Kolnai concludes that the reason we do not censure the second woman for not forgiving is that there is no obligation to forgive. We would be aghast if neither woman felt an injustice had been done. A definite obligation to affirm the value of justice does exist and to fail to affirm this value is a serious moral failing. But to fail to forgive is not itself a moral failing, at least not a failing of anything like the same degree. Put simply: to murder is a lot more immoral than failing to forgive. The most Kolnai is willing to say is that if someone beseeches forgiveness, and if that person has demonstrated a change of heart, then a quasi obligation to forgive surely exists. But only a quasi obligation exists, no more.

Though it is an idea in search of a definition, advocates of social justice understand it to wreak havoc on the distinction between negative and positive precepts. It is as much an injustice that I fail to feed you as that I kill you, according to the lights of social justice. It is no longer merely that I have a right to travel so that I might find work, there is an injustice if I am not provided work. Humanitarians, and sometimes church documents, cast social justice as an obligation on government. Social justice offers a rationale for government's administration of daily life. It invites the state to manage daily life through a psychological, educative, medical, and economic welfare bureaucracy. Kolnai can find no moral basis for government's insistence that we endorse social justice programs because positive precepts have weak emphasis. Humanitarian claims about "blood diamonds" ignore the varied emphases of the different acts involved in buying diamonds. It is on account of this confused moral basis that humanitarians demand legal and governmental administration replace diamond traders' self-regulation.

The role of moral knowledge is decisive for the moral emphases involved in diamond trading. Indeed, this trade shows there is a split between reality and our moral knowledge; that, on occasion, opacity shrinks our moral world. The criticism of blood diamonds would have us believe that the moral world is seamless and that from mining to final sale a "consistent ethic" applies, and equally, for all involved. But this is to ignore distinctions that must be made if we want to avoid the deformation of the moral world (MP2, 119).

The moral charge is that when I buy a blood diamond I break the negative precept "do not kill." I do not directly do this, of course, but my act of purchase is an act of complicity towards the act of someone else who does break the negative precept. An act of purchasing, through some causation, is an act of killing, so we are told. Consider the famous opening of Proudhon's book: "as slavery is murder so property is theft."[43] Whereas a thinker like Aquinas sees four very different moral objects here, and an ordinary language intuitionist like Kolnai sees four different moral phenomena, Proudhon sees but two, and, as the logic of his book develops, in fact one, theft. To Aquinas' mind, two *intrinsic* evils (murder and theft) are confused with a punitive evil (slavery) and a good (property). Where Aquinas sees moral variety, Proudhon monistically sees theft. Proudhon replaces sensitivity to moral phenomena with a logic that obscures the fact that myriad values, moral and non-moral, have some claim upon us and that low values, as much as high values, have a legitimate place in daily life. The problem is evident in Kant, one of the architects of humanitarianism. All motivation is suspect for Kant and must be strictly legislated *within* the human. Precisely because the ordinary motivations of human life are suspect as not in fact being human, merely *pretium vulgare*, the distinctions of moral emphasis disappear. This militates against political pluralism and invites totalitarianism:[44] hence, despite the putative liberalism of Kantians, the constant tendency of progressivism to heavily legislate ordinary life and constantly find it wanting.[45] Humanitarianism is a morality identified with an unvarying rationality and universalism based in mastery of appetite and thus customary ways of living.[46] By contrast, moral emphasis shows that moral values make a claim upon us that is "privileged and autonomous rather than all-embracing" (MP2, 100). Proudhon can only make his claim by slipping between the non-moral value of property and the moral disvalues of theft and murder. To visit a property and witness a murder is to see two different things. His thesis is startling for the same reason it is wrong: it is a slip between emphases. Similarly, buying a diamond in a mall in America does not *look like* pulling the trigger of a gun in Africa and—on account of the role of ignorance—it is not.

Dworkin's jurisprudence makes the same error when he argues that abortion must be legal. The state, Dworkin reasons, must treat its citizens equally. To do so, it must transcend any particular conception of the good life. Otherwise in choosing a conception it treats unequally those who cannot agree with that conception.[47] Moral emphasis shows why there is a sleight of hand here. Rejecting the privatization of homicide is not a matter of specifying the good life but recognizing a hard moral emphasis: the innocent cannot be intentionally killed. We know from our condemnation of tyranny that "not killing the innocent" is a proscription, a negative precept establishing, in Thomas' words, a "most strict duty." Dworkin cannot trade upon the idea of tyranny unless he concedes the *meaning* of tyranny. The precept "do not kill the innocent" has a greater claim upon us than even the powerful prescription, "To judge in favor of the orphan and lowly" (Ps. 10:18). Dworkin wants us to believe that we might as a polity dispute whether we are bound to aid the orphan and lowly *and equally* dispute whether we should kill the innocent. There is broad consensus on the former—and has been for millennia[48]—and near-unanimity[49] on the latter. Dworkin's "any conception of the good life" is just a sleight of hand to mask the power of the self-evidence of the distinction between negative and positive precepts. To claim that laws confirming the negative precept "do not kill the innocent" are laws that confirm us in dictatorship is the flabby intellectualism that does invite dictatorship. Dworkin's indifference to emphasis leads him to ignore the distinction and limitation basic to the very idea of constitutionalism.

Deference to ordinary life,[50] our time in schools, gyms, workplaces, churches, and shops (yes, it really is important to "keep going to the malls," as a famous and much ridiculed statement would have it) is basic to moral and legal order because it is amidst our daily concerns that we constantly relate to others and are *watched* relating to others. We are moral, as the Scottish School showed convincingly, because we stand under the judgment of others, the impartial spectator. On account of this attunement to others moral reciprocity develops. Kant's and Proudhon's intolerance of the compromises entailed by competing values, roles, and vocations intrinsic to ordinary life is fully on display in humanitarian or social justice ethics. Advocates exude grievance at the collective indifference to suffering, which is in fact the impartial spectator's rightful recognition of strong and weak emphasis, the priority of intrinsic evils over other kinds, the distinction between acts of commission and omission, the role ignorance can play in moral responsibility, and the local nature of justice, e. g., the order of charity.

Ordinary moral consciousness is alive to distinction and limit. It is alike the content of the Scottish School's impartial spectator, the *ius gentium* of Thomas and de Vitoria, Scheler's *ethos*, and Kolnai's "moral consensus." Scottish writers viewed the spectator as a sympathetic spectator, believing you and I are linked morally to one another through manifold emotional ties. I think this is right and so in the expression "moral consensus" stress is upon *sensus*, that is, the emotional register of human life. To greater or lesser degree, Smith, Scheler, Kolnai, Wojtyla, and (as I argued in EM) Thomas, all agree. Kolnai thinks a simple intuition of emphasis is possible, that values can appear unmediated to (emotional) consciousness. However, in the normal course of things, values make their appeal in and through social institutions that can run counter to, or foster, the appeal of moral sentiments. Following Smith (TMS, 110), Kolnai makes a stronger claim: moral consciousness is only rudimentary without this mediation. Moral intuition is, in any rich sense, social. In his essay, "The Concept of Hierarchy,"[51] Kolnai offers a fascinating example for why these supporting institutions of moral life must be institutions of privilege. Imagine, he asks, climbing a hill. On the flat, before climbing, various aspects of the landscape stand out. Even a little elevation, however, adds richness to what one sees. In particular, with the climb underway, one can come to see behind the buildings and copses that previously had blocked one's sight. The phenomenology of height suggests, says Kolnai, that civilizational values are only acquired atop elevated positions. Authors as diverse as Cicero and the writer of *Beowulf* attest that height is an attribute of public authority and, of course, we speak of being elevated to the bench and judges handing down decisions. Equalitarianism is, of course, a value. But it is most definitely a low value, tending in fact towards disvalue—for it tends to restrict our very capacity to recognize value, rejecting, as it does, raised positions.[52]

Atheism is, as de Lubac argued, a prop to totalitarianism because in striking out God fusion replaces distinction. Christianity is a defender of dignity, not because man as *imago Dei* is a straightforwardly moral idea (it is not), but because Christianity defends the moral significance of the raised position of the Cross, Resurrection, and Assumption. Moreover, constellations of words and social concepts in all cultures set the dignified at a height. If equalitarianism is fostered by modernity, and before it, by a certain strain within Christianity, then a politics of privilege is necessary to shore up institutions of height, the importance of which phenomenology, ordinary language, and social practice confirm. Unless shored up, equalitarianism will eat away at privilege and therewith dignity. Humanitarianism is contradictory: emancipating us from intrinsic moral claims it purports to enhance our dignity; yet we end up diminished and subject to arbitrary power.

An upshot of "consensual intuitionism" is the implication that no one is sovereign respecting morality; we rely decisively on others. The emancipation of progressive or humanitarian democracy does not have this character, however. Rather than showing deference to intrinsic moral claims, humanitarianism asserts the radical sovereignty of man and its banner is equality. Equality because only if one is equal to others is one free, unlimited. Intrinsic moral claims assert precedence over human will but finding this intolerable, Dworkin, for example, forsakes constitutionalism. The claims of the hierarchy of value are set socially in sites of privilege. Political subversion is moral subversion, unlimitedness hostile to intrinsicalism, limit, mutual accommodation, and pluralism. A constitution, no matter how formally perfect, is impotent if moral subversion is afoot. It is our daily accommodations to the spectator, as we busy ourselves in ordinary life, which is in fact the genuine constitutionalism upon which all constitutional documents and rule of law rest.

Notes

1.   H. Berman, *Law and Revolution: The Formation of the Western Legal Tradition* (Cambridge, MA: Harvard University Press, 1983), passim, but especially pp. 181-3, 190, 529, & 539 (hereafter = PR); European jurisprudence is "the child of the medieval school" (F. Schulz, *History of Roman Legal Science* [Oxford: Oxford University Press, 1946], pp. 22-23; 61). Lord Justice Brooke, [2000] H.R.L.R. 721, *786 (I discuss this case at length in the seventh chapter). Upholding the state bans on assisted suicide in 1997, the Supreme Court of the United States cited evidence that for the past 700 years "the Anglo-American common law tradition" forbade suicide and assisted suicide (WSJ, September 13, 2005 [A4]); "F. Swancara, "Medieval Theology in Modern Criminal Law," *Journal of the American Institute of Criminal Law and Criminology*, Vol. 20: 4 (1930), p. 489; S. Uniacke, *Permissible Killing: The Self-Defence Justification of Homicide* (Cambridge, MA: Cambridge University Press, 1994), p. 57; P. Nemo, *What is the West?* (Pittsburgh, PA: Duquesne University Press, 2006), c. 4.

2. There are deep reasons for this: see Schmitt's claim that so long as there is politics there will be theology (CP, 64-65).
3. W. Smith, *The Culture of Death* (San Francisco: Encounter Books, 2000), pp. 15 & 16.
4. H. Arkes, *Natural Rights & the Right to Choose*, p. 145; henceforth = NR.
5. A. Scalia, *McCreary County v. ACLU* (June 2005). Cf. J. Ratzinger, *Homily at the Mass for the Election of the Supreme Pontiff* (April 2005); Benedict XVI, *Regensburg Address* (September 2006); and the collection of essays from a *First Things* symposium, *End of Democracy?* (Dallas: Spence, 1997).
6. I present my understanding of Thomas'anthropology in EM where I show why his view is less violent that those of post-structuralist theorists.
7. This is a theme of the work of Manent, a thinker influenced by Kolnai. Amongst many titles, see, for example, his *A World beyond Politics?* (Princeton, NJ: Princeton University Press, 2006).
8. P. Singer, *Rethinking Life and Death: The Collapse of Our Traditional Ethics* (New York: St. Martin's Press, 1994), p. 190; henceforth = RLD.
9. And, actually, it is not so nice. Singer dedicates RLD to Helga Kuhse with whom he has written a book. She argues that dehydration is a painful way to kill, thus immoral, and so doctors should move to intentional killing by lethal injection (W. Smith, *Forced Exit* [New York: Random House, 1997], p. 65).
10. Cicero, *Murder Trials* (London: Penguin, 1990), pp. 34-7 amongst others.
11. Elders played an enormous role adjudicating proportionate response even in the Icelandic/Germanic revenge cultures, which permitted private killings (A. Smith, *Lectures on Jurisprudence* [Indianapolis, IN: Liberty Fund, 1982], pp. 106-12). Cf. W. Miller, *Eye for an Eye* (Cambridge: Cambridge University Press, 2005), p. 9; and Berman on *moots* (PR, 56 & 60).
12. See the stunning scenario by Richard John Neuhaus, "A Philosopher from Nowhere," *First Things*, No. 120 (February 2002), pp. 180-1: Parents exhausted through caring for their two-year-old autistic child take the child to be "put to sleep" at the hospital. These slippery slope scenarios are always dismissed as simple scaremongering. Why people react in this way to such arguments is baffling. You only need to read a court opinion to see the slope getting very slippery indeed; see the case examined in the seventh chapter, for example. A perfect illustration of how quickly law expands to take in new and significantly different cases is offered by the history of ATCA (see the article cited below at n. 32). For how quickly the Dutch have extended killing innocents to very different kinds of cases, see W. Smith, *Forced Exit*, c. 4.
13. P.J. Proudhon, *What is Property?* (Cambridge: Cambridge University Press, 2007), pp. 136-40. Some such logic probably underwrites Singer's well-known argument for the West's obligation to the world's poor. He certainly claims anarchist heritage for his overall philosophical position.
14. B. Akinrinade, "International Humanitarian Law and the Conflict in Sierra Leone," *Notre Dame Journal of Law, Ethics & Public Policy*, Vol. 15: 2 (2001), p. 397.
15. See L. Saunders, "Rich and Rare Are the Gems They Wear: Holding De Beers Accountable for Trading Conflict Diamonds," *Fordham International Law Journal*, Vol. 24 (2001), pp. 1402-76; hereafter, RR.
16. "Conflict Diamonds" www.zalecorp.com/corporate/corporate.aspx?pid=108 (12/28/2006).
17. "U. S. Officials, Alarmed by New Film, Call Efforts to Eliminate Conflict Diamonds Successful," www.news.findlaw.com/scripts (12/28/2006).
18. "Press Release from World Vision," www.csrwire.com/synd/business-ethics/article. cgi/7029.html (12/28/2006).

19. "Diamonds Whose Price Is Measured in Blood," *Guardian* (October 18, 2004).
20. B. Akinrinade, "International Humanitarian Law and the Conflict in Sierra Leone," p. 397.
21. "Between a Rock and a Hard Place," WSJ, February 4-5, 2006 (B1).
22. "Making a Killing: The Business of War," www.thirdworldtraveler.com/Weapons/Conflict_Diamonds_MAK.html (12/28/2006), p. 2; hereafter, MK.
23. "Action Update" www.amnestyusa.org/business/survey_press.html (12/28/2006).
24. "Amnesty Press Release (November 2006)" www.csrwire.com/synd/business-ethics/article.cgi/6951.html (12/28/2006).
25. "A `Good Deed' for AIDS Drug Hits Obstacles," WSJ, June 30, 2006 [B1].
26. A. Bryant Banat, "Solving the Problem of Conflict Diamonds in Sierra Leone: Proposed Market Theories and International Legal Requirements for Certification of Origin," *Arizona Journal of International and Comparative Law*, Vol. 19:3 (2002), p. 946.
27. RR, 1413-14.
28. Ibid., p. 949; citing a *Financial Times* article.
29. Ibid., p. 963.
30. Typical of the claims made: "Particularly, the United States, as the largest importer of cut diamonds, owes a duty of reform to the citizens of Sierra Leone" (A. Bryant Banat, "Solving the Problem of Conflict Diamonds in Sierra Leone: Proposed Market Theories and International Legal Requirements for Certification of Origin," p. 974).
31. There is enormous interest in using the 1789 Alien Tort Claims Act for legal remedy. The act is very interesting philosophically. Oftentimes described as "obscure," this old piece of American legislation is now drawing intense scrutiny. For how it might be applied to the diamond trade, L. Saunders, "Rich and Rare Are the Gems They Wear: Holding De Beers Accountable for Trading Conflict Diamonds," *Fordham International Law Journal,* Vol. 24 (2001), pp. 1402-76; hereafter, RR.
32. Contemporary Western invocation of the *ius gentium* warrants skepticism since it is typically nothing like the *ius gentium* as understood by de Vitoria. See the disturbing idea of the *ius cogens* and how some seek to employ it in international trade (T. Donaldson & T. Dunfee, *The Ties That Bind* [Cambridge, MA: Harvard Business School Press, 1999]).
33. Consider the case of Patricia Dunn, Chair of the Board of Directors at Hewlett Packard. Establishing a probe of directors, the private detectives used by Dunn employed borderline legal methods. In the controversy that followed, Dunn was forced to resign but not the CEO Hurd. He knew about the probe but, since he was not managing the probe, not about the details. Dunn was forced to resign because she failed to ask tougher questions about techniques used by the detectives. She was judged negligent, I suggest, because intuitively people grasped her ignorance vincible, Hurd's invincible. See the rash of articles in WSJ and elsewhere, September 2006.
34. The difficulties involved in the idea of being held responsible for complicity—to the point of capital punishment especially—is why Hannah Arendt's *Eichmann in Jerusalem* remains a classic work.
35. For example, it is true about Yuri the gunrunner in *Lord of War*.
36. An interesting example is the case of wine merchant, Louis Eschenauer. See the interesting chapter, "The Collaborator," in D. & P. Kladstrup, *Wine and War* (New York: Broadway, 2002).
37. "Between a Rock and a Hard Place."

38. On the importance of trust to the social fabric, see *De malo*, q. 13, a. 4, ad 13, and Kolnai's "Forgiveness," p. 223.
39. A Humean might deny even this, doubting the role causality is supposed to play.
40. For a recent Catholic example, see "Worthiness to Receive Holy Communion: General Principles" (Congregation for the Doctrine of the Faith [June 2004]).
41. For my understanding of Thomas' treatment of the moral object, and how it relates to value theory, please see my, "Two Case Studies in Schelerian Moral Theology: The Vatican's 2005 'Instruction' and Gay Marriage," *Nova et Vetera: The English Edition of the International Theological Journal*, Vol. 6: 1 (2008), pp. 205-17.
42. Kolnai is probably right that over time a constant failure to live up to the positive precepts will diminish our capacity to do even the strictest duties. See his essay, "Are There Degrees of Ethical Universality?" *Exploring the World of Human Practice: Readings in and about the Philosophy of Aurel Kolnai* (Budapest: CEU Press, 2004), pp. 83-94.
43. P.-J. Proudhon, *What is Property?* (Cambridge: Cambridge University Press, 2007), p. 13.
44. The way was prepared for Hitler by German intellectuals constantly belittling ordinary life. For defense of this thesis, see L. Strauss, "German Nihilism," *Interpretation*, Vol. 26:3 (1999): 353-78.
45. Miller's characterization of much contemporary leftism strikes me as just right (*Eye for an Eye*, pp. 168-88).
46. Just consider the disappointment with the *ius gentium*, a record of customary human life globally, and the fascination with the *ius cogens*, an attempt to build international law from elite centers of opinion.
47. R. Dworkin, "Liberalism," *A Matter of Principle* (Oxford: Oxford University Press, 1986), p. 191.
48. See the kingly code of Ur-Namma, circa 2100 B. C. (W. Miller, *Eye for an Eye*, pp. 56-7).
49. Singer is refreshingly honest that abortion is the killing of the innocent but argues, not as a matter of freedom, but as a matter of justice, that the innocent should sometimes be killed and that a ready community standard exists to help us understand when—utilitarianism (RLD, c. 5).
50. For a study of the ordinary in Aquinas' ethics, see T. Hibbs, *Aquinas, Ethics, & Philosophy of Religion* (Bloomington, IN: Indiana University Press, 2007).
51. In his collection *Ethics, Value and Reality* (New Brunswick, NJ: Transaction Publishers, 2008).
52. For Bentham's hostility to elevated positions, see J. Bentham, *A Fragment on Government* (Cambridge: Cambridge University Press, 2001), p. 13.

2

State Privilege to Kill

Whether It Is Lawful to Kill Sinners

Aquinas argues that public authority alone may intentionally kill the guilty but never the innocent. Departing radically from this Thomistic principle, defenses of abortion and euthanasia request that public authority permit individuals to kill innocents on private authority. Indeed, when these defenses claim that abortion and euthanasia are "rights" they make no request of public authority at all but assert a right to kill on private authority alongside the public authority to kill.[1] Though this chapter discusses (and wonders at) Catholic pressures on Thomas' second article, it comes as no surprise that liberalism wants to see the dismantling of the privilege of public authority. The heart of liberal theory is the dissolution of the hierarchical relationship between ruler and ruled. Modern liberalism aims to make each individual simultaneously ruler and ruled.[2] What more profound way to do this is there than to grant individuals the private authority of intentional killing and thereby make them equal, or even superior, to the state? Russell Hittinger's response to liberalism is that political order cannot endure when authority to kill passes from public to private.[3] Is this convincing? From abortion to dehydration of very sick patients, homicide permitted on private authority is common throughout the Western world and yet political order remains.

Hadley Arkes wrestles with this phenomenon in an interesting way. Agreeing with Hittinger, Arkes argues that America remains, in outward form, a republic but in its essence it has slid into tyranny.[4] Arkes' approach to the conflation of public and private authority to kill is fascinating. But it is puzzling that Arkes does not seem to appreciate the most basic principle upon which his argument rests. Nor, I fear, and this will be the focus of this chapter, does the Catholic critique of Aquinas on capital punishment. A natural law theorist like Hittinger is very Thomistic in seeing the problem with our political order as an unjustifiable transference of the public authority to kill to private individuals. Hittinger stresses the *consequence* of this transference but is less clear about exactly why in principle the transference is illicit. Arkes approaches the problem with, if one can put it this way, a nativist logic.

Taking his cue from American Revolutionary jurisprudence, Arkes argues that since American government rests on the premise that "all men are created equal" government can only be by the consent of a free people. Any law or legislation that would entail the enslavement of a part of the people, and even more obviously, any legislation that would kill some is fundamentally at odds with the foundational political logic of the American republic.[5] It would not be government but tyranny.

Applying the argument, Arkes claims that the "new regime's abortion jurisprudence" (Hittinger) is thus not merely "something radically new in the western tradition" (NR, 67) it is nothing less than treasonable (NR, 147). Abortion law, through which innocents are killed on private authority, is not law to which a free people "created equal" can consent. Arkes argues that because abortion jurisprudence must reject natural rights, for these attach to humans *on account of their being*, abortion jurisprudence has annulled in principle the foundation for all rights. Since rights are now positive law rights, in the gift of the state or the majority, "partisans of the 'right to abortion,'" Arkes concludes, "cannot protect any longer my life, my freedoms, my rights, against the most arbitrary takings and restrictions" (NR, 173). Under such government a people has ceased to be a free people.

As a matter of dark fact, of course, Arkes points out that Americans have never consented to the abortion jurisprudence. As doctrine of the court, which in 1973 flew in the face of all but three states' laws,[6] the legislatures of the people have been prohibited (directly) to consider the issue as open. Arkes explains:

> ...looking back on the 1960s and 1970s...the threat to the lives of unborn children did not come principally from the laws in the states. It would become clear that the threat did not emanate from the states, but from the federal government: It emanated from that branch of the federal government whose decisions went unnoticed as interventions of the federal government and the flexing of federal power. (NR, 214)

Rejecting legal positivism, Arkes seeks limited government on the basis of man as a political creature who requires a certain political order to serve his nature. Unsurprisingly, Arkes is as vulnerable at this point as Thomas, and for the same reason. Arkes is clearly critical of privilege. His defense of Lockean natural rights is to insist on a basic equality between adult and child: equality rejects a scenario wherein "the mother decide[s] to confer upon her [child] the privilege of living" (NR, 179). Yet, as Peter Singer points out, rights thinking based upon a theory of human essence is "speciesism," that is, a theory of privilege. As shown in the fifth chapter, liberty requires privilege and Arkes is right to sense this (albeit confusedly). He does not name the privilege upon which his own jurisprudence depends, however, and this makes his work vulnerable to Singer, there is an unexamined, and undefended, assumption.

It is not only Arkes' criticism of privilege which inadvertently under-mines his own position, for I fear that when contemporary Catholic social thought denounces privilege it manages to do the same. The concerns of Hittinger and Arkes are at one with Catholicism's reservations about liberalism and its supporting ethic, humanitarianism. Catholicism is wary because, as Chapter 3 and chapters 5 through 8 show, humanitarianism oftentimes stimulates more killings. A Thomist can hope to limit the damage humanitarianism causes by defending the principle that only public authority has the privilege to intentionally kill. Increasingly, Catholic thinkers have opted for a different strategy: deny that there is a private *or* public privilege to intentionally kill. Are Thomists now squeezed between humanitarians and other Catholics? Other chapters of this commentary are devoted to debating humanitarianism. Here, I engage Catholic criticisms of Thomas on state privilege. The typical arguments relied on by Catholics to alter the church's traditional support of capital punishment are not coherent. As far as I can see, there is not (yet) a *Catholic* basis for departing from Thomistic principle.

Not that Thomists have never had to fend off criticism from within the church. This is not a new problem. For example, in his Scotistic commentary on Aquinas' *Summa*, the Franciscan Hieronymus de Mon-tefortino (d. circa 1740) in a brief discussion of Question 64 disagrees with Thomas' jurisprudence. Montefortino's argument has the flavor of contemporary Catholic humanitarianism. Commenting on Aquinas' third article—whether it is licit for a private person to kill a sinner—he first raises the bar for killing as such and then lowers it to allow anyone to kill the sinner. Thomas considers an objection where it is argued that it is worse to kill a sinner than someone who is innocent. If those guilty of murder can be killed they will have no time for repentance and redemp-tion denied them. With a theological sentiment that can only outrage today, Thomas tersely responds (a. 6, ad. 2) that when it comes to terrestrial justice how someone stands in relationship to judgment in heaven is beside the point. Montefortino insists, by contrast, that no one should will the bodily death of a sinner for to die a sinner closes off the possibility of conversion to a love of God. However, Montefortino continues, it is possible to will the bodily death of a sinner *sub conditione*, namely, if one believes the life of the sinner is shut up amidst evil (*si credat eum clausum vitam in malitia*). This condition sets up a higher threshold for homicide than the Thomistic "for the common good" principle (a. 2, ad 2), and it is common to hear this reasoning today (EV, para. 56). Yet, with a subtle change of words, and a most unscholastic failure to invoke distinctions, Montefortino promptly lowers the bar. Montefortino gives de Vitoria's interpretation of Scotus—which is interesting in that de Vitoria comments that unnamed Scotists dispute his reading (H, 139-41)—namely, homicide is prohibited by God save in those cases where God gives an exception (*nisi excipiatur casus*).[7] There is, thus, no *natural* law justification for homicide but divine positive law can grant a legitimate power to kill (*iuste homo occiditur per legitimam potestam*). Here, perhaps, the idea of legitimate power is supposed to carry *the sense of* public authority but nowhere is this said and no distinctions invoked. Indeed, Montefortino closes his comments with the classic test case of whether one can kill on private authority—tyrannicide—and with little nuance he affirms such a homicide.[8] Having abandoned the restrictions of natural law for humanitarian reasons, the Franciscan concludes on a revolutionary note with (God's) positive law standing surety.

In his 2006 Regensburg Address, Benedict XVI re-affirmed the role of natural reason in moral theology and expressed grave concern about revolutionary application to (divine) positive law.[9] A warning to the Montefortinos of the world then, requiring us to ask: Has Catholic criticism of Thomas developed compelling and coherent *reasons* for rejecting the principle that public authority has the privilege of intentional killing?

The *Catechism* states it is an absolute moral law that it is gravely immoral to deliberately or directly kill the innocent (para. 2258 & 2261). In a somewhat odd formula, the *Catechism* says it is "the murder of the innocent that constitutes intentional killing" (para. 2263). Is it implied that one cannot intentionally kill the guilty? The *Catechism* immediately follows this definition of intentional killing with a quote from Thomas' famous passage on double effect in the seventh article. Doing so seems to suggest that war and capital punishment are always matters of self-defense, the intention being protection of the self and the death of the guilty a non-intended but foreseen side effect. Thus later (para. 2268) the fifth commandment is said to forbid *"direct and intentional killing* as gravely sinful."* If this is the claim, it is not in continuity with the argument of Thomas and Vitoria. Humanitarian wars are wars of choice,[10] and many of the justifications Vitoria gave for war (e.g., trade) are not matters of self-defense. And Aquinas argues that punishment, including capital punishment, concerns expiation not self-defense. The root justification of punishment is not the same as most wars. Indeed Scheler, and I discuss this later, offers an argument that punishment for the sake of self-defense cannot be moral.

The *Catechism*'s formulation sits ill with Question 64 itself: Why would Thomas only introduce double effect theory in the seventh article when, according to para. 2268, it is basic to understanding his second article? Thomas turns to double effect in the matter of self-defense (the only place Thomas uses the idea in his treatise on homicide and nor is it found when he treats of war) because killing in self-defense does not fit the logic of his basic contention that public authority is necessary for killing.[11] It is especially odd that the *Catechism*—but all these same problems are present in the famous paragraph 56 of *Evangelium Vitae*—relies on Thomas' treatment of self-defense as though it were definitive for state action. Thomas' discussion of self-defense as a killing on private authority concerns cases where the state is absent. It is strange in the extreme to transfer Thomas' analysis for action when the state is absent to a model of state action. I explore all these problems more below.

I do not think it outlandish to say that I imagine the authors of the *Catechism* did not mean to be out of step with Aquinas, but they are. Thomas does clearly argue that public authorities may intentionally kill. Question 64 begins by asking: May one kill animals? The answer is "yes" because the imperfect are for the sake of the perfect. The same hierarchical principle acts as the premise of the second article. Now unless someone wants to argue that Thomas did not tolerate the direct and intentional killing of animals it must be conceded that Thomas clearly envisioned the direct and intentional killing of guilty humans. The premise of both arguments is identical, as Thomas himself reminds us. Animals can be killed because they are imperfect. A guilty person makes himself imperfect by alienating his human dignity (*decidit a dignitate humana*) and can be killed on the grounds one kills an animal; hence, Thomas' words, "it may be good to kill a man who has sinned, even as it is to kill a beast." Alienating his dignity, a man enters "into the slavish state of the beasts, to be disposed of according as he is useful to others" (a. 2, ad 3). Having lost dignity, the criminal comes to have a use value that is impossible for one having dignity.[12] The importance of Thomas' words regarding dignity is discussed later—they are easily misunderstood—but it is enough for the moment to conclude that, for Thomas, there is no role for double effect when we kill an animal and nor, therefore, a guilty man. This is why Thomas does not mention double effect until the seventh article and nowhere in de Vitoria's fascinating discussion of hunting is it mentioned. Thomas does think we kill criminals directly and intentionally.

Perhaps I am wrong, and despite quoting Thomas in places, the *Catechism* does mean to imply that Thomas is just mistaken. There are clear trends within contemporary Catholic commentary denying the tight association between intentional killing and public authority. I consider these trends in the four arguments that organize the rest of this chapter.

1. The first concerns John Paul II's justified reservations about Scheler, especially his concept of the person. I agree with the criticism that Scheler's is too "thin" a personalism. Prescinding from the ontological question,[13] I nonetheless argue that even following Scheler's social phenomenology examples exist that challenge his personalism. Arguing that Cain and Christ are a biblical response to the idea of the Greek *atimetos*, I contend that Scripture is the principal basis of the rule of law. However, the argument is also to offer a different theological reading of a part of *Genesis* used by John Paul II to support his opposition to capital punishment.

2. Catholic versions of the argument that no one may intentionally take human life are not cogent. I consider two versions: (ii a) capital punishment is forbidden by divine positive law or Evangelical law and (ii b) by the dignity of the human person. The argument of (ii a) is longstanding (PW, 296-7) but plays no direct role in EV 56. If (ii b) is the basis of EV 56, then—given other stated imperatives there, like public safety—the passage is contradictory. It fails Wojtyla's "personalist norm" (cf. *Love and Responsibility*) *unless* John Paul II relies heavily on double effect or stays closer to Thomas on dignity than typically appreciated. If the former, then Schmitt and Scheler both, though for very different reasons, harry his argument. Should the latter underwrite the passage then Aquinas holds the field and John Paul II's concerns are prudential only and not a matter of principle.

3. Finnis' two arguments for why Thomas' position is contradictory both fail. Thomas' argument is far stronger than detractors suppose and, since it stems from Thomas' deepest convictions about action and morality, dissenting from the argument is really to disagree with Thomistic ethics *tout court*. One can do this, of course, but Thomas' argument does lend rational support to a moral consensus view that the *ius gentium* recognizes the licitness of capital punishment.

4. This moral consensus view can also claim support from (iv a) the theory of punishment Scheler and Thomas share. What is strange about EV 56 is its failure to clarify a general theory of punishment. I argue that Thomas and Scheler share a theory of punishment as bodily retribution. Moreover, such a theory is congruent with John Paul II's *Theology of the Body* and *Veritatis Splendor*. This theory (iv b) refutes two arguments against capital punishment made by Camus. Against Camus, the theory argues that his Stoic downgrading of the role of emotion in moral knowledge is unwarranted and that he confuses law and morality, on the one hand, state and person, on the other. It might be put graphically, but there is some truth to de Maistre's comment that but for the hangman, "order yields to chaos, thrones collapse, and society disappears" (RG, 196-7). Camus mocks de Maistre's comment, yet if privilege sustains good social order, de Maistre makes a better point than might at first be thought. In short, in EM, I showed the pivotal role privilege plays in Catholic sexual politics. I wonder here whether John Paul the Great's 1995 critique of capital punishment does not inadvertently obscure basic hierarchies that he wants, and desperately needs, to support.

Arguing against relativism (1) Scheler insists that the *ethos* of every society—the fundamental moral tenor of a social order rooted in acts of love or hate (OA, passim)—is at one in regarding murder gravely immoral. It is not enough to note that different cultures have different rules about who can be killed, and when, for the crucial question always is: What does each culture think about killing a man—a creature in which "the value of the person" is given (F, 312)? Persons stand highest in the value hierarchy (F, 109) and so cannot be instrumentalized. Affirming the highest value when ethical decision is required, is, says Scheler, to choose the good. Persons cannot be made instruments of utility (profit) or vital values (nationalism) because these values are lower in the hierarchy. Crude utilitarianism or biologisms of different stripes fail this test but not Singer's preference utilitarianism. Surveying cultural norms, consensus exists, says Scheler, for all cultures agree that to kill a creature where this value is present is gravely immoral. Again, Singer would agree with Scheler: of course, I imagine him startled by Scheler's social phenomenology approach to identifying persons rather than Singer's cognitive psychology approach. Social phenomenology shows that warfare is not murder because to kill "the enemy" is to destroy a "vital value" not a personal value: the person does not straightforwardly emerge in the enemy (*hostis*) or the stranger (*hostis*).[14] In capital punishment, "the value of the person" is given but given under the perspective of immortality. Capital punishment, argues Scheler, has always been understood not as an annihilation of the person but the removal of a good from the person, earthly existence (F, 313-314; RG, 223).[15] For this reason, when Europe was Christian capital punishment was not viewed as murder. Scheler has undeniably captured something of the essence of murder. In another example, Scheler notes that abortion has never been punished as murder (F, 315) because personality or "the value of the person" is not given in our experience of the unborn.[16] In later Victorian England, maternal killing of children under the age of one often only led to convictions of manslaughter or even just concealment of birth.[17] In the common law, abortion is punished *as far as the mother is concerned* as a misprision: a wrongful act.[18] Of course, in England, since the introduction of statutes permitting and promoting abortion even the direct intentional killing of *born* children is now permitted: crucial justifications being found in abortion.[19] Scheler's observation is also the basis of Peter Singer's attempts to have the laws of homicide relaxed for a variety of categories of humans, though not persons (of any species).

Scheler certainly has identified some important social phenomenological evidence for his contention. Missing from Scheler's account, however, are some complicating factors: What role do the values of innocence, the privilege (or otherwise) of public authority, and rule of law play in shaping the value of personality? There appears to be little appreciation (and this is surprising) that the values of personality, innocence, and public authority, are intricately woven. Ancient Greece supplies an interesting confirmation of Scheler's claim but also points beyond Scheler to the complexity involved in the ascription of the value of personality. The Greek *atimetos metanastes* (*Iliad* 9, 648 & 16, 59)—"an alien wanderer, with no relatives at hand to demand the atonement"—though a freeman, could be killed, outraged, and oppressed with impunity.[20] Cast from the rule of law, the *atimetos* is punished by being placed outside of revenge networks where proportionality flourished: it flourished because families were well aware of the cost of pressing an exaggerated claim and also because elders acted as a public authority.[21] Assuming Scheler's thesis, here, it must be the case that personality is tied to kinship, a matter of being able to give pedigree (think here of Beowulf's long introduction of himself to the Danes or how this theme is seen in Tolkien's *The Hobbit*). Even more basically, personality is tied to the protections afforded by revenge networks (TMS, 220). Interestingly, the Greek *atimetos* is akin to a concept of ancient Scottish law, the *landlouper*, where personality is tied even more dramatically to place.[22]

Though early Greek culture seems to have been relatively little bothered about homicide,[23] to outrage the guest with pedigree was censured vehemently as the *atimetos* counter-concept testifies.[24] Here is the beginning of something developed thoroughly in Judaeo-Christianity. The sanctity of human life, and especially care for the lives of infants, is, we are reminded by Peter Singer, "a distinctively Judaeo-Christian attitude rather than a universal ethical value" (PE, 125). Whilst he desperately wishes us to jettison this parochial way of thinking, we may pause. For if Western culture is a combination of Athens and Jerusalem, the contribution of Jerusalem must be weighed. For in contrast to the Greek *atimetos metanastes, Genesis* begins with Cain in despair at God's punishment for his murdering Abel, "and I shall be a fugitive and a wanderer on the earth, and whoever finds me will slay me" (Gn 4: 14). This does not happen for God anoints Cain, "the Lord put a mark on Cain, lest any who came upon him should kill him" (Gn 4: 15). If we have here an Hebraic rejection of the Greek *atimetos metanastes*—and the concept of the *atimetos* must have been a common cultural form (PR, 61) for becoming such is what Cain himself fears—a deep significance of the *Genesis* passage emerges.

In *Evangelium Vitae*, John Paul II sees in this passage a general prohibition of killing and, in particular, a biblical basis for reservations about capital punishment (EV, para. 9). John Paul II quotes Saint Ambrose's *De Cain et Abel*: "God, who preferred the correction rather than the death of a sinner, did not desire that a homicide be punished by the exaction of another act of homicide." Perhaps the meaning of *Genesis* 4:15 is not so sweeping: Might not *Genesis* cast the anointing as a protection from homicide on private authority? Note that Cain's worry is that "*whoever* finds me will slay me" and God's anointing is a protection "lest *any* who came upon him should kill him." The scope of the "whoever" and "any" is not all persons but specific to those who just happen across the wanderer's path. It is possible—indeed, the most likely reading is—to cast Cain's anointing as an early cultivation of the privilege of killing only on public authority: an outlawing of the killing of the murderer by any who might chance upon him; a prohibition of vigilantism. This is how Blackstone reads the passage.[25] At the same time, the anointing is an extension of the protection of the law to the stranger, the *landlouper* who has no pedigree of family or place, no testimony to give of his origins. It is an amplification of the Greek sacrality of the guest to a new sacrality of the stranger.[26]

A central focus of Christ's teaching is the welcoming and aiding of the stranger (Dupuis) but it is little appreciated to what degree Cain is an early figuring of Jesus himself. Augustine emphasized the figuring of Jesus in Abel but, in a certain respect, the same can be said of Cain.

It is not, of course, that Jesus is a murderer but the Incarnation makes him like Cain. He is a "wanderer on the earth," a *landlouper* provoking wonder: "We do not know where he comes from" (Jn 9: 29). Christ tells us His kingdom "is not of this world" (Jn. 19: 36) and "the Son of man has nowhere to lay his head" (Luke 9: 58). For this reason he becomes the *atimetos metanastes*, outraged and slain, "and the world treated him as a stranger" (Jn. 1: 10). But his homicide is a new anointing. For "his blood be on us and on our children" (Matt. 27: 25) is not a blood libel but a protection, a repeated promulgation of *Genesis* that the stranger has protection at law. His blood-anointing, the outraging of God, is a vouch-safing of the protection afforded the stranger; it is a new, universal, and definitive formulation of the hospitality principle. Even the guilty whose personality is gainsaid without pedigree or family receives protection of law.[27] The raised position of Easter is an extension of law so that no one now is a stranger to the law. A reflection of Easter, the raised position of public authority, elevates the stranger to the dignity of person. In no way is this elevation an obscuring of innocence and guilt: rather now the public trial of dignity can begin. Examined and cross-examined at trial, dignity intensifies both the value of the person and the disvalue of the *atimetos*, the *personal* forsaking of worth.

Henceforth public authority must be invoked before we may be slain (note in Luke Christ warns that divine condemnation will be prefaced with the words, "I don't know where you come from") and so this is also a biblical rejection of the Greek and early Germanic practice of private killing, or homicide as tort. Agreeing with Singer that there is something distinctively Judeo-Christian about this idea it might still be the case that a universal moral value is here announced, perhaps for the first time, but nonetheless a universal value at that. As Scheler shows, it is possible for an objective value to be given in "private revelation" (R, 97-8), in this case, a revelation in and through the church. For, does anyone seriously question that the protection of public authority extend-ing to the guilty and innocent stranger—changing *hostis* to *persona*—is preferable to the concept of the *atimetos*? More importantly, is this not what we mean by the rule of law? The role of the *atimetos metanastes* underwriting abortion law, for example, is clear enough, and its forma-tive role in abortion jurisprudence helps expose the corruption of the rule of law at the "heart" of humanitarianism.

The unexamined relationship between personality and the privilege of public authority causes difficulty in one of Scheler's own examples. He notes in certain combats the value of chivalry required "the person

expose himself to the same kind and degree of danger as he affords."
This was required whenever the value of the person was given with the
enemy combatant. Indeed, if the enemy fought well, one would "*affirm
the favour* of the *person* of the enemy" (F, 314; emphasis original).
Exactly what Scheler says was formalized in old naval sea battles. Both
captains would stand on their quarterdecks, typically a raised part of the
ship, and oftentimes before hostilities would acknowledge one another by
removing their hats or even waving them. If the enemy ship was taken,
and assuming a gallant fight, upon surrender the sword of the enemy
captain (if he lived) would be ceremonially returned to him. Scheler is
right, but the example is problematic. For by his theory, given that the
captain's person is so evidently present,[28] to kill him in battle ought to
be counted morally as murder. Yet, such was obviously not the case: the
King's officers did not regard themselves as murderers and no one else
did either. One might argue that Scheler's point is similar to his comments about capital punishment. The enemy captain was deprived of the
good of life under the aspect of immortality. But this only helps reinforce
what is missing from Scheler's account: a privilege of intentional killing
was exercised by the king's officers such that battle or execution is not
murder. The presence of the value of personality may have something to
do with the essence of murder but it is essential to know what cultural,
other moral, and institutional factors, *genetically* enter the value of the
person. The point is recognized by another phenomenologist. Soldiers,
Sokolowski notes, do not "establish the original moral categoriality" by
which they are ordered to hurt the enemy. This is established by government and public authority. Hence, old enemies might meet at a reunion
to chat about an old battle, quite without resentment, whilst there would
certainly not be some jolly old reminiscences with someone who had
attempted to murder you on the street.[29]

So far demonstrated is that Gen. 4:15 does not have the significance
thought by John Paul II. Instead of a biblical prohibition against capital
punishment, the passage points to a theological intensification of the rule
of law, extending the value of personality to the stranger, that is, the raised
position of public authority increases the dignity even of the guilty.

(2) John Finnis takes capital punishment as the benchmark of whether
public authority can intentionally kill. Thomas thinks such authority exists (A, 280)[30] but, according to Finnis, he is wrong (A, 282-3). Police
action and soldiers use lethal force but the intention is self-defense even
though the lethal side effect is foreseen (A, 284 & 286). "It seems clear,"
states Finnis, "that if choosing to kill—killing with intent to kill—cannot

be justified as a form of capital punishment, it cannot be justified at all" (A, 286). Finnis expresses a fairly common sentiment found in much Catholic commentary. Oftentimes this sentiment yields the argument (a) that the ethics of killing cannot be understood in isolation from Christ. Some observe that Aquinas' account of just war falls within his treatise on charity. Evangelical law guides war, they conclude, and so, strictly speaking, there is no *natural* theory of war at all. I examine critically the basis of this approach to Thomas—it rests upon a particular understanding of nature and grace—in the fourth chapter.

Noted already is Thomas' use of the same premise for his arguments why humans can kill animals and why public authority can kill the guilty. If the "evangelical insight" argument is right, it seems reasonable to expect Thomas to justify hunting by "evangelical insight." He does not do so: surely, Singer is right that Jesus shows a Jewish indifference to animals so concerned is He for humans.[31] Vitoria shows that the licitness of hunting cannot be separated from issues in property law. Does Thomas have a treatise on property law? Do theologians write property law textbooks on the basis of the New Testament? Does Thomas' famous comment at ST II-II, q. 66, a. 7 stem from evangelical insight? Rather, the argument is that "extreme necessity" suspends ordinary property law and the natural law principle that lower things are for the sake of higher—physical goods for persons—excuses theft. I discuss the necessity defense in relation to homicide in the seventh chapter. What is important here is Thomas' excuse of theft in crisis on the same hierarchical principle used to justify killing animals and criminals. Even if Thomas' argument had an origin in evangelical law, it would still be crucial to note that the ordinary course of property is suspended in crisis. But the extreme, crisis moment does not *define* the ordinary course of human, or property, relations (CM, 70-1).

This idea of "evangelical insight" sits ill with the praise Aquinas thinks due to the brave soldiers who fight for the common good. Following Aristotle, he observes a moral consensus in republics as well as monarchies that soldiers, "who fight bravely in battle are honored both while they live and after death. But honor is the reward of virtue." For "virtue is concerned with what is greatest and best...fortitude especially deals with death that takes place in battle" (Comm. NE, III, l. 14, n. 538-9). This argument from moral consensus, de Vitoria repeats in relation to hunting (H, 125). A consensus exists, he says, that hunting is "honorable"—it stands amongst the *res honestas*, and more particularly, *inter honestas voluptates* (H, 122-4). As I argue in the fourth chapter, this sort of "evangelical" argument seeks to reduce law to one kind of law, but it ignores the variety of law accepted in Catholic tradition. As de Vitoria points out, different human activities, their occasion and scope, fall under different kinds of law, and thus emphases: eternal, natural, common, positive law divine and human, custom, and the law of nations.[32]

This is only one type of argument used to challenge Thomas' conviction that capital punishment is "praiseworthy and advantageous" (*aliquis homo...laudabiliter et salubriter occiditur* [ST II-II, q. 64, a. 2]). EV 56 relies heavily, as do statements of the Catholic Bishops of the United States,[33] on (b) "the dignity of the human person" as a control on the use of capital punishment. This phrase is taken from the *Catechism*'s para. 2267 where the argument also continues: When non-lethal means are "sufficient to defend and protect people's safety," lethal means must not be employed. John Paul II adds that executions should only happen "in cases of absolute necessity...when it would not be possible otherwise to defend society" (EV, para. 56).

How can EV 56 combine human dignity and public safety arguments coherently? The argument is incoherent if human dignity is an ontological invariant of absolute value. If lethal means are necessary, does public safety trump human dignity? Human life is made to serve "safety," which is not even a *moral* value. Schmitt is surely right when he uses the idea of public safety as a norm for sovereign decision and understands it to have no reference whatsoever to morality (PT, 6 & 9). The exact reasoning of EV 56 is never stated, but at this point one could imagine an application to double effect theory. Uncanny is the similarity with the position of John Finnis: human life is a basic good; on *his* Thomist theory no one can ever intentionally destroy a basic good (no preference between basic goods can rationally be made);[34] so it is gravely immoral to intentionally kill; and for public security demands, a promiscuous recourse to double effect theory is possible. The promiscuity, of course, stems from taking Thomas' use of double effect in the case of an absence of government and making this case definitive for government action. Naturally, Thomas' logic of homicide is utterly twisted out of all recognition. Howsoever this maybe, the reasoning is extremely vulnerable to Anscombe's chilling words. About those who maintain an absolute prohibition on intentional killing but allow public authority nonetheless to have recourse to killing through some use of double effect, she wrote, "someone who can fool himself into this twist of thought will fool himself into justifying anything, however atrocious, by means of it."[35]

This sort of argument suffers from a pincer movement by philosophical opponents. Schmitt turns one flank, questioning whether the idea of public safety has any moral content, and Scheler turns the other, questioning how persons can be instrumentalized. A case requiring capital punishment would be, John Paul II says, when the community could not otherwise be protected. This reasoning is a marked departure from Wojtyla's own "personalist norm." Wojtyla's principle for how to correctly judge relations amongst persons rests on recognizing the "distinct personal ends" of those with whom one is interacting and thus excludes using the other as a means or instrument to an end (LR, 27-8; VS, para. 48). Of course, it is possible to salvage John Paul II's argument that "when push comes to shove" capital punishment is permissible. Coherence is gained if one argues that human dignity rightly understood is an absolute control on lethal state action, i.e., innocence, and for those who alienate their dignity capital punishment is permissible. Adopting Thomas' position is more coherent and saves one from a Finnis-like collapse into Schmitt's realism or rank instrumentalization.

(3) So many commentators point out the problems with Finnis' Thomism that I will only address his two arguments on why Thomas is wrong that public authority can intentionally kill. He points out that, for Thomas, it is licit for public authority to kill (A, 280) and also to enslave, beat, and mutilate (A, 281, n. 43). Thomas, he says, tightly ties injustice to punishing or harming the innocent. Finnis is irked by Thomas' claim that some guilty of crime have alienated their dignity. Thomas says that a man who "departs from the order of reason" alienates "the dignity of his manhood"—immediately explaining, Thomas continues, "in so far as he is naturally free, and exists for himself" (a. 2, ad 3). Coming under the criminal law, a man no longer exists for himself. As Thomas puts it (ScG II, c. 47, para. 4), a man's lordship of himself is a matter of rational liberty. At the heart of Thomas' personalism is the distinction between *actus humanus* and *actus hominis* (AP, 66-7; 70; De malo, q. 2, a. 4). A person does moral evil when he departs from the order of reason, that is, reason no longer shapes his appetites, and failure in virtue follows. Finnis objects to the claim that a man who loses dignity comes to the "status of the beasts" (A, 282). Yet, if at the heart of Thomas' entire action theory is the human act, and if crime destroys virtue making genuinely human acts impossible, then Thomas seems to be right, the human is reduced to appetite and thus animality. Thomas, of course, views humans as another kind of animal.[36] So far as I can see, Finnis takes this idea of alienation as establishing the *authority* to kill, but this is wrong, because it only

works to pick out who can be killed. Privilege gives authority, loss of dignity the target, to speak bluntly. Target and not authority because in war, given its different rationales, authority to kill remains but the principles of target selection differ (PW, 295-327).

I think it inevitable that Finnis radically misunderstands Thomas at this point because he thinks that liberty is "not inseparably connected to basic human goods."[37] Thomas thinks just the opposite: liberty is the basic human good. Churchill is closer to Thomas than Finnis. Read Churchill's haunting passage—he was a POW at one time—on imprisonment and its conclusion: "a death sentence [is] far more merciful than a life sentence."[38]

To Finnis' mind, Thomas' dignity argument is wrong for two reasons. Thomas contradicts himself twice. First, dignity must remain if, as Thomas himself says, the sinner may not be killed without public authority (a. 3, ad 2). This counter-argument is a non-starter: public trial *establishes* that the criminal alienated his dignity, not the mob. And, if so, the criminal forgoes liberty, and like a beast is at the command of another. Not just of anyone, of course, but of the owner. Property law governs who can use a beast (a. 1, ad 3)—de Vitoria develops this point at length—and the criminal is the property of public authority. Property, not dignity, is the control. Aquinas ties punishment to vengeance (*vindicatio*) and is acutely aware of the connection between vengeance and property covered by the root *vindico*.[39]

For a second argument why Thomas contradicts himself, Finnis marshals the claim that dignity must persist in the criminal because the convict, even when sentenced to death, has moral liberty (human rights, according to Finnis). He derives this claim from Thomas' statement that those condemned to starve to death can eat smuggled food. The example does not have the implication Finnis thinks. Finnis claims that for Thomas the criminal may not resist punishment (A, 282, n. 45), but then falsely credits Thomas with the position: "In short, they [those condemned to death] are morally at liberty ['retain important human rights'] to avoid any act or omission which would contribute to their own death." Finnis relies on ST II-II, q. 69, a. 4. Treating the same problem (H, 179), de Vitoria's example is the Socratic one of a man condemned to death who has the possibility of escape. It is lawful for the prisoner to escape, but, adds de Vitoria, there is no obligation to do so, "and this is not to kill himself, but rather to patiently bear the sentence imposed upon him for his crime." It is this choice that Finnis casts as proof of the convict's dignity. According to de Vitoria, following trial public authority can pass a sentence of death on account of radical moral failure. This loss of dignity may well, at some later date, give way before a change of heart *and a retrieval of a life of virtue.* In de Vitoria's reasoning, it is the virtue of patience, a form of courage (ST, I-II, q. 61, a. 3), that points to the capacity for choice. Courage enables a choice about alternatives and the *virtuous* man awaits execution even though he might escape. Oddly, but predictably, Finnis' argument trades on a voluntarist theory of will. Camus argues that Greek law was more humane than our own for the condemned could choose suicide over execution (RG, 202). Finnis knows *this* "moral liberty" does not exist for Aquinas (a. 5; cf. I-II, q. 94, a. 2; II-II, q. 69, a. 4, ad 2). The choice countenanced by de Vitoria is a choice from within a life of virtue. Due process (a fourteenth-century phrase) is not invalidated on account of a change of heart. That someone re-attains a life of virtue, and thus dignity, after sentencing—which is all Thomas and de Vitoria imagine in these passages—does not warrant the idea Finnis trades upon. Thomas contradicts himself, says Finnis, because if in the jail a convict has the dignity of moral choice then he has always had this dignity of choice. Only a voluntarist could presume such, and not a virtue theorist, as the likes of Thomas and de Vitoria.

Bill Miller gives voice to something very deep (4) when he wonders how we ever came to think punishment needed a philosophical defense. Rather, he suggests, the shoe is on the other foot: it is for whoever doubts the morality of punishment to provide arguments.[40] There is, as Miller's comment suggests, something primordial about punishment. It is the body that speaks in punishment. Thomas and Scheler (iv a) share a theory of punishment as embodied justice; a theory that offers *support* for the moral consensus that capital punishment is (sometimes) licit.[41] I think EV 56 is so confusing because *Evangelium Vitae* is obscure on the question of punishment. Certainly, EV 56 speaks of "the primary purpose of punishment" being to "redress...disorder." This is in continuity with Thomas' idea that temporal power is commissioned with God's retribution and has the responsibility of restoring political, legal, and moral order once disturbed. Drawing on long tradition himself, Thomas cites Romans 13 in support [ST II-II, q. 108, a. 1, ad 1) and gives as a rationale of punishment that it operates *ad justitiae conservationem* (ST II-II, q. 108, a. 1). Absent completely from EV 56 is Aquinas' linking of vengeance and punishment (cf. de Vitoria [PW, 297-8]). Vengeance is medicinal, says Thomas, healing the sense of injury. This argument figures prominently in Scheler.

Thomas thinks that some types of sins are dangerous and must be punished (*Sed poenae praesentis vitae sunt magis medicinales; et ideo illis solis peccatis poena mortis infligitur quae in gravem perniciem aliorum cedunt* [ST II-II, q. 108, a. 3, ad 2]). What does he mean by "grave danger?" Certainly, a public safety argument suggests itself, though Thomas thinks there are limits to the role punishment plays in deterrence, some not being afraid of punishments (ST II-II, q. 108, a. 3). Perhaps "grave danger" points more to the question of *moral* order, and punishment to healing lesions made in this order. For the idea that the protection of society is the norm of punishment, one Catholic document turns to Aquinas: "[the] good of society, which becomes more peaceful through punishment of sinners" (ST II-II, q. 68, a. 1).[42] A very different understanding of Thomas emerges if we read "peaceful" as the pacification of emotion. This is Scheler's understanding of punishment. Crime stirs hatred, he argues, and the lesion in sympathy only healed by reprisal. Aquinas—and I say more about this in the sixth chapter—prefers to argue that crime stirs wrath (De malo, q. 12, aa. 2 & 4) but he shares Scheler's general point.[43] Thus, the criminal punished loses that liberty Thomas places at the heart of dignity: constrained both by being an object of wrath and, at a deep ontological level, by the nothingness of evil.

To examine the worth of Thomas on this matter is not to dissent from papal teaching. John Paul II's reflections on capital punishment are just that, reflections. In no way does he promulgate a new claim upon conscience in this regard, although *Evangelium Vitae* does include a number of claims upon conscience put in the strongest possible terms. At the end of his discussion of capital punishment there is no statement even coming close to one like the following:

> Therefore, by the authority which Christ conferred upon Peter and his Successors, and in communion with the bishops of the Catholic Church, *I confirm that the direct and voluntary killing of an innocent human being is always gravely immoral.* This doctrine, based upon that unwritten law which man, in the light of reason, finds in his own heart (cf. Rom 2:14-15), is reaffirmed by Sacred Scripture, transmitted by the Tradition of the Church and taught by the ordinary and universal Magisterium. (EV, 57; emphasis original)

This confirmation reaffirms the center of natural law homicide. For our purposes, of particular significance is the phrase "man, in the light of reason, finds in his own heart (cf. Rom 2:14-15)." For this phrase links three sources of moral knowledge: reason, heart, and scripture. It is an especially interesting phrase in light of Scheler's thesis on the role of the heart in moral cognition and Wojtyla's place in the Munich School.

Wojtyla's early book on sexual ethics, *Love and Responsibility*, relies heavily on Scheler's theory of value, and in particular the theory's hierarchy of value (LR, 121-5; 147-53).[44] Although Wojtyla always had reservations about Scheler's philosophy[45]—he regarded him as an "emotionalist" (AP, 233; 245)—he never abandoned his commitment to a hierarchy of value (*Laborem Exercens*, sections 9 & 13; *Dives in Misericordia*, section 5; CA, para. 45 & 47). At the center of Scheler's value ethics is the claim that our moral life is guided by a logic of the heart: that moral value is uniquely revealed to a moral sense of sentiment (OA, 98-99). Wojtyla agrees that the heart is a source of moral knowledge, and a source[46] that is "unique" (AP, 234). In 1969 Wojtyla writes: "The differentiation of feelings is not merely quantitative but also qualitative, and in this respect they come in a hierarchical order" (AP, 52; 232). The prohibition against intentionally killing the innocent is derivable from multiple sources of moral knowledge. Still, an important source is the moral logic of the heart.[47] The experience of values, says Wojtyla, is "a function of man's sensitivity," but he warns that human action must sometimes be "taken in the name of *bare truth* about good, in the name of values that are not felt" (AP, 233).

Significantly, the source of value in feeling is omitted in John Paul II's discussion of capital punishment. Like other followers of Scheler (e. g., Kolnai), Wojtyla had adopted a "moral con*sensus*" view of morality: without feeling, or what Wojtyla likes to call "sensitivity," there could, ultimately, be no right cognition of value (AP, 234; 247-8; 251). This omission in EV 56 is odd because John Paul II was surely aware that there is a continuity between Thomas' and Scheler's theory of punishment as embodied retribution and his own *careful* valorization of the body in *The Theology of the Body*. Most especially, his claim that the body—repeated in VS 48—is an anticipatory sign and expression of the moral law. What a contrast this is to Finnis who argues that though all cultures share "the basic values of human existence" (NL, 59)[48] nonetheless these values are not even "pointing to" a set of inclinations (NL, 91) true of human nature. These values present no hierarchy, but "each is equally self-evidently a form of good" (NL, 92; 94), and about Thomas' famous ranking at ST I-II, q. 94, a. 2, it is, Finnis says, "pertinent in a metaphysical meditation…[but] in ethical reflection the threefold order should be set aside as an irrelevant schematization" (NL, 94-95). In EM, I show that Thomas' ranking—preservation of life, procreation and education of the young, knowledge of God and others, and so social life generally—is a description and prescription for moral life expressing the moral intuition *bonum diffusivum sui est*. I also show there the central place this vision of moral embodiment plays in the *Theology of the Body*.[49]

EV 56 is all the more intriguing if this background is kept in mind. Much of *Evangelium Vitae* is given over to a theological account of homicide. In particular, following the Christological account of moral theology and natural law given in *Veritatis Splendor, Evangelium Vitae* articulates a profound theory of sacrificial service to the stranger. How EV 56 is tied to this broader account, and why John Paul II did not pursue the connections, is unclear. John Paul II relies heavily upon a rational account of punishment. Might this be a case of "bare truth" correcting false emotional impulse? For this to be true, John Paul II would then be arguing against his earlier "moral consensus" view of moral embodiment. And yet he does appear to ignore Scheler's account, despite the fact it largely tracks Aquinas' own account of punishment, and both accounts make much use of a moral embodiment that the *Theology of the Body* relies upon.[50]

Scheler (iv b) identified four regions of value and placed them in strict order: values of pleasure, vital values, spiritual values, and the holy. He argues that punishment is a response to a vital value, the "sense of reprisal," a felt need for expiation, that stands warrant for criminal law (F, 365 & 367, n. 154).[51] Punishment is not a felt value of the highest realm of value, the holy, where one would rather expect forgiveness (F, 360 & 367), but nor is the value response to crime of a vital need for expiation a disvalue, something disgusting. Rather, it is more likely the other way, that the moral consensus that capital punishment is appropriate is rooted in an appeasement of moral disgust.[52] Anger at a felt injustice is quieted through retribution (De malo, q. 12, a. 4, ad 3), says Thomas, and Scheler concurs: "Punishment diminishes the hatred in the world" (F, 365). What is most important in Scheler's argument is his claim that punishment as a response to vital value is not the use of a person for some ends of public safety. No human can be used as a tool or an instrument. True, a *consequence* of expiation may be certain social benefits—security, deterrence, example—but these can never serve as moral justifications (F, 365). Expiation reconciles a community (F, 365). It may also serve the person of the criminal (F, 364-6): Scheler thinks that punishment, as Francis Dunlop puts it, purifies "the evildoer by forcing his attention inwards, so that he is confronted by his own spiritual state."[53] Not only is there plenty of phenomenological evidence for the structured role emotion plays in moral judgment (moral disgust) but to ignore how these emotions sustain the moral life of a community invites disaster. I show in detail at the end of the sixth chapter that Thomas and Scheler are agreed that ignoring the felt demand for expiation and *the limits it imposes* upon our moral appetites twists our moral sense so that we become hateful, cruel, and indifferent all at once.

To Aquinas' mind, Camus is right that capital punishment is the taking of vengeance, rooted in emotion. Camus, however, thinks that vengeance is "related to nature and instinct" and "not to law" (RG, 198). With a gesture typical of the Stoic, Camus downgrades emotion as a disturber of the peace. Aquinas' criticism of Stoicism is well-known: it fails to observe—and this is especially true of anger which under-writes retribution—the internal connection between reason, emotion, and the body. Scheler, of course, following the Scottish School, goes further. Stoicism completely fails to grasp the moral cognitive power of the emotions and the rigorous order that exists amongst them. All punishment is related to anger, thinks Thomas, and he obviously rejects the splitting of nature and law. *Vindicatio* or revenge is accomplished through a penal evil inflicted upon the sinner (ST II-II, q. 108, a. 1).[54] It is a virtue (and following Aristotle virtue builds on natural propensities without contradicting them) perfecting a natural inclination for repelling evils (De malo, q. 12, a. 1, s.c.). Citing Cicero, Thomas observes that *vindicatio* is an inclination belonging to natural justice (*ad ius naturale*) (ST II-II, q. 108, a. 2). Similarly, Scheler roots law in the "feeling of right" belonging to human nature (F, 367, n. 154). Vengeance is a virtue because naturally integrated into the order of reason: it is a pursuit, not an avoidance, and the will pursues the good and avoids evil (De malo, q. 12, a. 2 & 4). Thus, Thomas denies that retaliation "comes down to us from the primitive forests" (RG, 198)—because Camus' Stoicism is wrong[55]—and, for many reasons already given, he also rejects the major premise, and minor, of Camus' anthropology: "If murder is in the nature of man, the law is not intended to imitate or reproduce that nature" (RG, 198).

Camus thinks that the Catholic position on capital punishment is intimately linked with its view on the divine right of kings. The king can kill because he is *in persona dei* and like God a master of life and death. The secular state can claim no such justification (RG, 225-6).[56] Thomas does argue that retribution is not in opposition to charity (ST II-II, q. 108, a. 2, ad 2) and oftentimes springs from love (*secundum quod importat fervorem amoris, importat primam radicem vindicationis*): zealous for justice, some, from charity, view an injury to their neighbor as an injury to themselves (*ex caritate reputat quasi suas*). Still, Camus is not right. Thomas' position derives from natural law, namely, the hierarchical principle that the lower is for the sake of the higher. As Vitoria explains, the evangelical law is called the "law of liberty" because it does not prohibit what is licit at natural law (PW, 297). In Cajetan's terse formulation, the point is put thusly: matters of killing and property "Jesus Christ left to moral reason" (In Comm. II-II, q. 64, a. 2).[57]

This explains why another argument of Camus' is wrong and one often heard in Catholic circles today. Camus argues that no one can be punished absolutely because no one is absolutely guilty. Without denying individual responsibility for acts, each of us nonetheless comes "into the world laden with the weight of an infinite necessity," (RG, 210) an inheritance of a general disorder and so only ever a "relative culpability." Scheler's answer is that Camus has confused two *depths* of feeling (F, 360). Punishment speaks to "*vitally conditioned* reason" (F, 364) whilst the religious insight of a collective responsibility for evil in the world is an insight of holiness (F, 363; R, 100-1; OA, 104-5). At this "depth of feeling," persons respond to values of holiness and morality and return evil with good. Punishment is a value response of another level of feeling entirely; one not divorced from Smith's "animal resentment." The Stoics make the same error, argues Thomas, when they confuse the "unconditionally best and the best in a particular case" (De malo, q. 12, a. 1). Absolutely speaking, for example, it is better to philosophize than to have money, but, continues Thomas, in the particular case where one needs to eat or have other necessities, it is better for this person to make money. In the particular case of a dog, it is good to be ferocious whilst this is not good for humans. Following these examples, Thomas points to the particularity of the human, a composite of soul and body, and reasons:

> Therefore, since human nature is a composite of soul and body, and of an intellectual nature and a sensory nature, *it belongs to the human good* that the whole composite as such be subject to virtue, namely, both regarding the intellectual part and the sensory part and the body. And so the virtue of human beings requires that a desire for due vengeance belong to both the rational part of the soul and the sensory part *and the body itself*, and that the body itself be moved to observe virtue. (De malo, q. 12, a. 1; emphasis added)

These orders of value—the intellectual, sensory, and bodily—are not unconnected and moral life is twisted and destroyed if one tries to supplant the licit role of the lower in favour of the higher.[58] In the sixth chapter, I give the example of humanitarian war as a fine illustration of the dangers here and the parallel between Thomas and Scheler on this point is remarkable. To collapse levels of feeling and value is also to collapse person and state. The state, as Scheler points out, is not equal to all of the acts a person can do (F, 545). It even sounds odd to say that I look for forgiveness from the state, but not at all from a person. As I now show, there is a sense in which one can look to the state for mercy, but mercy is still not forgiveness. Double jeopardy, I argue, is a structure of mercy built into the law at the behest of theology, but to speak of a "structure of forgiveness" could only be a falsification of the value.

Notes

1. There are even extreme formulations where a right to private homicide against the self (assisted suicide) is cast as a liberty to free the innocent from state oppression. Wesley Smith talks about these sorts of claims in *Forced Exit*, p. 10. Camus wanted the abolition of the death penalty since he viewed it as a means of state oppression. See A. Camus, "Reflections on the Guillotine," in *Resistance, Rebellion, and Death* (New York: Alfred A. Knopf, 1961), pp. 226-7; hereafter = RG.
2. C. Delsol, *Icarus Fallen*, trans., R. Dick (Wilmington, DE: ISI, 2003), pp. 19-21; cf. P. Manent, *A World beyond Politics?* (Princeton, NJ: Princeton University Press, 2006), p. 177.
3. R. Hittinger, *The First Grace: Rediscovering the Natural Law in a Post-Christian World* (Wilmington, DE: ISI, 2003), pp. 135-162.
4. H. Arkes, *Natural Rights & the Right to Choose* (Cambridge: Cambridge University Press, 2002), p. 151; hereafter NR.
5. For an argument along similar lines respecting embryonic stem cell research, please see Diana Schaub, "How to Think about Bioethics and the Constitution," AEI Bradley Lecture, June 7, 2004.
6. R. Hittinger, "Abortion Before Roe, " *First Things* (October, 1994), pp. 14-16.
7. Cf. Cajetan, *In Comm.* II-II, q. 64, a. 2.
8. H. de Montefortino, O. F. M., *Joannis Duns Scoti Summa theologica*, Pars. II (Rome: Ex typographia Sallustiana, 1902), Appendix, q. 64, pp. 878-82.
9. See Benedict XVI's reservations about Scotism and revolution in his Regensburg Address. Cf. Cajetan's *scholastic* quip against Scotism: "Et propterea non oportet expectare bullam ab Auctore naturae, sed scrutari *secundum lumen signatum ab eo super nos*, quando occidere hominem peccatorem est malum, et quando non" (*In Comm.* II-II, q. 64, a. 2).
10. John Paul II, *Message of Pope John Paul II for the Celebration of the World Day of Peace*, (January 1, 2000), para. 11.
11. Pointed out by many is the disturbing near-constant recourse to double effect analysis in much contemporary moral theology. For an excellent account of why this promiscuity is disturbing, see S. Jensen, "The Trouble with *Secunda Secundae* 64, 7: Self-Defence," *The Modern Schoolman*, Vol. 83 (January 2006), pp. 143-162.
12. "Occidere hominem in sua dignitate manentem, id est, bene viventem, sit secudum se malum… tamen hominem peccatorem occidere ei qui habet auctoritatem est bonum" (St. Anthony of Florence [1389-1459], O. P., *Summae Sacrae Theologiae, iuris pontificii et Caesarei* [Venice, 1571], Part II, Book 7, c. 8, f. 273va).
13. For a remarkable Catholic treatment of the ontology of the person, see D. G. Leahy, *Beyond Sovereignty (pro manuscripto)*.
14. Cf. C. Schmitt, *The Concept of the Political* (Chicago: The University of Chicago Press, 1996), pp. 28-9. See also Smith's brilliant example about why weaponry is often used decoratively in homes, TMS, 36.

15. Strangely, Frings claims that Scheler here calls for the abolition of the death penalty because it is murder. Not only does this contradict the point being made by Scheler, that capital punishment is not straightforwardly murder, but in footnote 99 on p. 314 Scheler expressly states that he is not here addressing whether capital punishment is moral or not. Moreover, as he indicates in his discussion of the issue, the entire question has to be discussed alongside the *ressentiment* of humanitarianism for where the grave immorality of the prisoner is rejected then, of course, capital punishment must be viewed as ethically murder (F, 313).

16. Testy disagreement exists amongst Scheler scholars respecting the nature of person. Frings insists that person is a center of act-consciousness. "What is called "person" exists only in and through the execution of acts. "Act" has the common phenomenological meaning of an activity of the mind in which there is "consciousness-of-something" (M. Frings, *The Mind of Max Scheler* [Milwaukee, WI: Marquette University Press, 1997], p. 43). He is alive to the problems this raises for a pro-life ethics. Whatever Scheler thought about the nature of the unborn the unborn still represent a "vital value" and so, argues Frings, abortion would still be immoral for Scheler since such a vital value trumps an instrumental or quantifiable value, or values of pleasure (p. 48). Frings is clearly nervous that his understanding of Scheler's theory of person plays into the hands of a utilitarian understanding of person. He is surely also aware that Scheler's definition conflicts with the condemnation in *Evangelium Vitae* of any mentality "which carries the concept of subjectivity to an extreme" (EV, para. 19). And also, he knows that many advocates of abortion would defend the practice as a personal value trumping a mere vital value (for example, Singer's preference utilitarianism). Nota sharply rebukes Frings for casting Scheler as Heidegger and ignoring Scheler's definition of the person as an act-substance (*Aktsubstanz*). Nota points out that Scheler speaks of "the metaphysical substantial existence of the spiritual person" (J. Nota, S. J., *Max Scheler: The Man and His Work* [Chicago, IL: Franciscan Herald Press, 1983], pp. 47-48). This is more compatible with Boethius' definition already stressed by Wojtyla in 1960.

17. A. W. B. Simpson, *Cannibalism and the Common Law* (Chicago: The University of Chicago Press, 1984), p. 243.

18. "To kill a child in its mother's womb is now no murder, but a great misprision" (W. Blackstone, *Commentaries*, Book 4, c. 14, *198). Blackstone says "now" it is no murder but a misprision because earlier he notes that a law of James I is repealed.

19. This is not an exaggeration. Please see the court record cited in my commentary on Aquinas' seventh article.

20. G. Calhoun, *The Growth of Criminal Law in Ancient Greece* (Westport, CT: Greenwood Press, 1973), p. 67

21. W. Miller, *Eye for an Eye*, p. 9.

22. Blackstone observes that kinship remained important in English law until the time of Edward III (1312-77) when homicide law no longer recognized distinctions between Danes, Normans, and English (W. Blackstone, Commentaries, Book 4, c. 14, *195). Smith thinks commercialism vital to weakening kin revenge networks and bemoans in 1759 that highland Scots still defer to such networks (TMS, 220-4).

23. G. Calhoun, *The Growth of Criminal Law in Ancient Greece*, p. 17. Cicero says the same about early Roman history, *Murder Trials*, p. 36.

24. M. Gagarin, *Drakon and Early Athenian Homicide Law* (New Haven, CT: Yale University Press, 1981), pp. 119-20.

25. W. Blackstone, *Commentaries*, Book 4, c. 1, *8.

26. The Roman *hospitium* was a part of the household reserved for military guests and later the one who lived in the *hospitium* had the same privileges as other members of the household. See Cicero's, *Murder Trials*, p. 38, n. 1.

27. An extremely interesting point, one I would have to address elsewhere, is whether the stranger also includes the enemy. Blackstone thinks not: see his comments on the *ius gentium* (W. Blackstone, *Commentaries*, Book 4, c. 5). Schmitt agrees: see his interesting observation about the language of the Bible, CP, 28-9. The question is obviously important for a Christian understanding of the legal issues connected with the "global war on terror."

28. An interesting question is to what degree it is the privilege of the officer class that humanizes war rather than straightforward humanitarian sentiment. This theme is touched on in Schmitt's essay on the partisan.

29. R. Sokolowski, *Moral Action: A Phenomenological Study* (Bloomington, IN: Indiana University Press, 1985), pp. 109-110.

30. J. Finnis, *Aquinas: Moral, Political and Legal Theory* (Oxford: Oxford University Press, 1998); henceforth = A.

31. P. Singer, *Animal Liberation*, pp. 194-200.

32. Respect for variety in law is one of the great bequests of the Middle Ages to constitutional government, according to Berman (PR, 395).

33. The *1980 USCCB Statement* relies on the argument in this telling phrase, "sanctity of human life *in all its stages*." The emphasis is mine but I will not comment on the disturbing view of criminality as passivity. The argument is basic in *Responsibility, Rehabilitation, and Restoration: A Statement of the Catholic Bishops of the United States* (Washington, D. C.: United States Catholic Conference, 2000), p. 32.

34. J. Finnis, *Moral Absolutes* (Washington D. C.: The Catholic University Press of America, 1991), pp. 54-6.

35. G. Anscombe, "War and Murder," *Ethics, Religion and Politics* (Minneapolis, MN: University of Minnesota Press, 1981), p. 54, n. 2.

36. A. MacIntyre, *Rational Dependent Animals* (Chicago: Open Court, 1999), c. 1.

37. J. Finnis, *Moral Absolutes*, p. 80.

38. W. Churchill, *A Roving Commission* (New York: Charles Scribner's Sons, 1930), p. 260.

39. Those aghast at the suggestion that a human can be property ignore the reality of imprisonment and I refer readers to the eloquence of Churchill on this point.

40. W. Miller, *An Eye for an Eye*, (Cambridge: Cambridge University Press, 2006), p. 206, n. 5. As he observes, the prevalence of revenge throughout the world's laws, languages, and cultures across millennia, "solves the intersubjectivity problem" (p. 61).

41. Lots of evidence exists but illustrative were the polls respecting Saddam Hussein's execution. See the numbers cited in the Preface.

42. U. S. Catholic Bishops' Statement on Capital Punishment, November 1980.

43. To fail to grant this point is, I think, to make a classic of Catholic imagination like Tolkien's *The Lord of the Rings* unintelligible; and it is not.

44. The very deepest structural principles belong to Thomism, however, and Wojtyla's relationship with Scheler is not straightforward: please see my *Ecstatic Morality and Sexual Politics*.

45. See M. Waldstein's introduction to his new translation, *Man and Woman He Created Them: A Theology of the Body* (Boston: Pauline Books & Media, 2006), pp. 63-76.

46. K. Wojtyla, "Act and Experience," *Analecta Husserliana*, Vol. 5 (Dordrecht: Reidel, 1976), pp. 271-3; K. Wojtyla, "The Problem of Experience in Ethics," (PC,

122-5). See also K. Wojtyla, "On the Metaphysical and Phenomenological Basis of the Moral Norm," PC, especially pp. 88-90.

47. Cf. E. Burke, "A Philosophical Enquiry into the Origin of our Ideas of the Sublime and Beautiful," *Pre-Revolutionary Writings* (Cambridge: Cambridge University Press, 1993), p. 70. See Adam Smith's remarkable pages on the prohibition against murder arising from the heart's horror at witnessing a murder (TMS, 76-7; 159).

48. J. Finnis, *Natural Law and Natural Rights* (Oxford: Oxford University Press, 1980); hereafter, NL.

49. For an excellent summary of contemporary Catholic thinking on inclination, see M. Levering, "Natural Law and Natural Inclinations: Rhonheimer, Pinckaers, McAleer," *The Thomist*, Vol. 70: 2 (2006): 155-201. For a discussion of my Thomist interpretation of John Paul II, see F. Kerr, *Twentieth-Century Catholic Theologians* (Oxford: Blackwell, 2007), pp. 180-82.

50. Also relevant here is that we now know from the work of Michael Waldstein that the *Theology of the Body* was finished before 1979 and written in Poland. This means less than a decade stands between it and the 1969 *Acting Person*. Since *Veritatis Splendor* (1993) uses important ideas of the *Theology of the Body* I see no grounds for thinking some major intellectual change overcame Wojtyla before 1995 and the writing of *Evangelium Vitae*. About Scheler's influence, see Waldstein's pages cited in n. 45 above.

51. A good account of Scheler on punishment is F. Dunlop, "Scheler's Theory of Punishment," *Journal of the British Society for Phenomenology*, Vol. 9 (October, 1978): 167-74.

52. For how thoroughly structured are some of our moral emotions, see A. Kolnai, *Disgust* (Chicago: Open Court, 2004). For disgust as grounds for war, see PW, 209-10.

53. F. Dunlop, "Scheler's Theory of Punishment," p. 173.

54. Scheler does not discuss Thomas on this issue. Had he done so, he would accuse Thomas of a *certain* superficiality. *Vindicatio*, to his mind, is a composed phenomenon. Most basic to punishment is reprisal and atonement. Justice, the idea of a proportionate response to the injury, guiding the reprisal, is analytically distinct (F, 361-2). Because Thomas thinks that anger is intrinsically related to the good, reason, and law, he runs these analytically distinct parts together. Scheler prefers the careful language of reprisal, Thomas, vengeance, but I do not think their positions are significantly different.

55. Consider Smith's remarkable analysis that we "reverence" humans because we "dread that animal resentment" should we harm the innocent. "Animal resentment" renders the innocent "holy, consecrated" (TMS, 106-7). Cf. Miller's comments on Germanic *mund* and its importance for the idea of dignity (W. Miller, *An Eye for an Eye*, pp. 132-9)

56. This argument is recently repeated by J. Bottum, "Christians and the Death Penalty," *First Things* (August/September, 2005).

57. "And so also particular negative and affirmative precepts are contained in the natural power of reason and in the divine law, which ought to govern our actions" (*De malo*, q. 2, a. 1).

58. Cf. H. Arendt's fine observation in *Eichmann in Jerusalem* (London: Penguin, 1994), p. 296.

3

Victims' Rights and Double Jeopardy

> *The mystery of pietas is the path opened by divine*
> *mercy to a reconciled life.*
> —*John Paul II[1]*

> *The world of grace and the world of rebellion.*
> *The disappearance of one is equivalent to*
> *the appearance of the other.*
> —*Albert Camus[2]*

Whether It Is Lawful for a Private Individual to Kill a Man Who Has Sinned

A right of resistance is basic to the idea of revolution. The idea is perhaps most famously linked to Locke and to Jefferson's use of Locke's philosophy in the Declaration of Independence. Aquinas rejects any such right and in the tradition of Aquinas, Aurel Kolnai is quite correct to speak of the American War of Independence as the "original sin" of the United States: his sense that rebellion is a grave sin is a thoroughly Catholic intuition (PM, 204). Only public authority has the privilege of intentional homicide and rebellion is the usurpation by private individuals of a lethal authority that is not theirs. Aquinas acknowledged the licitness of tyrannicide but, as Cajetan forcefully points out in his commentary on Thomas' third article, tyrannicide must be understood as the *continuation* of a war publicly declared and now continued by partisans upon the collapse of their nation's public authority (*In Comm.*, q. 64, a. 3; cf. H, 161). Implicit in Locke's political philosophy is a theory of homicide and, as Albert Camus has convincingly shown, few great modern thinkers have ignored the problem of homicide entirely. However, it is Camus' 1960 *The Rebel* that is the first book explicitly devoted to the topic in modern times. The book, which is remarkable and worthy of far more scholarly attention than it has so far received,[3] is really only known as the final provocation that enraged Sartre to publicly denounce Camus and thoroughly sever the friendship the two men had enjoyed. *The Rebel* is far more than some frisson in the history of French letters, however, for its theory of rebellion is an outright rejection of Aquinas' restriction of homicide to public authority. As such, it is a major theoretical statement of the moral necessity to privatize homicide.

Camus is no legal positivist (indeed, he is some sort of natural law theorist) but the reason he threw his lot in with the Benthamites is of perhaps unique interest to moral theology. Camus is often credited with formulating the most incisive arguments against capital punishment. From this, however, one should not suppose he opposed killing: Camus, more than Singer even, is a great theoretician of killing for justice. Justice requires that the innocent be protected through killing the unjust. Objecting to *state* killing as a great oppression, Camus is nonetheless a great advocate of the privatization of homicide.

Camus is especially challenging to Thomism, and moral theology more broadly, because he thinks that acts of mercy condone murder. Throughout *The Rebel* he insists that the "age of grace," the Christian era of the West, was at root, and through and through, a matter of privilege: the "secret mercy" of God (R, 250). Privilege, Camus claims, is no less murderous than modern ideas of political order that have led to nihilism (R, 287). For Camus, Christianity is a politics of privilege because a politics of love (R, 56) and his theologically-minded critique is potent against the argument developed in this book: natural law homicide relies on a platform of privilege and any social order that hopes to avoid totalitarianism must embrace privilege in its law and politics. Camus also wished to avoid totalitarianism. To do so, he relied on a version of natural law that is radically equalitarian and the primary content of which is a metaphysical law of violence in the service of justice. As Miller puts it, "if mercy has to play more than a rare role it is not a good sign for the state of law or of the polity."[4] In the eighth chapter I combine parts of Camus' analysis with Thomistic natural law to assess the morality of the humanitarian air war over Kosovo. Here, I want to assess his claim that mercy is collaboration with murder, a useful avenue to a discussion of the deep significance of the doctrine of double jeopardy.

Camus objected to capital punishment but he equally objected to mercy as little more than condonation, acquiescence in the criminal's act that is no better than a self-enslavement. *The Rebel*—a remarkable intellectual protest at philosophical ideas that give the nod to murder—does not include a single mention of mercy or forgiveness. Only the harsh edge of the sword of justice figures and Camus does not pretend otherwise: "God or the sword" (R, 287). He makes it clear in the opening pages of the work that what is of concern in rebellion is to see established "the unitarian reign of justice" (R, 24). Mercy has no place in Camus' politics because it offends our natural sense of justice: when the murderer goes unpunished, the dignity of the victim is diminished. The logic of mercy, for Camus, perpetuates injustice.

The Pauline "how much more" (Rom. 5: 9, 10, 15, 17), Ricoeur says, highlights a divine logic whereby "the logic of superabundance bursts the logic of equivalence." The moral equivalence of sin and death (capital punishment) is destroyed by Christ, who is the bodying forth of the good news of the "how much more" by which we are saved from wrath. Punishment must not then be directed at vengeance and expiation but rehabilitation and improvement. "Because on which side is the gospel?" asks Ricoeur.[5] But is Ricoeur's claim that the Gospel destroys the moral equivalence of sin and death also to concede Camus' point (and Kolnai's in "Forgiveness") that mercy is tantamount to condonation? Is it also the conflation of the holy and the vital that destroys moral order, which Scheler warns us about? Is it perhaps to have misidentified the place of the superabundance of grace? Pardon, someone like Kolnai might argue, as an exuberance of privilege, does not relativize or problematize the order of justice but acts as a hinge linking the natural and the supernatural. It appears to be an assumption on the part of Ricoeur that there is something *wrong* with the order of justice. As Kolnai points out, condonation "means silencing and neutralizing the retributive attitude to moral disvalue" (FG, 215) and such cannot be done without rending ordinary moral consciousness. An obvious Christian rejoinder—"But what's ordinary about Christian love"—will not do: Christian love is not utopian and basic to the utopian mood is replacing morality with *something else* (I, 234). The Gospel "how much more" appeals for a conversion of heart, an appeal to the world of spiritual acts, in Scheler's sense, and not a transvaluation of the moral order as such.

For a less dialectical approach, consider the medieval philosopher-theologian Giles of Rome who wondered how the church might promote the asylum suggested by the Lord's command to Israel in the Book of Numbers (35: 6; 12):[6]

> The cities which you give to the Levites [the priestly caste] shall be six cities of refuge, where you shall permit the manslayer to flee...a refuge from the avenger, that the manslayer may not die until he stands before the congregation for judgment.

I want to show that the plea of double jeopardy is an approximation to this Scriptural ideal. It answers Camus if we keep in mind the discussion of emphasis in the first chapter. Defending the plea—and a defense is required—demands that Catholic social thought take a critical distance from certain currents commonly found in jurisprudence today, including motifs in the church's own jurisprudential thinking. The church must defend the plea, for justice depends upon it. No meaningful reform of the criminal justice system is possible without a correct understanding of the plea of double jeopardy for "no other procedural doctrine is more fundamental or all-pervasive" to criminal procedure.[7]

A focus of this chapter is the development in the English understanding of the meaning of double jeopardy over the last four decades but the import of these developments is not parochial. Over these decades the protection afforded by the *autrefois* plea has weakened and this for two connected reasons. One of these reasons, well identified by American jurist, Michael Moore, is the prevalence of a philosophical skepticism about what we know about reality. Embracing this skepticism, judges and legal scholars argue that statutory descriptions of actions have legal significance, not actions themselves. Real actions matter less than the actions "read off" events by means of statutory descriptors. G. Thomas is a fine example,[8] he writes, "the legislature creates substantive blameworthiness..." and "with the role of defining crimes comes the role of defining jeopardy offenses. It is that simple" (DJ, 21 & 20).[9] That simple—if you are a legal positivist willing to believe that morality ("substantive blameworthiness") is created! Even where there are constitutional guarantees that no one will be placed twice in jeopardy—as in American law—skepticism facilitates an "end run" around those protections. After all, as Peter Westen points out, "the terms of the double jeopardy clause are not self-defining."[10] In English law, this skepticism has proved corrosive of doctrine itself and not merely practice. Whilst the plea is protected in the Fifth Amendment to the U.S. Constitution, and all fifty states have protections as well, debates around English law clearly hold lessons also for America.

John Paul II issued vivid denunciations of the corrosive effects of skepticism on law. The moral realism of his Thomistic moral theology is an antidote to skepticism and how it can help in double jeopardy adjudication is a topic of my commentary on Thomas' third article. John

Paul II was also a strong advocate of human rights. The second reason weakening the protections of the *autrefois* plea is human rights. Recent English legal thought shows that human rights thinking is, at the very least, *sometimes* antithetical to the basic commitments of moral theology. By the lights of moral theology, serious crime tracks a hierarchy of objective evils. Such a hierarchy relies on a confidence in reason to make careful distinctions between good and evil. Aquinas' *De malo* is probably Exhibit 1 of such reasoned distinctions. As Chantal Delsol has observed so acutely, the contemporary West has experimented so often, and so disastrously, with conceptions of the good shaping the social order that no confidence in reason remains. What seems left is the conviction that suffering alone is an evil.[11] Human rights are not a conception of the good but a set of prohibitions on suffering. Recent reflection on double jeopardy in England shows that assuaging suffering is now a structural principle of law. The basic argument of this chapter is that a victim's right not to suffer expands punishment and cancels out the high moral value of mercy. Appeasing the human right not to suffer has severely distorted the *autrefois* plea and certainly removed any idea of the law as an asylum. This institutional cancellation of the high value of mercy is an immorality. Since English law reform is ongoing in a broader European context—the European Convention on Human Rights—it is perhaps time for Catholic social thought (and Vatican policy) to express even broader reservations.[12] If I can put it this way, the commitments of moral theology to the innocent, mercy and reconciliation—and these are the deepest meanings of the plea—"trump" Catholicism's commitment to human rights where these show evidence of weakening the plea's protections. After all, the Kingdom of God is not a kingdom of human rights but reconciliation.

There are five stages to the argument. Asking whether (i) a human rights or victims' rights criminal law is compatible with moral theology's contribution to law, I suggest "no." A victims' rights criminal law obscures the hierarchy of objective wrongdoing. Moral theology's contribution to law stems from a realism about acts and morals, however, (ii) nominalism expresses a skepticism about whether acts have natures. An analysis of double jeopardy in recent English law shows (iii) the role of skepticism in shaping doctrine. The claim is made that moral realism once shaped doctrine explaining the plea. The argument continues (iv) that Catholic jurisprudence requires a robust version of the plea and resources are abundantly available in the moral realism of John Paul II. Finally, this argument is deepened by showing (v) that relying on

Providence is *essential* to defending the plea and an implication of (v) is that any public philosophy that excludes a providential God of mercy cannot deliver justice. The chapter closes with some speculative concluding remarks on why the plea no longer has intuitive appeal.

At the behest of the Blair government England's Parliament (i) recently abolished the plea of double jeopardy[13] for thirty-two crimes.[14] Anyone anxious for liberty must be deeply troubled but ought the church be especially concerned? The plea is at least 800 years old in English law with Thomas à Becket credited with its introduction (DJ1, 72-6; cf. DJ2, 5-6). For aid in one of his struggles with Henry II, Thomas à Becket turned to St. Jerome's commentary on the Book of Nahum (1:9): "For God judges not twice for the same offence."[15] This places the plea's origin firmly in Christendom. The plea's place in English law had long been prepared by Canon Law, which had preserved the idea from Roman law, and Greek law had the notion too (DJ, 73). Is the plea's abolition another indication of the creeping post-Christian organization of European society? More, is, as Berman might suspect, its abolition another indicator of the West's departure from rule of law since Becket's remarkable story laid a foundation stone of constitutionalism (PR, 268)?

The change in English law has a troubling proximate cause but the more remote should cause grave concern to Catholic jurists. None of the documents hide the fact that change in the law was prompted by the "racist murder" of Stephen Lawrence as proximate cause.[16] Writers of the left and right were equally disturbed by the use of the Lawrence case, variously accusing government of "a most cynical exploitation of the case" and of operating "under the cloak of sanctity provided by the martyrdom of Stephen Lawrence."[17] As to the remote cause, a recent piece of English legal scholarship argues that human rights advocacy of victims' rights is the primary engine behind the legislation. The authors of the chapter celebrate the way that human rights concerns allow judges "to break free from the shackles of legal precedent" (RDJ, 4) all the while acknowledging that the *autrefois* plea has never been the object of sustained academic study (RDJ, 2). Throughout deliberations, Parliament gave close attention to human rights issues, especially the European Convention on Human Rights (hereafter ECHR).[18]

There is a marked difference of opinion amongst Catholic intellectuals about human rights. The encyclical tradition is an advocate (VS, para. 51). Endorsing Maritain's argument that rights can be derived from natural law,[19] this tradition argues that rights stem from obligations or duties specified by natural law (CA, para. 34). The liberal account of rights, by contrast, views them as expressions of a liberty from obligation. The encyclical tradition argues that this individualistic idea of rights is incoherent because rights defended by liberals as part of the rule of law as often as not subvert that rule, removing protections from the innocent (EV, para. 18-20). An important Catholic thinker like Finnis also defends rights. Putting matters more strongly than Maritain, he argues that Aquinas actually had a theory of rights that closely tracks his natural law theory.[20] He then explains what human rights are by his "basic goods" interpretation of Aquinas.[21]

MacIntyre, however, heads a group of Catholic critics of human rights. Rather cleverly, MacIntyre shows the goals of the encyclical tradition are securable without recourse to rights. In my opinion, his *Rational Dependent Animals* is a rewriting of paragraphs 18-20 of *Evangelium Vitae* where the virtues do the work of rights. Besides this positive proposal, MacIntyre, amongst others, thinks the idea of human rights either incoherent or pernicious.[22] Recent thinking in England about double jeopardy suggests MacIntyre might be in the right.

Double jeopardy has a foundation in moral theology because Catholic jurisprudence is fundamentally guided by the idea of the protection of the innocent. A review of government documents about the proposed change in ancient English law shows that in the mind of the Blair government (1) the primary objective of criminal law is "to bring criminals to justice" for harms done (RP2, 22) and (2) criminal law has its authority from victims' rights. Catholic jurisprudence cannot accept either proposition. The idea that criminal law is first and foremost about securing justice for victims is by no means obvious. For a Catholic, I suggest, the primary objective of criminal law is safeguarding the innocent and, for someone like Michael Moore, retribution is basic.[23] Nor is it obvious that the authority of criminal law stems from the human rights of victims. Bracton understood the victim of serious crime in medieval England to be the "country" (DJ, 78) and Aquinas cast Bracton's point in terms of a common good served by a hierarchy of objective wrongdoing. Far removed from Aquinas is a member of the Parliamentary Select Committee that refined the legislation before the vote in Parliament. Martin Linton, M.P., argued that the initial proposal of the Law Commission (the body of legal experts asked to review existing law and make recommendations for reform) that the law remove protections of double jeopardy for murder trials only, mistakes the issue of victims' rights. The parliamentarian described the thinking of the Select Committee: rape is a greater harm than murder since the murder victim is no longer suffering, hence, the case for retrial in a rape case is stronger.[24] Humanitarianism—the desire to reduce suffering—is here offered as a structural principle of law. Murder, the taking of innocent human life, is no longer a uniquely malicious act: though the Law Commission argued that English law has always held this to be so.[25] Indeed, since the victim does not live with the suffering, it is not necessarily the worst criminal offence. Certainly, with regard to criminal procedure, murder is not privileged, which the Law Commission had suggested. Ultimately, government's "relaxation"—a favored expression—of double jeopardy protections extended to thirty-two offences, including murder, arson, terrorist offences, and a remarkable number of sexual crimes (RP2, 29). To think in terms set by Bakunin,[26] to cause suffering is political theology's equivalent of the sin against the Holy Spirit: the sin for which forgiveness is impossible.

Aquinas' jurisprudence is based on the idea of privilege, that only the state has the authority to intentionally kill. This position respecting the role of privilege is dialectically about as far as one can get from the idea that victims' rights sustain the authority of criminal law. To the Thomist, the "relaxation" of double jeopardy strictures at the behest of humanitarian sentiment is but a further collapsing of the distinction between private authority and public authority. This distinction, which assumes government can correctly distinguish between good and evil, John Paul II strongly reaffirmed in the second part of *Evangelium Vitae* where he traces the lineaments of Aquinas' theory of homicide. Catholic ideas of law rely heavily on this distinction but since the 1960s, and probably before, the privatization of legal authority has been ongoing. This trend is easy to spot when one considers the change in the exercise of lethal authority, what with the decriminalization of suicide, abortion, and euthanasia.[27] Here, the measure of law is private suffering not a common good served by knowledge of good and evil. As commentators point out, the Blair government had a "mantra" of modernizing criminal justice (RDJ, 6). "Tony Blair talks about creating a victim justice system rather than a criminal justice system" (RP1, 18). Government argued that "social justice" requires nothing less than a "sweeping away" of obstacles to a justice that favors victims, and so a "root-and-branch" reform of the justice system is necessary (RP1, 8, 10-11).[28] Legal commentators think it evident that European Convention jurisprudence is a victims-based jurisprudence such that "national laws must allow and muster continued efforts to bring criminals to justice so as to respect the rights of victims" (RDJ, 8).

Bizarrely, in government documents acknowledgement is made that "the double jeopardy rule is long-standing and well-founded" (*Third Report*, para. 64) and with great British understatement, "it may be significant that no such proposal has been made before" (*Third Report*, para. 14). The Criminal Bar Association argued at the time of the reform that there was no evidence at all that the plea was "working in a way contrary to the interests of the community" and certainly none sufficient to abandon a plea found around the world in all "sophisticated" legal systems (*Third Report*, para. 14). What underlying principle animates the change? I am the last person to favor a "hermeneutics of suspicion" (Ricoeur) but in this case some speculation as to what is really desired by the change seems warranted. God forbid that we ever return to Saint-Just's "dictatorship of justice"[29] but what are we to make of phrases like "the wider interests of justice" (*Third Report*, para. 64) determining which cases shall be prosecuted for a second time? Might John Paul II be right that "the present-day mentality" is more opposed to mercy than in time gone by?[30]

The Western phenomenon of skepticism (ii) has nominalism as its partner in law. *Veritatis Splendor* begins with a remarkably severe condemnation of relativism and skepticism. The opening page recalls the biblical identification of Satan as the "father of lies" and then gives the examples of relativism and skepticism as Satan's fruit (VS, para. 1). The culture of death, John Paul II argues in *Evangelium Vitae*, is a consequence of Satan's cosmic struggle with Christ (EV, para. 28) and one of Satan's central supports is subjectivism (EV, para. 19-20). These condemnations appear severe and strident to those of us in the academy. So many of our colleagues are proud of their skepticism, relativism, and subjectivism. Dominant forms of theoretical analysis rest on these pillars: Legal Realism, legal positivism, conventionalism, hermeneutics. Nonetheless, skepticism is hostile to moral theology and if, as I will show, double jeopardy has a basis in moral theology as the history of the doctrine suggests, then skepticism is hostile to justice. Strong language aside, it is John Paul II who shows how to make this argument.

In England, when government proposed legislation the Bar Council argued that the change to the law sought was the "wholesale abolition" of double jeopardy protections.[31] Government documents constantly speak merely of a "relaxation"[32] since all that is desired is an "exception" to the plea made for persuasive new evidence (*Third Report*, para. 57).[33] These same documents argue that the dangers of the relaxation are hedged in by constraints set by the European Court of Human Rights

(ECHR). Yet, as the Law Commission pointed out, the constraining clause, Article 4 (1) of the Seventh Protocol, prohibits new proceedings for the same offence as the old but may well permit prosecution for a slightly different offence based on same the facts (CP 267, 5).[34] Case law suggests at least two ways to read the clause. One double jeopardy case has already been adjudicated on appeal at the European Court of Human Rights in a way to well justify Michael Moore's concern that an "end run" around double jeopardy protections is positively encouraged by skepticism in legal theory.

The well-known Scottish Dominican theologian, Fergus Kerr, recently noted that John Paul II's *Fides et Ratio*, whilst a major engagement with philosophy, shows little appreciation of Analytic or Anglo-American philosophy.[35] Others have recently wondered why Catholic thought is so captive to European ideas when it is only analytic philosophy that still takes seriously large metaphysical claims that traditionally rooted Catholic speculation about the world.[36] Respected as a leading authority on the relationship between law and philosophy, Michael Moore is very much an analytic philosopher. The curious thing about him is that two of his principal interests, moral realism and action theory, are principal interests of John Paul II and the Munich School of phenomenology in which Karol Wojtyla did his early work. In Moore's treatise on action theory and criminal law he explains the skepticism surrounding double jeopardy.

Moore argues that legal commentators enamored of "interpretivism"— a host of contemporary theories of language that all concur that reality is basically unknowable and that law is entirely conventional[37]—have expressed skepticism about double jeopardy. In particular, they have challenged the idea that there is such a thing as an action independent of the "actions" described by statutory language. As one of the great authorities in law, John Salmond, puts the point, "An act has no *natural* boundaries...Its limits must be artificially defined for the purpose in hand."[38] Differences in statutory "actions" generate different acts rendering the central claim of double jeopardy void:[39] no subsequent prosecution for the same act tried and acquitted. What *same* act? In a "skeptical ontology" (Moore) there is no such thing in reality independent of statutory description. Combing through statutes, prosecutors can frame multiple cases as need be on the basis of variations in act descriptions. Moore is well known, and much criticized, for the roles a strongly realist metaphysics and morals play in his jurisprudence. I suggest that Moore's use of realism as a response to skepticism is one that, with certain necessary modifications, Catholic jurists can employ.

A recent tussle amongst the justices of the U. S. Supreme Court amply demonstrates Moore's broader point. In *Rapanos v. U.S.* the role of nominalism in statutory interpretation is fully on display. The case concerned property rights and much hung on the definition of "navigable waters." At stake is the scope of federal jurisdiction over "wetlands" through the Clean Water Act. Justices of the Supreme Court varied on what the definition might be. One suggested using the ordinary dictionary definition (Scalia), while another argued that water that has a "significant nexus" to navigable water or water that once was or could "reasonably" become navigable (Kennedy) is a "wetland." The dispute centered on a property regarded by the state as "waters of the United States" but Justice Scalia could see no more than "land with sometimes saturated soil conditions."[40] Rather wittily, Epstein has suggested that "verbal alchemy" won't change land into water.[41] Similarly, about the change in double jeopardy in English law, one commentator said, "what we are seeing now is a strange postmodernist kind of law reform."[42] In fact, it is the continuation of a voluntaristic nominalism that has a philosophical pedigree stretching into the High Middle Ages.[43] G. Thomas exhibits this philosophical position: "A king is no different from Moses or God. Sovereigns can define blameworthiness to be what they wish" (DJ, 82). *Pace* Epstein, will, with a bit of "verbal alchemy," *can* change land into water.

In English law (iii) few cases have probed the plea of *autrefois* but those that have all turn "on whether the earlier trial was in fact for the same offence and on the same facts" (*Third Report*, para. 6). A crucial test to adjudicate this matter is the "same evidence" test, which dates to the English common-law case of 1796 in *King v. Vandercomb*.[44] Judge Buller wrote in *Vandercomb*:[45]

> ...and if crimes are so distinct that evidence of the one will not support the other, *it is as inconsistent with reason*, as it is repugnant to the rules of law, to say that they are so far the same that an acquittal of the one shall be a bar to the prosecution for the other. (DJ2, 97; emphasis added)

I take the highlighted phrase to be realist: reason can discern the character of crimes imposed by acts themselves. Reason is an independent resource for adjudication with "the rules of law." The same insight, I suggest, is found in a 1962 draft of the *Model Penal Code*. Evoking *Vandercomb*, it runs: "...each requires proof of a fact not required by the other and the law defining each of such offenses is intended to prevent *a substantially different harm or evil*" (DJ2, 109; emphasis added). The highlighted phrase is clearly realist and establishes a limiting framework for legal definition. This formulation is strikingly similar to Moore relying on "morally salient act-types" in his effort (discussed below) to explain "the same offence" aspect of double-jeopardy doctrine. Moore claims the *Vandercomb* test was integrated into the defining case of American judicial reflection on the plea *Blockburger v. United States* (1932).[46]

In English law, the landmark case is from 1964, *Connelly v. DDP*. A majority of the judges (3-2) argued the plea gave protection against a subsequent prosecution for *any* offence if the facts supporting the offence are the same or substantially the same. If the facts change at all, say through new evidence or witnesses, then the case can be reopened or a new charge brought (RDJ, 3). Lord Morris of Borth-y-Gest dissenting in 1964 provided a detailed review of case law across four centuries to show that the plea had always been understood to mean more: no matter the evidence, if the second offence charged is substantially the same as the first, the plea gives protection. That is, the legal properties of statutory "acts" are less important than the nature of the action itself (CP 267, 9, n. 4).[47] The act itself puts a restraint on prosecutors' creativity in deploying the statutory descriptors of "acts."[48] In 1591 the King's Bench declared:

> If a man commits murder, and is indicted and convicted of manslaughter, he shall never answer to any indictment of the same death, for all is one and the same felony for one and the same death, although murder is in respect of the circumstance of the forethought malice more odious. (DJ1, 78)

Murder and manslaughter are here regarded as substantially the same and protection afforded under the plea. Lord Morris argued the same understanding is found in military law. The Army Act of 1955 has it that (in some circumstances) a person "shall not be liable in respect of the same or substantially the same offence to be tried by court-martial" (CP 267, 9, n. 8).

Beedie (1998) argued that Lord Devlin's speech in *Connelly v. DPP* is defining. Lord Devlin had argued that the plea is both narrow and broad. The plea is narrow because the "same offence" means *precisely* the same offence as per definitions and wording in statutes, and not "substantially" or "effectively" the same, as Lord Morris would have it. The plea is broad, however, in that no new offence can be brought before the court based on the same facts. Lord Morris showed that across centuries there are dozens of cases where the plea was rejected even though subsequent (though significantly different) charges were brought on the same facts. He argued that basing the protection on facts was contrary to case law.[49] The majority followed Devlin, thinking that the weight of the protection afforded by the plea rests on sameness of fact.[50]

However, Lord Devlin allowed that under "special circumstances," a subsequent prosecution for the same (or different) offence on the same facts is possible but left unclear what circumstances might justify this (CP 267, 13). Nevertheless, in principle, the *autrefois* rule was no longer binding. CP 156 points to an example found in *Attorney General for Gibraltar v. Leoni* (1998). Here a "new event" served to justify a subsequent prosecution. Smugglers prosecuted for jettisoning cargo were subsequently prosecuted for possessing and importing cannabis once the dumped cargo was finally recovered. The Appeals Court upheld the further prosecution as an example of "special circumstances" and the three former judges of the English Appeals Court drew an analogy between "new event" and discovery of new evidence (CP 267, 13-14). If in 1964 the court majority had followed Lord Morris such would not be possible. He argued that English tradition, no matter the facts now in evidence, prohibits a prosecution for an act the same *or substantially the same*; that is, it prohibits prosecution for a different offence (massaged) at law.

Following Lord Devlin's 1964 speech and *Beedie*, the 2001 proposal of the Law Commission after the consultation process was that double jeopardy protection shall be: no subsequent prosecution for the same offence (*autrefois* rule) and no prosecution for *any* offence based on the same or substantially the same facts (*Connelly*) with the caveat of "special circumstances,"[51] which can include new evidence (*Leoni*) (CP 267, 74 & 84; CP 156, 6). This proposal was formalized in the 2003 Criminal Justice Act. What the Law Commission gave with one hand (no subsequent prosecution for *any* offence) they took with the other—excepting special circumstances. For the law now allows a case to be reopened on new facts in evidence *and* prosecution of a different offence (massaged) in law. No wonder the Criminal Bar Association declared that double jeopardy was "abolished wholesale."

Yet, from the perspective of moral theology, the error in English law was introduced in 1964 not with the 2003 Criminal Justice Act. The brouhaha in England during 2000-2003, on announcement of the government's proposal respecting double jeopardy, was misplaced. All government suggested was codification of a change in the law that had been emergent since 1964 when the essential moves were made. As the Law Commission explained its own logic, making a new exception to the *autrefois* rule was based on such an exception accepted in *Connelly* (CP 267, 85). The unraveling of double jeopardy is a consequence in part of a philosophical proposition in Lord Devlin's speech:[52] the "legal characteristics" of actions are highly specific and a change in these legal properties is a change in the nature of the action itself. Having learned his lesson from Sir John Salmond, that there is no such thing as a *natural* action, he concluded that a new charge with new properties is not *at law* to be prosecuted for the same offence. As the Law Commission points out, Devlin's analysis is now accepted as definitive. This is a fine example of Moore's rightful concern with "interpretivism" where any attempt to access a rational or moral discrimination of acts so as to control the ingenuity of legislators or prosecutors is abandoned. That there is no *nature* to action but only nominal kinds is vividly on display in another observation of the Law Commission: though acquitted overseas a person may be tried again, for the "definition of offences… may not be described *in exactly the same way* in the legislation of other jurisdictions" (RP2, 31; emphasis added).

Moore's concern is plainly on display in current European Convention jurisprudence, as well. At the time of the public defense of the change to English law, political advocates made much of the fact that the change is compliant with the ECHR. Matters are not helped by the ECHR as it is beset by the same problem. Protocol 7, Article 4 concerns the plea. Already cases exist that read Article 4 very differently. In *Oliveira v. Switzerland,* the offence charged at the second trial was different from the first though based on the same facts. Raising Moore's concern of statutory abuse, the judges at the appeal argued that Article 4 was not violated if successive prosecutions relate to "a single act constituting various offences." In this case, the offences arising from a road accident were "failing to control a vehicle" and "negligently inflicting physical injury" (CP 267, 31). However, in *Gradinger v. Austria* the same appeals court argued that change in the "legal properties" of the crime is no grounds for a second trial, at least not if the facts are the same or substantially the same. Of course, new evidence changes matters entirely (RDJ, 7). *Oliveira* is a nominalist judgment with the different descriptors in law carrying weight whilst *Gradinger* is a realist judgment. The Law Commission concludes that as European human rights law stands currently there is a fundamental conflict on how to understand the "human right" of double jeopardy (CP 267, 33). *Gradinger* is certainly a better way to read Article 4 (1) than is *Oliveira,* but the "new evidence" latitude extended to prosecutors is fatal to the protections of the *autrefois* rule, nonetheless. As *Leoni* shows, the menace acting in *Oliveira*—nominalism—is only encouraged by the "new evidence" clause. Without a robust realist understanding of action, such that, for instance, prosecuting smugglers for dumping cargo cannot leave room for prosecuting them for attempted importation of contraband, the *autrefois* plea basically dissolves. As is evident from the speech of Lord Morris, a realist understanding of action does not prohibit subsequent prosecutions of criminals. It simply requires that the prosecution be for a significantly different act or, as the Model Penal Code draft of 1962 had it, a prosecution for "a substantially different harm or evil."

Moral theology (iv) requires of Catholic jurisprudence a robust conception of double jeopardy. As John Paul II says, piety is the path to a reconciled life. In this case, Catholic jurisprudence should advocate the old understanding of the plea as described by Lord Morris. This understanding can be justified philosophically by Moore's idea of the "morally salient act-type." Before explaining Moore's idea, and ultimately discussing reservations with his version of moral realism, my first proposition needs defending: Catholic jurisprudence needs a robust conception of double jeopardy.

Theological language may appear singularly unhelpful in developing arguments about law in the contemporary, pluralistic university. Yet, categories of moral theology are essential to appreciate the significance of double jeopardy. In the *Acting Person* (1969), Wojtyla argues that human dignity rests on the self-possession of persons (AP, 117-8 amongst others). The nominalist reading of double jeopardy doctrine means that anyone tried and acquitted of a serious crime can no longer feel secure that she will not be tried in the future, and who knows how many times. Being under prosecution, or the threat of prosecution, like punishment itself, alienates the person. She is less a person because now *suspect*. Double jeopardy, said by Blackstone to be a "universal maxim of the common law of England,"[53] is a structural element of law that seeks to preserve dignity.

The doctrine of double jeopardy also serves to institutionalize reconciliation. It used to be that social and personal peace was promoted by getting "your day in court." Prosecution and trial once fostered justice in England *and* acts of resignation.[54] If the verdict was not what the victim or her family hoped, at least the "day in court" had finality to it. The Law Commission thinks otherwise—"accuracy of outcome is more important than finality" (CP 267, 36). The commission argued that where the credibility of the justice system as a whole would be damaged by an "outcome" of a trial, exception to double jeopardy must be made. It also suggested that inaccurate verdicts in murder cases were alone of such sufficient seriousness to override double jeopardy protections (CP 267, 40-43). As previously noted, the limits of this recommendation were rejected by the government. I will return to the issue of reconciliation shortly.

Crucially for the church, the doctrine affirms the absolute significance of the value of innocence. The doctrine assumes that the asymmetry between the resources of the prosecution and those of the defendant requires balancing. Should the state pursue a defendant the likelihood is that a prosecution will succeed at some point. The threat to the innocent is obvious. The core fear that prompted *Evangelium Vitae* is that in much of the world innocence is no longer a protection against being killed *even at law*. The abolition of double jeopardy is the removal of another legal protection for the innocent. Double jeopardy protects the innocent in part by making the law an asylum. The plea, I suggest, is a formalization of mercy at law. I defend this idea below but to appreciate the deepest meaning of the plea as mercy it is well to consider Moore's jurisprudence in more detail.

Instead of conceding that criminal cases are inescapably tied to "the nominal properties each criminal statute creates" (AC, 337) double-jeopardy adjudication can rely on the moral properties realized in an act. A criminal act, argues Moore, is always a "morally salient act-type." First- and second-degree murder, for example, as well as manslaughter and negligent homicide, are the same morally prohibited act-type, the killing of a human being (and I add, but Moore does not) on private authority. Thus, "the same morally wrong act-type is referred to by each such statute…and no matter how such act-types may be described in the differing statutes," for double jeopardy purposes the offences are the same (AC, 337-8).[55] I think this is the logic of Lord Morris' position and that of the common-law tradition he documented.

The broader metaphysical and epistemological support of the idea of the "morally salient act-type" is found in a number of Moore's other works. Catholic jurisprudence cannot accept Moore's ontology of moral properties and besides it has its own sources for defending the existence of such properties. Catholic social thought can nevertheless accept Moore's analysis of double jeopardy adjudication on account of its natural law foundation.

In a few very fine pages, Moore usefully makes clear some of the basic commitments of a natural law jurisprudence. Such jurisprudence is committed to the claims that there is a necessary connection between law and morality, that there are objective moral truths, and that the truth of legal propositions depends in part on the truth of moral propositions.[56] Intriguingly, an atheist, he nevertheless claims an Augustinian patronage for his basic commitments on the relationship between law and morality. A legal moralist theory, such as Moore's, makes moral wrongdoing central to legal wrongdoing (PB, 669) and legislators can legitimately try to make law reflect their best estimations of moral truth (PB, 69-70). In a number of places, Moore develops a theory as to what these extra-mental moral qualities are and how we access them. There is some, but only some, continuity here between Moore and moral theology. Moore thinks that *malice*, *wrongness*, and *justice*, for example, are properties out in the world that can be known. "We have," writes Moore, "moral intuitions in response to a moral reality."[57] His own view is that moral properties supervene upon realist metaphysics. That is, moral qualities are not exactly reducible to, but never separate from, or other than, natural events of causation and intentionality (LFK, 296 & 301; MR, *1127-8). Moral qualities are a type of "natural kind" where "natural" is taken in the extremely strong sense of, in fact, a physical event happening in the world (MR, *1144).[58] His basic argument is that moral properties relate to natural events just as mental states to brain events: mental states are not other than physical states of the brain yet possess a "subjective" character not similarly part of the character of the physical states (MR, *1137; MRR, 2442).

Moore thus rejects both the idea of a non-natural realm of objective moral qualities and the idea that what is morally right is specified by certain aspects of human nature (LFK, 296-7). The former is the position of the British intuitionists of the twentieth century and certainly had an earlier life in the Scottish Enlightenment. It is also found in the work of Scheler. The latter is oftentimes the position ascribed to Aquinas: norms are derived from the inclinations of human nature. In my opinion, the ethics of Aquinas and Wojtyla are a synthesis of the two. Besides having in Catholic tradition their own well-established theories of moral realism, Catholic jurists cannot accept a basic assumption Moore makes, and from which follows the peculiarities of his own realism (and perhaps its incoherence)—namely, there can be no such thing as a value reality. Value reality is, in Scheler's much-loved phrase, an *ordo amoris*: a hierarchy of values *structuring* reality.[59] Value reality is an expression of exemplary causality: simultaneously, a making manifest and imitating of the generosity of God's creative mercy (DM, section 4). Thus John

Paul II, with the judges of the European Court of Human Rights in the audience, can point to their human rights abortion jurisprudence and say, "This radical contradiction is possible only when freedom is sundered from the truth inherent in the reality of things…"[60] For Moore, moral value must ultimately be derivative of changes in physical reality—a reductionist in a "weak sense," as Moore calls himself (MRR, 2442), is still a reductionist. In no way does he accept that values are more primordial than nature and structurally active. In other words, he rejects exemplary causality: "Have I been with you so long, and yet you do not know me" (Jn 14: 9)?

John Paul II's Thomism and his phenomenological realism (v) are congruent with Moore's metaphysical realism. Each affirms that moral reality is most basically a latticework of intrinsic evils. Some acts are intrinsically evil "by reason of their object," the "objective content" of the chosen act (RP, para. 17). What is the "origin and the foundation" of a norm specifying an act as intrinsically evil (VS, para. 50)? All basic norms specify a conversion to or departure from the exemplary causality of the Supreme Good (PC, 90). The Supreme Good, God, is ecstatic: God is gift. The world, and the world of spirit especially, is rooted in, shot through by, and an example of the causality of gift (PC, 88-89; cf. LR, 126). The natural law describes *and protects* man's "primordial nature," as a personal unity of body and soul (VS, para. 50). The natural law affirms and protects man as gift. It demands that man nourish this gift by becoming a gift to others and demands that the gift be restored when human acts have caused a departure from the order instituted "from the beginning" by the Exemplar.[61] This vision of man explains why *Humanae Vitae* argues that contraceptive acts are intrinsically evil acts (acts which always must contradict the order of gift instituted "from the beginning") and why *Evangelium Vitae* argues that the (direct and voluntary) killing of an innocent human being is an intrinsically evil act (EV, para. 57)—such an act always destroys the gift offering that is a basic property of innocent life (EV, para. 58).[62]

Moore thinks that the morality addressed by criminal law is a set of prohibitions directed at each and every agent, that is, an agent-relative morality (PB, 74). Although, and here traditional moral theology must be critical, he has what he calls a "complex agent-relative" morality as opposed to that of "absolutists," as he calls them (PB, 75). He explains this theory most thoroughly in an article on the morality of torture and law governing interrogations.

Moore argues that there are no convincing arguments for the role of God in natural law. On the face of it, he seems to have an important point against a central theme of John Paul II: that a public philosophy without God will not contain robust protections for innocents. John Paul II speaks frequently of the need to recognize God's sovereignty as a restraint upon human ambition to render (an inevitably cruel) justice (RP, para. 14). Moore can respond that his moral realism acknowledges sovereignty beyond and restraining man, but there is no need to accept that this sovereignty is ultimately secured by a personal God. Moore comments that Finnis, having very ably elaborated a natural law thesis without God, ultimately introduces God's providence. Commenting on Finnis' claim that law without God leaves us with a "debilitating subjectivity," Moore struggles to see why there is any such anxiety. Finnis is quite right, says Moore, that God is not required for "making out the objective existence of moral qualities" or motivating us to action. He sees no good reasons for supposing the moral order requires anything else, however.[63] But Moore mistakes Finnis' point and also John Paul II's. Despite the seeming rigor of Moore's moral objectivism, his jurisprudence collapses into decisionism. Moore confirms the infamous jurist Carl Schmitt's claim that political order ultimately rests on the extra-moral foundation of decision.

Considering the role of torture in government intelligence gathering, Moore argues that torture is an intrinsic evil but reasons of state, that is, knowledge that a horrendous evil will be perpetrated unless intelligence derived from torture victims is found, allows one to relax the requirements of the intrinsic evil. Moral order limits action for the most part but a balancing of evils test is, in some cases, necessary. Moore offers this test as an elaboration of the necessity defense.[64] The basic mistake here is that Moore thinks human action can reconcile all things. Finnis and John Paul II do not. Reconciliation "is principally a gift of the heavenly Father" (RP, para. 5) and it is Christ alone in whom all things will be reconciled (RP, para. 7). Torture and killing of innocents is sometimes necessary, says Moore, and, of course, he has no *principled* way of saying when necessary and when not. Schmitt's point is that if there is no principled way then why claim that statecraft is governed by moral truth at all or a natural law theory of intrinsic evils or the rule of law. Moore has no answer to Schmitt: he is prompted to instrumentalize some innocents for the sake of some others—to do evil that good might come of it—because justice *must* prevail. Quite cogently for an atheist, providence is rejected by the desire for, as Camus puts it, a "unitarian reign of justice"

(R, 24). And this desire, as John Paul II notes, is the desire of Babel but no solution to "the tragedy of humanity today" (RP, para. 13). Rejection of God's providential action, a rejection of the cross, an act that brings to fruition cosmic reconciliation of justice and mercy,[65] is also suicidal: humanitarian sentiment contradicts itself in an instrumentalization of the innocent.[66] Indeed, John Paul II—and the similarity with Camus here is remarkable—casts this collapse of humanitarian sentiment into crime as "an objective law and an objective reality" (RP, para. 15).

Justice cannot reconcile the world and the attempt to make this so issues in an unprincipled intrumentalization of the innocent, hence, Finnis' talk of a "debilitating subjectivity." Humanitarianism is homicidal and without forgiveness (RP, para. 17-18). Mercy rises above injustice; it does not cancel it out. The biblical story of the Prodigal Son, with which John Paul II's *Reconciliatio et Paenitentia* begins, is a fine example of the point (RP, para. 6). John Paul II argues here that the Eucharist, a sacramental renewal of the *mysterium crucis*, is rightly called the "sacrifice of reconciliation" (RP, para. 7). At the cross, Christ responds to the injustice wrought in His body with the mercy He channels from His father (DM, section 1). With the cross, the Innocent shields all with His mercy: "this blood, which flows from the pierced side of Christ on the Cross (cf. Jn 19:34), "speaks more graciously" than the blood of Abel; indeed, it expresses and requires a more radical "justice," and above all it implores mercy..." (EV, para. 25). The cross is then a protection to innocence and guilt alike—"The Just One who offers himself for the unjust" (RP, para. 20). The plea of double jeopardy has its deepest moral theological foundation—and can this be a surprise?—in the cross. The plea is an institutional recognition that law aims at reconciliation but sometimes *because truly human* settles for resignation. This resignation is a wounding, the suspicion of injustice persisting, but it is a wound founded on an institution of reconciliation. To observe piety in respect of the ancient plea is in fact to enter into that "mystery of *pietas* [which] is the path opened by divine mercy to a reconciled life."

By way of concluding, the whole of revelation, says John Paul II, is a demonstration that mercy is more basic than justice (DM, section 4). With Kolnai, we might say that mercy is a higher value than justice but with weaker emphasis. Like Aquinas, John Paul II thinks that a person can alienate his dignity—this is part of the content of the parable of the Prodigal Son (DM, section 5). Yet, another content of that same parable is the mercy of the father, "totally concentrated upon the humanity of the lost son, upon his dignity" (DM, section 6). The doctrine of double jeopardy is an effort to make mercy present in criminal procedure. It is an asylum for the guilty and the innocent who is suspect; it aims at restoring dignity. John Paul II reminds us that the generosity of the father "so angers the elder son" (DM, section 6). It is a remarkable feature of all of the documents leading up to the 2003 Criminal Justice Act how focused they are on people "getting away with stuff." They are written entirely from the perspective of making people "pay." If the review of the law had been from the perspective of protecting the innocent, these documents would read differently; and this would even be true if written with an eye to the idea of asylum. I will add here that I see no reason to accept that the plea is just a matter of being "soft" on crime. The point is to find a place for mercy in the law and this is entirely compatible with, say, a defense of capital punishment as one finds in Aquinas. The logic of the defense of the plea is not also an argument against capital punishment. This is just to ignore the role of emphasis. How would this entire review of the law look if the Law Commission was first and foremost concerned with sensational cases *from another perspective*? Verses from the *Book of Numbers* began the commentary on this chapter; these verses speak of the "manslayer" seeking refuge from judgment, even capital. Moral theology's defense of the *autrefois* plea is not fundamentally about giving the guilty time to reform but protecting the innocent from the stalking avenger in sensational cases—sometimes, even the innocent need the protections of mercy.

Why do the documents betray so much anger with the generosity of the plea? John Paul II observes that the "present-day mentality" tends to "remove from the human heart the very idea of mercy" (DM, section 2). In this case, the clue to the "mentality" at play is making law derivative of human rights. There is something truly shocking to a victim who, told he is the source and reason for law, observes the law to privilege a few: the tried. Double jeopardy is a special protection, a unique "place" of asylum in the social order. This is completely unsurprising: Saint Thomas à Becket advocated it as a privilege of the clerical *status*. The shield offered by double jeopardy is an inequality stemming from the law's generosity, which cannot but offend a democratic egalitarianism.

Some commentators argue that the recent abolition of double jeopardy is a destruction of basic English liberties at the behest of efforts on the part of the Blair government to integrate English into European law. Benedict XVI's engagement with a Europe he fears is increasingly post-Christian might, at one level, be misconceived. If there is a foundation in moral theology for double jeopardy doctrine, and if it is true that its protection of innocence has no place in the emerging skeptical European human rights jurisprudence, how ought the Holy See react? The Holy See has welcomed European integration. John Paul II famously reversed long-standing Vatican policy towards the Eastern bloc: Might Benedict need to change policy also? Most basically, what is required is that the church defend privilege. It is not a matter of rejecting democracy or wholesale abandonment of the idea of human rights. Aware of the egalitarian dynamic of democracy and de Tocqueville's warning that it can sometimes be pernicious, Catholic social thought needs to re-affirm the value of those sites of privilege that still remain from the inheritance of Christendom. After all, Berman argues that when the church insisted on its privilege in the twelfth century over against the state, the Western legal tradition was born (LR, 85-8). Aurel Kolnai saw this as the most essential task of contemporary politics. I have argued elsewhere (EM) that this is precisely the role played by John Paul II's sexual politics. If criticism is now heard of theology's captivity to European ideas might not the same be said of Vatican policy on law? Double jeopardy is a provision of the U. S. Constitution. The greatest jurist of the twentieth century, Carl Schmitt, regarded Anglo-American law as *sui generis*—a conception of law, he thought, intimately tied to American sea power. Might Rome be wise to look towards the Atlantic for future policy on law? Might Mary, *Stella Maris*, beckon?

Notes

1. John Paul II, *Reconciliatio et Paenitentia*, para. 22; hereafter, RP.
2. A. Camus, *The Rebel*, trans., A. Bower (New York: Vintage, 1991), 21: (= R).
3. Please see my essays: "Contemporary Jesuits! You Have But Two Choices: The Politics of John Paul II or Ultramontanism," *Budhi: A Journal of Ideas and Culture*, Vol. 4, Summer 2000, pp. 283-297 [co-authored with Jamey Becker]; "Rebels and Christian Princes: Politics and Violence in Camus and Augustine" *Revista Filosófica de Coimbra*, Vol. 16, October 1999, pp. 253-267.
4. W. Miller, *An Eye for an Eye*, p. 83.
5. P. Ricoeur, "The Logic of Jesus, the Logic of God," *Figuring the Sacred* (Minneapolis, MN: Fortress Press, 1995), pp. 279-283.
6. Giles of Rome, "On Ecclesiastical Power," in *Medieval Political Philosophy*, eds. R. Lerner & M. Mahdi (Ithaca, NY: Cornell University Press, 1983), p. 397.
7. M. Friedman, *Double Jeopardy* (Oxford: Oxford University Press, 1969), p. 3; hereafter, DJ2.
8. G. Thomas, *Double Jeopardy: The History, the Law* (New York: New York University Press, 1998). A legal positivist who thinks theology warrants the idea that there are no intrinsic evils—and, therefore, no moral constraint on legislative will. I disagree with his potted theology (pp. 72-3). He rejects Michael Moore's analysis of double jeopardy (though he admires Moore's efforts [p. 87]) but he and Moore are really ships passing in the night. Thomas is a thoroughgoing nominalist and

does not engage the realist foundation of Michael Moore's position; a position defended with modifications in this chapter. Thomas' book hereafter = DJ1.

9. Lord Devlin rejects this position of legislative liberty out of hand in *Connelly* (1964): "The courts cannot contemplate for a moment the transference to the Executive of the responsibility for seeing that the process of law is not abused" (as cited by DJ2, 90). Nonetheless, as becomes apparent later that Lord Devlin, like G. Thomas, is a nominalist respecting acts.

10. P. Westen, "The Three Faces of Double Jeopardy: Reflections on Government Appeals of Criminal Sentences," *Michigan Law Review* (1980), p. 1001.

11. C. Delsol, *Icarus Fallen* (Wilmington, DE: ISI, 2003), especially Chapters 5 & 7.

12. Speaking about, and to the judges of, the European Court of Human Rights, John Paul II noted, "the Holy See has been especially interested in the jurisprudence of the Court." In the context of an overall welcoming, John Paul II expressed strong reservations about that Court's family and abortion law (John Paul II, *Address of John Paul II on the Occasion of the Commemoration of the Fiftieth Anniversary of the European Convention on Human Rights*, para. 3.)

13. For recent discussion, see J. L. Malcom, "Mad Dogs and Englishmen," WSJ, June 17-18, 2006.

14. See "Schedule 5," *Criminal Justice Act* (2003).

15. Ironically, contemporary biblical scholars understand the passage to be about the "tenacity" of God as an avenger. See *The Jerome Biblical Commentary* (London: G. Chapman, 1978), p. 294.

16. A. James et al., "The Reform of Double Jeopardy," *Web Journal of Current Legal Issues* (2000), p. 5; hereafter, RDJ.

17. S. Broadbridge, "The *Criminal Justice Bill*: Double Jeopardy and Prosecution Appeals," *House of Commons Research Paper 02/74* (2 December, 2002), p. 36; hereafter RP2.

18. A. Thorp & S. Broadbridge, "The *Criminal Justice Bill*" *House of Commons Research Paper 02/72* (2 December, 2002), p. 13; hereafter, RP1.

19. J. Maritain, *Man and the State* (Washington, D.C.: The Catholic University of America Press, 1998), Chapter 4.

20. J. Finnis, *Aquinas* (Oxford: Oxford University Press, 1998), Chapter 5.

21. J. Finnis, *Natural Law and Natural Rights* (Oxford: Oxford University Press, 1980), Chapter 4.

22. A. MacIntyre, *After Virtue* (Notre Dame, IN: University of Notre Dame, 1981), pp. 66-7; and perhaps most provocatively, R. Kraynak, *Christian Faith and Modern Democracy* (Notre Dame, IN: University of Notre Dame, 2001), pp. 172-80. Cf. T. Roland, *Culture and the Thomist Tradition: After Vatican II* (London: Routledge, 2003).

23. M. Moore, *Placing Blame: A Theory of the Criminal Law* (Oxford: Oxford University Press, 1997), p. 29; hereafter, PB.

24. Martin Linton, M.P. "Second Time Unlucky?" *Guardian Unlimited* (July 17, 2001), pp. 1-2. For similar sentiments expressed in the official record, see *The Double Jeopardy Rule: Third Report of the Select Committee on Home Affairs*, para. 18; hereafter, *Third Report*.

25. "In law, as in morals, deliberate killing will be marked off as a special category of act" (CP 267, 43). Please see n. 34 below for full bibliographical information on document CP 267.

26. For Bakunin's insight into the theological character of modern politics, see his *Statism and Anarchy* (Cambridge: Cambridge University Press, 2005).

27. In England, the dates of these respective decriminalizations are 1961 and 1967. The crucial date for English understanding of double jeopardy is a 1964 case. Recently, English doctors *en masse* have asked the Blair government to withdraw its legislation decriminalizing euthanasia.

28. Admittedly, the Blair government had been under enormous pressure to do something about crime in Britain. No other industrial nation has as high a violent crime rate, homicides have increased dramatically in the last decade or so, and a day does not go by without political commentary on the fact.

29. J. Talmon, *The Origins of Totalitarian Democracy* (New York: W. W. Norton & Co., 1970), p. 116.

30. John Paul II, *Dives in misericordia*, section 2; hereafter DM.

31. "Re-balancing the Scales of Justice," *Guardian Unlimited* (November 22, 2002), p. 2.

32. Amongst many other places, see *Third Report*, para. 1.

33. Finland appears to be the only other European country with such an exception.

34. *Double Jeopardy: Law Commission Consultation Paper No 156* (October 1999) = CP 156. After the provisional proposals of this document were reviewed widely amongst professional and political bodies, a refined document appeared, *Double Jeopardy and Prosecution Appeals: Law Commission Consultation Paper No 267* (March 2001); hereafter, CP 267.

35. F. Kerr, "*Fides et Ratio*, Analytic Philosophy, and Metaphysics of Goodness," *John Paul II & St. Thomas Aquinas*, ed. M. Dauphinais & M. Levering (Ann Arbor, MI: Sapientia Press, 2006), pp. 187-207.

36. See R. Reno, "Theology's Continental Captivity," *First Things*, 162 (April 2006), pp. 26-33.

37. Amongst other essays, see Moore's "The Interpretive Turn in Modern Theory: A Turn for the Worse?" in *Educating Oneself in Public: Critical Essays in Jurisprudence* (Oxford: Oxford University Press, 2000), pp. 335-423.

38. J. Salmond, *Jurisprudence*, 12th edition, (London: Sweet & Maxwell, 1966), p. 355. Salmond's nominalism is the philosophical foundation of G. Thomas' treatise on double jeopardy. This from G. Thomas: "I conclude that since the legislature creates statutory criminal blameworthiness…the legislature is the ultimate source of guidance on when offenses are the same and when the first jeopardy has ended" (DJ, 6).

39. The position of Westen, for example. See his "The Three Faces of Double Jeopardy: Reflections on Government Appeals of Criminal Sentences," *Michigan Law Review* (1980), p. 1004.

40. WSJ (June 20, 2006), A3, A13, & A20. The Leader article is appropriately called "Parsing the Waters."

41. R. Epstein, "Trust Busters on the Supreme Court," WSJ (July 12, 2006).

42. Baroness Helena Kennedy, QC, "Second Time Unlucky?" *Guardian Unlimited* (July 17, 2001), p. 4.

43. The classic discussion is found in S. Pinckaers, O. P., *The Sources of Christian Ethics* (Washington, D. C.: The Catholic University of America Press, 1995).

44. 2 Leach 708, 720, 168 Eng. Rep. 455, 461 (1796).

45. According to Lord Morris of Borth-y-Gest this decision came from an appeal where all the judges of England were present (*Connelly* [1964] A.C. 1254, *1309).

46. M. Moore, *Act and Crime: The Theory of Action and Its Implications for Criminal Law* (Oxford: Oxford University Press, 1993), p. 314; hereafter AC.

47. Lord Morris of Borth-y-Gest, *Connelly* (1964) A.C. 1254, *1310; 1323-4.

48. Lord Morris of Borth-y-Gest, *Connelly* (1964) A.C. 1254, *1309.

49. Lord Morris of Borth-y-Gest, *Connelly* (1964) A.C. 1254, *1330. Cf. Lord Hodson's speech, *Connelly* (1964) A.C. 1254, *1337-8.

50. *Regina v. Beedie* (1998) Q.B. 356, *360-1. Cf. Lord Reid's speech, *Connelly* (1964) A.C. 1254, *1295-6.

51. "The *Connelly* principle, on the other hand, allows a second prosecution where a different offence is charged on the same or substantially the same facts, because it counts as a 'special circumstance' " (CP 156, 6). Cf. CP 156, 12.

52. Lord Devlin, *Connelly* (1964) A.C. 1254, *1340.

53. W. Blackstone, *Commentaries*, Book 4, c. 26, *4.

54. On the moral and spiritual importance of acts of resignation, see M. Scheler, *Ressentiment*, p. 35.

55. Moore offers a similar analysis of a variety of other crimes over a number of pages (AC, 337-44).

56. M. Moore, "Law as a Functional Kind," in: *Educating Oneself in Public: Critical Essays in Jurisprudence* (Oxford: Oxford University Press, 2000), pp. 294-7; hereafter, LFK.

57. M. Moore, "Moral Reality," *Wisconsin Law Review* (1982), *1124; hereafter, MR.

58. "...even though not type-identical, there can be no change in one without a change in the other" (M. Moore, "Moral Reality Revisited," *Michigan Law Review* (1992), p. 2441); hereafter, MRR.

59. For a detailed analysis of value reality see A. Kolnai, *Early Ethical Writings of Aurel Kolnai* (Aldershot: Ashgate, 2002).

60. John Paul II, *Address of John Paul II on the Occasion of the Commemoration of the Fiftieth Anniversary of the European Convention on Human Rights*, para. 3.

61. For John Paul II's famous reflections on *Matthew* 19:8 see *Theology of the Body*, Part One; cf. VS, para. 51.

62. See my earlier discussion of capital punishment and Aquinas' claim about the alienation of dignity. A more biblical image is that such a person has become like the Leviathan of the Book of Job (41: 23) whose scales are so tightly drawn together that the creature is monstrous, unnatural as anti-gift.

63. M. Moore, "Good without God," in *Natural Law, Liberalism, and Morality*, ed. R. George (Oxford: Oxford University Press, 1996), pp. 251-259.

64. M. Moore, "Torture and the Balance of Evils," *Israel Law Review*, 23 (1989), pp. 280-344. For caution in applying the necessity defense, please see the seventh chapter below.

65. Cf. M. Levering, *Christ's Fulfillment of Torah and Temple* (Notre Dame, IN: University of Notre Dame Press, 2002).

66. For the general argument that a public philosophy without a role for Providence is inevitably nihilistic, see M. Levering, *Biblical Natural Law: A Theocentric and Teleological Approach* (Oxford University Press, 2008).

4

Political Theology and the Law of War

*Our spirit is made hierarchical so that it may
continue upward.*
                                    —*St. Bonaventure*

*[Jesus Christ] introduces into our history a univer-
sal truth which stirs the human mind to ceaseless
effort.*
                        —*John Paul II,* Fides et Ratio *as
                        quoted in* Dominus Iesus[1]

Whether It Is Lawful for Clerics to Kill Evildoers

Commentary on Thomas' fourth article aims to counter recent Christian efforts to deny that there is a natural law justification for war. These efforts are variously the attempt to show that theological ethics has no place for autonomous morality and that the vital reduces to the holy and the natural to the evangelical.[2] Whatever the terms, the logic is to deny the ordered hierarchy amongst values, and it contrasts sharply with how the "papal revolution" (Berman) related to Germanic law (PR, 82-3). There is a tendency to deny low values the status of value because the "height" through which distinctions amongst values is made is opposed by equalitarianism. The theories of nature and grace introduced mid-twentieth century by de Lubac and Rahner especially hamper Christian thinking about value hierarchy. This is the thesis I defend now.

In his commentary on Aquinas' question on homicide, Cajetan forthrightly acknowledges that evangelical law is one of mercy and so foreign to the punishment of blood (*poena sanguinis*) that is regularly imposed by civil authorities. The New Law does not remove civil power, however, for whilst the passion of Christ revokes the judicial precepts of the Old Law the moral precepts are eternal. Crucially, it falls to natural reason to

85

discern in what way, where, and when these moral precepts are binding in human affairs ("...these things Jesus Christ left to moral reason" [In Comm. II-II, q. 64, a. 2]). The moral law does not have its content on account of something having been prohibited but on account of some things being evil; and this moral content human reason can discern (De malo, q. 2, a. 4; H, 79-83). Many Christian ethicists believe that Jesus was a pacifist. The Renaissance Cajetan agrees, but the dispute, to put it a little paradoxically, is whether everyone else ought to be (PR, 148).

Cajetan's paradoxical formulation loses some of its character once his reliance on hierarchy is appreciated. The point is very evident in Thomas. Addressing an objector's argument that slaying the innocent is less harmful to the innocent than is slaying the guilty—for the innocent go straight to glory—Thomas replies that the innocent are protected by both charity and justice, and whether a person can "be received by God into glory" is "accidental" to the moral significance of the slaying (ST II-II, q. 64, a. 6, ad 2). Although the objector relies on a man's supernatural standing, Thomas denies that the question of friendship with God is relevant to the question at hand: "In weighing the gravity of a sin we must consider the essential rather than the accidental." Thomas argues here that there is an autonomous morality that human reason can know. To his mind, the Christian moral hierarchy presupposes the integrity of this natural order without denying it can be *supplemented*, even dramatically.

Thomas held that priests cannot kill. De Vitoria observes that Thomas held to an ancient prohibition, but, subsequent to Thomas, debate on the issue intensified. Vitoria concludes his article speculatively: if a priest kills he becomes "irregular," needing purification, although the pope may well have authority to suspend the prohibition (H, 163-9). Both insist that the sacrament of Holy Orders divides clergy from laity in the matter of killing. The priest's hands are smeared with the sacrificial blood of Christ, and he must not mix that blood with another's by homicide, insists Thomas. With the famous declaration of *Gaudium et Spes* (para. 22), that Christ is the revelation of the meaning of being human, some doubt now whether Thomas' distinction between clergy and laity, the sacramental ordination to the evangelical and a layperson's closer proximity to the world of Aristotle's natural virtues, is still viable.[3] A recent work on just war by the distinguished Anglican theologian Oliver O'Donovan relies on this doubt. Very briefly below, I describe his central thesis. I will not address his work on war directly but will consider the broader theory of nature and grace that, in my opinion, sustains this doubt. This broader theory stems from the enormously influential work of the Jesuits de Lubac and Rahner. It presupposes an equalitarianism that fosters monism: monism being unacceptable for all the reasons discussed at length in the first chapter. Monism adopted, totalitarianism flourishes. If grace evacuates nature, theology acts as a leveling agent against this order and provokes a falsification of morality.

O'Donovan's interest in an evangelical devaluing of war diminishes moral order and (unwittingly) extends an invitation to totality. To defend his claim that there is no Christian natural law theory of just war but only an evangelical critique,[4] O'Donovan argues that peace is the moral good, which makes war a disvalue. This is evidently Thomas' thinking, he argues, not so much from what Thomas says as from the place of the discussion of war in the structure of the *Summa theologica*. There, war is ranged alongside various disvalues contrasting with positive values. Since peace is a value that contrasts with war as a disvalue, it cannot be that Christianity views war as a good able to serve statecraft but, at very best, an evil requiring toleration ("war serves the end of history only as evil serves the good, and the power to bring good out of evil belongs to God alone").[5]

By contrast, Augustine argues that war and peace are in a certain *continuity* with one another as values found in the service of good social order. Augustine does not posit an absolute opposition between the city of man and the City of God, with the peace of the church opposed to all violence of the power of the city of man. Reprising Cajetan's formulation, are we right to think that Augustine believes the peace of the church ought to be the same sort of peace of worldly government? He speaks favorably of the Christian prince who uses domination to bring order.[6] This worldly order, albeit a low value, is an ally of the City of God on earth. This is to say that political power, including domination and violence, is not an evil demanding toleration but a value with its own proportionate place. This premise is basic to Thomistic political theory, as well (PW, 9-11; 92). Might it then not be that war, for Thomas, is a lower value than peace, but not a disvalue? This logical possibility O'Donovan does not consider.

Respecting the central thesis of this chapter—that removing the hierarchical relationship between nature and grace fosters denials that low values have autonomous standing as values—it is well to note that the Catholic Church claims that it is the spouse of Christ, and because this marriage is monogamous, the church has a uniquely close relationship with God that no other religion can rival. The church says it is closer to the inner core of reality and goodness than any other institution on earth. If the world and supra-sensible reality meet at all, then they meet in the church. This privilege generates other privileges: the male priesthood, a unique diplomatic corps, and a universal spiritual authority. It is on account of a spousal intimacy with God that the church is a bastion of conservative causes. Despite the media firestorm, the church is an outspoken defender of heterosexual marriage and the traditional family. It is part and parcel of family life that parents seek preferential treatment for their own children, they pursue privilege for them, and so unsurprisingly the church is a defender of private schooling and school choice. The pursuit of family privilege, the church explains, is but an instance of the order of charity in which one loves what is closest. For this reason, the church expects a preferential regard for one's own nation and peculiar concern for its political, military, and economic robustness. The church is not the guardian of the just war tradition merely because it wants justice in the world: the church acknowledges as completely appropriate the patriot's keen desire to protect the division of land without which social order and preferment are impossible.

The church's social philosophy is conservative. Persons are born into a community with origins in privilege—family life, property, national resources, character, and prestige. The church in no way accepts that persons are born as isolated individuals facing one another as equals and ready to consent to a contract in which goods and pleasures will be distributed according to a rationally conceived plan. If Catholicism's conservatism goes back to the core theological idea that the church is *married* to God, might it not all unravel? Everyone knows that sexuality is not only the most contested political issue today but that the Catholic Church is one of the principal battlegrounds. Surely, the theological center of the church might give and with it, all the conservative positions generated from that centre. It is no surprise that the only book of political philosophy written on the topic of divorce is by Louis de Bonald, a French Catholic who was a member of the Bourbon restoration government following Bonaparte's dictatorship. To preserve the center of the church, Thomists must ward off the threat to privilege posed by equalitarianism.

A basic and wholesale shift in Catholic thinking occurred around the 1950s when Catholic theologians accepted as seminal the work of the French Jesuit Henri de Lubac. In his 1946 *Surnaturel*, de Lubac criticized one of Catholicism's theological giants, the Renaissance cardinal Thomas Cajetan (1469-1534). Despite the passage of 400 years, Cajetan remained a dominating presence in Catholic theology. His stature rested on two pillars. In the earliest years of the twentieth century, Cajetan's commentary on Aquinas' *Summa theologica* was printed right alongside Thomas' own words in the definitive Vatican edition of the *Summa*. Apart from this privilege, Cajetan's fame derived from a profound intervention he had made in Catholic theology. On the face of it, the problem so famously addressed by Cajetan seems too piquant to be little more than a theoretical curiosity. However, the problem—what did Aquinas mean by saying that there is a natural desire in humans to see God?—turns out to be so basic to how a Catholic views the world that there is no corner untouched by any answer given. As I hope to show shortly, the answers given to this question in the twentieth century included a political orientation replete with consequences for how one thinks about the person, politics, and law.

Cajetan's answer to the problem, the *duplex ordo*, generated a consensus amongst Catholic theologians that lasted for over 400 years. It was this idea de Lubac so famously, and until recently,[7] successfully attacked. Aquinas barely mentioned the idea of a natural desire to see God but what little he did say posed the very definition of a mind-bender. How can the supernatural, God, provoke a natural desire? Wouldn't the provoked desire be supernatural in some sense? And if humans can respond to the supernatural, wouldn't this mean that humans are in some sense already supernatural? Yet, if humans all have some sort of supernatural orientation what of God's initiative respecting salvation? It is axiomatic to Christianity that salvation is granted to any of us only through an utterly gratuitous act of mercy on the part of God (DCE, para. 1). But Thomas' idea of natural desire seems to place some of the initiative on the side of human nature. Yet if humans can initiate salvation do they really need it? And if they don't need it, what need have they of God? It was to stop this disturbing train of questions in its tracks that Cajetan came up with the idea of the *duplex ordo*. Put bluntly, Cajetan insisted that human nature is indeed completely natural and all that Thomas meant to say was that man could be lifted out of the natural order by a completely gratuitous and merciful act of grace: elevated by God to the supernatural order man "naturally" comes to have a desire to see God. Insisting on a discontinuity between the two orders, the natural and the supernatural, Cajetan could preserve God's privilege and liberty in the matter of salvation.

For the next 400 years, Catholic theology tweaked and finessed the language and concepts used by Cajetan but no one doubted the explanatory elegance and suitability of the *duplex ordo*. This consensus not merely ended in the mid-twentieth century, it was positively buried and forgotten in the aftermath of de Lubac's work. De Lubac rightly observed that any defense of the gratuity of salvation had to balance another fundamental Catholic theological intuition. Expressed most famously by Augustine, man has a restless desire for God. De Lubac argued that Cajetan eviscerated Thomas' formulation of Augustine's point, giving no real explanation of how a nature possessing a natural end could at the same time have a desire for a supernatural end, an eternal life suffused by a vision of God. Catholic theology had to return to Thomas' problem again, insisted de Lubac, and re-explain it in order to end two disastrous consequences that flowed, unintentionally, of course, from Cajetan's theory.

Cajetan's theory made the life of grace extrinsic to the operations and actions of human nature, claimed de Lubac, and a fatal consequence of so severing humans from any dynamic of intimacy with God was secularization—for Cajetan had all too ably articulated a concept of human self-sufficiency in which humans have a nature and an end without any reference to God at all. Catholicism, argued de Lubac, helped engineer Enlightenment ideas like autonomy and individualism and therewith rejection of the idea of responsibilities and duties to family and community. Embracing Cajetan's mistaken analysis of nature and grace, Catholicism actually fostered Enlightenment anomie and willful self-assertion culminating in the late Western phenomenon of atheism and its murderous filiation, totalitarianism. Atheism's abolition of God was also an annihilation of man, argued de Lubac, and it was Cajetan, however unwittingly, who helped make it all possible. Thus, in an effort to regain Christian culture and then to *extend* it against a murderous opponent, de Lubac re-worked Thomas' notion of the natural desire for God. He wanted to be able to argue that in all of their operations and actions human persons are at root animated by their natural desire for intimacy with God. He was convinced, as was John Paul the Great, that unless God is re-established at the center of human life no true humanism can be sustained.

It is undeniable that de Lubac's cultural theology, so to say, helped Catholicism think through how to reassert itself markedly in the public life of nations. John Paul the Great's description of the cultures of life and death, and indeed his own life, are perhaps the most brilliant formulations yet of de Lubac's call to a Christian re-engagement with culture. All the same, just as Cajetan's work appears to have had peculiar unforeseen consequences, so too it now appears de Lubac's own work may do so as well. Perhaps it is true that Cajetan's theology helped foster atheism, but perhaps it is equally true that de Lubac's theology has made Catholics unable to identify as an opponent a subtle creature indeed, humanitarianism.

What if de Lubac was wrong and Catholicism's most dangerous adversary is not atheism but humanitarian love? In identifying atheism as the principal enemy, what if de Lubac merely focused on certain secondary characteristics of the enemy and missed the fact that the basic disputed issue is not a matter of *belief* but, as Scheler contends in his *Ordo Amoris*, a matter of *how best to love*. Sacrifice is the essential content of Christian love, yet this idea of love can only strike the humanitarian as a perversity. The humanitarian is utterly convinced that if there is real human love—that is, the realization in the world of a just and equal order—there will be no place for sacrifice, for a just love precludes the very possibility of sacrifice. Many examples would point up this difference but simply consider the bewilderment and outright rage humanitarians feel towards Catholicism's rejection of condoms as a solution to the spread of AIDS in Africa and other places. The core of love is the sacrifice of self-donation, says the church, and so no matter what the cultural mores may be regarding male liberty for many partners, the solution to the spread of AIDS in Africa relies on sexual self-restraint, devotion to a partner, and the sacrifice this entails. By contrast, humanitarian love concedes the pull of cultural mores and so seeks to equalize the health situation of men and women when they have sex.

Because de Lubac so spiritualized or divinized human nature by arguing that the natural and supernatural are entwined[8] one is left to wonder both whether this elevation of human nature doesn't play right into the hands of humanitarianism and whether Catholicism has been basically disarmed to contest the idea that humans standing alone are equal to the task of moral and political life. De Lubac was so concerned that theology make sense of Augustine's claim that human desire is restless till it rests in God that he seemingly ignored a far more chilling thing Augustine once said, "No one is good." Much might be said in the *Confessions* about the desire for God but much is also said about the constitutive perversity of the will's fascination with evil. Thus, Augustine's pronouncement "No one is good" became the axiom from which the Catholic political theorist Donoso Cortés fought against humanitarianism in the mid-nineteenth century but this axiom has now simply been forgotten, worse, made incomprehensible on de Lubac's theory of the relationship between nature and grace. Theology's spiritualization of the human person has seemingly confirmed the Kantian rejection of human nature and the finitude it includes. Thus, theology's divinization of the human person runs seamlessly into Kant's universalization of the person. Kant famously rejected human nature as a perversion of the universal aspirations of man, deeming it nothing more than a *pretium_vulgare*, a vulgar commercial thing. But it is in the natural order that one finds the family, the patriot, markets, the need for expiation that is the foundation of criminal law, national character, and sovereignty. Humanitarians are aghast at each of these phenomena, preferring population control, international law, social management of the economy, therapeutic treatment of criminals, and world government. Humanitarianism as a moralizing, universalist credo depends on a radical spiritualization of nature for in this way only can the particular claims of nature be usurped.

It is, of course, the particular claims of nature that orient us in the world. The division of land by borders establishes a terrestrial order in which persons can find the geography of their daily concerns, and ultimately, their moral bearings (I take this theme up again in the sixth chapter). The particularity of these divisions privileges some places in our lives, and whilst every privilege encourages excellence, it also suggests a certain indulgence. No one is good, said Augustine, echoing the rebuke of Jesus, "Why do you call me good? No one is good but God alone" (Mark 10: 18; and Paul's comment, "nothing good dwells within me, that is, in my flesh" [Romans 7:18]). And so if the world is to know peace it can only be the peace of Augustine's *tranquillitas ordinis*, an order inescapably reliant upon the particularities of our natural orientation with its moral positives and limitations both. Jesus' rebuke at Mark 10: 18 is the premise of his saying at Matthew 10: 37: "He who loves father or mother more than me is not worthy of me; and he who loves son or daughter more than me is not worthy of me." Hence, as seen in the second chapter, when dealing with the question of vengeance Aquinas confirms Cicero's claim that it is a natural virtue. Vengeance might not be the finest thing about human nature but it is the indispensable support of our sense of expiation upon which good public order depends.

No one can deny or underestimate the influence of de Lubac on theology's divinization of man but he was not alone, the towering figure of another Jesuit in this story is inescapable. Between de Lubac's work of the 30s and 40s and its millennial reassessment stands Karl Rahner. It is impossible to read Rahner and not be in awe of the man: his theoretical acumen is stunning but even so it takes second place to his erudition; Rahner knew everything there is to know about theology. But it is in Rahner's work that a political assumption submerged in de Lubac's work comes plainly to the fore, an assumption that has desensitized Catholic theology to the threat it faces from humanitarianism. This assumption is equalitarianism. To see how far this equalitarianism has been pushed consider what Milbank has to say about the *visio dei*. Milbank very much wants to be a part of "the real theological revolution" started by de Lubac and Rahner. The revolutionary aspect befits his sense of himself as a "socialist Christian." Rahner and de Lubac have made the supernatural dynamism of human nature so evident, he claims, that human nature "demands as of right fulfillment" by God.[9] Thus, Aquinas' talk of a natural desire to see God now stands as a warrant for the claim that humans have a right against God. Aquinas insisted that God owes nothing whatsoever to creation, that there is no relationship of justice *from* God *to* creatures (ScG II, c. 28, para. 4). Of course, Milbank is not thinking of Thomas, but Rahner's equalitarianism. So imperious are the demands of equality that Milbank claims that the *visio dei* is nothing less than "the elevation of our being *into* the divine substance" (emphasis added).[10] Man made the equal of God! With such a claim one is very far from Aquinas. Aquinas argues that the human attains to a new intimacy with God in the *visio dei*, an intimacy made possible by the *lumen gloriae*. The light of glory is a *created* act gifted to the human by God, which fully realizes the human potential for knowledge and love and which allows the human a perduring *experience* of the interior life of the loving triune God. The point is crucial: the light of glory, according to Aquinas, is a created act divinely gifted out of privilege and liberty that allows an experience of the uncreated order that is the lived relationship of the three divine persons of the Christian God. In the *visio dei* the human never leaves the created order despite a perduring experience of the essence of God, for as Thomas insists, there is an infinite distance in being between the created and uncreated (ScG III, c. 54, para. 3; 50, para. 5). Aquinas never jeopardizes the "height" of God and the privilege of action given by the distinction of being the uncreated Lord of the created order.

Convinced of the moral claim of equality, even its claim on God, some contemporary (or is that revolutionary?) theologians begin their theology from the same premise as humanitarianism: equalitarianism. To appreciate how some theologians could claim to explain Aquinas' idea of the *desiderium naturale* and yet end up saying that humans have a right's claim against God, which Thomas utterly rejects, it is necessary to see the pedigree of these sorts of ideas in Rahner's theology. A little miffed perhaps at being beaten by his confrere to one of the greatest changes in Catholic theology in four hundred years, Rahner acknowledges the importance of de Lubac's *Surnaturel*, "even if," he says, "it is a little on the gloomy side."[11] In trying to expose the inadequacy of de Lubac's analysis Rahner introduced his now famous concept of "the supernatural existential."

As stated, the critique of de Lubac is epistemological, but of course, it really stems from the fact that Rahner developed a genuinely innovative theory of the relationship between nature and grace. This theory radicalizes de Lubac—about a decade after his ideas gained general acceptance de Lubac came to have grave reservations about the direction Catholic theology was moving—and begins with Rahner arguing that de Lubac has no way of knowing that the powerful spiritual yearnings experienced by people actually belong to human *nature*. Crucially, the fundamental oversight of de Lubac, says Rahner, is "that the possibility of experiencing grace and the possibility of experiencing grace *as* grace are not the same thing" (NG, 300). In restating the Thomistic natural desire, de Lubac had assumed that our basic "yearnings" are *not* supernatural because not actually experienced *as such*. This is a fatal assumption, insists Rahner, for grace can be operative and yet unrecognized. While Rahner's point could hardly be gainsaid, the positive leap to the supernatural existential that he next makes on the basis of this point surely could be. As Rahner introduces his innovation, the ostensible context is again epistemological, and even scientistic, with Rahner asking: Who could "prove" that grace is only present as "already stirred into faith and love?" Rahner's suggestion is daring indeed. Instead of the classical theory that the natural desire of the human for God is elicited by God freely infusing the theological virtues of faith, hope, and charity—divine gifts that humans can in no way generate—Rahner casts the supernatural existential as a "permanent dynamism of grace" that does not belong to "the substance of the *nature* of man" (my emphasis) but is a structure of *uncreated* grace belonging to each and every human *person*. Aquinas argued that a natural desire for God grows at the behest of the theological virtues gifted by God. These gifts and the supernatural bearing they give rise to are confirmed by *spiritual acts* of the persons involved, acts which are supported by, and in turn solidify, an *achieved* moral and spiritual life. Instead, Rahner argues that in the very creation of each and every human person God has always and already installed a *structure* of grace, which is both nothing less than "God's self-communication in love" (NG, 307) and intrinsic to the human person and so not a matter of a person's acts. The daring of Rahner's theory is matched by its brilliance for the installed grace remains unexacted because it is "something given in just the same way as nature and *with* it"; thus, the initiative stands with God, yet God and the human are drawn into profound intimacy.

Although Rahner insists that this theory preserves the distinction between nature and grace, still, in centering the site of this distinction at a point interior to the very constitution of the human person (though not human nature), Rahner has placed God and creatures in the same genus. Aquinas' absolute *ontological* division between man and God is here abandoned. The supernatural existential, the uncreated grace of "God's self-communication in love," says Rahner, is "not just a juridical decree of God but precisely what man *is*, hence not just an imperative proceeding from God but man's most inward depths" (NG, 302). And so the problem is not so much that he has not preserved a distinction between nature and grace but that Rahner has obscured the distinction between the human and the divine. God may not have been erased from human life but the "height" of God has been, and therewith the warrant of hierarchy, privilege, and the diversity of gifts, all of which result in thoroughgoing *spiritual* distinctions amongst humans, between "carnal" man and "reborn" man, as Augustine puts it.

Thus, the idea of the supernatural existential guts the church of its privileged standing in relationship to God. Having once implanted the supernatural existential as a universally held dimension of human persons, it seems incongruous to suppose, indeed untenable, that only Christianity amongst the world's religions has experienced and articulated the ever-present reality of "God's self-communication in love." That is, the supernatural existential encourages a *strong* form of pluralist theology in which many world religions should be said to contain genuine divine revelations, and not merely rich natural wisdom. It is implicit in Rahner's theory of nature and grace that the privilege that love supposes, and that marriage expresses, is no longer the foundation of a relationship with God: and so the church is no longer the spouse of Christ, for God's love is now a universal and egalitarian *regard* in which the church shares just like everyone else. Like humanitarianism, the universal regard for man proffered by the idea of the supernatural existential destroys any particular love for some and not all.

In eliminating the "height" of God and the distinction that separates God from man, a definite problem with Rahner's theory emerges. The basic difficulty to be addressed by any theory of the relationship between nature and grace is how to ensure that nature does not exact grace from God. Rahner sidesteps this question by positing a structure of grace given, and thus not exacted, with the other gifts of personhood and nature. Yet, he cannot avoid another question: How can the uncreated grace of the supernatural existential fail to exact a justifying grace, that is, fail to exact salvation itself? The essence of grace, Rahner tells us, "is God's self-communication in love." Once God has begun His self-communication in love, could His grace become discontinuous? And note the peculiar problem Rahner faces: he has defined the supernatural existential as *uncreated* grace, that is, he has defined it strongly. This is quite different from Aquinas, who conceives God's call to humans to join in His triune life as a series of infused theological virtues that perfect a moral order amongst the natural Aristotelian virtues. The theological virtues are habits divinely *created*—and so not "God's *self*-communication in love"—and gifted to some by God and eliciting from them spiritual acts of righteousness. So, the problem to pose to Rahner is not whether grace can be discontinuous, as clearly Aquinas thinks, but whether God's very own life—Uncreated Grace—could be discontinuous. Since the answer must be "no" the supernatural existential entails salvation. Rahner himself writes:

> One might with justice say that a gift of such a divine order and the communication of personal love are essentially unexacted. But all that follows from this is that a disposition cannot subsist on the human side which would inevitably draw this divine self-communication of personal love after it, *or that if it did*, the disposition must likewise be unexacted. (NG, 307-08; emphasis added)

Rahner does not then exclude that a constitutive part of what it is to be a human person can "inevitably" require of God a "divine self-communication of personal love." I suspect that he makes this admission because having once elevated the human into a partaker of God's personal love it becomes hard to see what a limited "divine self-communication" would be. For it is hard to see what divine love might be except total self-donation, the founding image of Christianity being the Father's mission of Christ's love displayed on a cross. Does not Rahner's strong formulation of the supernatural existential as "divine *self*-communication" expose that at the heart of Rahner's concept of grace is an equalitarianism? Written into the supernatural existential is the presumption of human righteousness and therewith the basis of humanitarian ethics. And so what Jesus once said is not true, "no one is good but God alone." Yet, the Christian is subtly disarmed, for what Jesus said remains true, only God is good: but because humans are in some sense the equal of God, in some sense *are* God, what Jesus said of God can now, without contradiction, equally as well be said of humans too. In Rahner's theology, God has lost His privilege and liberty. And if God has no privilege, nor does the church, nor can social privilege claim any warrant in theology.

De Lubac hoped to reinvigorate Catholic engagement with culture by refocusing Catholic attention on Thomas' concept of the natural desire for God. If human nature is always already directed to God political culture must always be a certain reflection of that propensity to God; and if reflecting God confusedly, Catholics have an obligation to engage politics in the hope of redirecting politics to God in a more immediate fashion. De Lubac's optimistic conception, one might say, of the relationship between politics and the natural desire for God may owe something to Augustine's oft-repeated comment in the *Confessions* that, "all who desert you and set themselves up against you merely copy you in a perverse way." What if the relationship between politics and natural desire is not even as indirect as the twisted image Augustine suggests? Augustine's pear tree example and his discussion in the *Confessions* of the three lusts suggest the relationship might be very indirect indeed. John Paul the Great's characterization of the conflict between the cultures of life and death as a bitter contest between two personal but cosmic opponents suggests that, to his mind at least, the relationship between the two is extremely vulnerable. In the last decade of his life, he argued repeatedly that the culture of death is becoming yet more ominous as it begins to corrupt the very structure of conscience itself, leaving culture unable to distinguish good from evil. If you like, the new problem of political culture is not that it offers little encouragement to develop the moral virtues but rather that it has begun an assault upon the capacity of the intellectual virtues to rightly know both moral truth and the true nature of what it is to be human. Not only perhaps is there no especial intimacy between the natural desire for God and culture but culture can take on a certain character whereby it becomes inimical to natural desire. If this is so, Catholic engagement with politics might be better served by a theory of nature and grace in which indeterminacy is posited.[12] Such indeterminacy is part and parcel of Cajetan's position. Political culture will show a desire for God only once that desire has been elicited (*appetitus elicitus*) by Christian teaching and practice.

Stretching from Augustine through Scotus and Donoso Cortés and up to Carl Schmitt is a tradition of Catholic thinking which, because "No one is good," holds that human desire has no particular affinity with, or regard for, God. Others, like Kolnai, argue that human desire is not intrinsically set *against* God but nor is there any dynamic movement toward God. This is a position somewhat similar to that of Scotus but Kolnai acknowledges there is a basic pro-attitude to humans, an attitude favoring the good. Thomas insisted that the will has a natural inclination to the good. For this reason, the will has no need of an internal virtue ordering it to reason and the good, unlike the appetites of fear and pleasure. Justice is an external virtue that links the will in a well-ordered manner to others. Rahner and de Lubac avidly build on this metaphysical optimism. Baroque Thomists were more cautious and, for reasons just given, rightly so. The Dominican Domingo Bañez (1528-1604) offers his theory quite self-consciously as drawing out the implications of Cajetan's analysis of Thomas. In this sense, a return to Bañez is a return to Cajetan. Affirming (with de Lubac) that there is a natural propensity in the human mind to a knowledge of the divine essence—and Bañez, unlike some other Baroque commentators, insists that this propensity to know the divine essence would be to know God as the Triune Persons and not merely as First Cause—he nevertheless argues that such a desire exacts nothing from God since of itself such a desire (against de Lubac now) is inefficacious, being conditional upon, and elicited by, created effects (*qui excitatur ex cognitione effectuum*).[13] This Baroque doctrine[14] is well suited to the needs of a contemporary theology of culture. It suggests itself as the theoretical basis for John Paul II saying that the Gospel "does not spring spontaneously from any cultural soil; it has always been transmitted by means of apostolic dialogue..."[15]

The universal natural desire for God does not then simply generate articulations and other desires that are directed at and foster a knowledge of the essence of God. This, it seems to me, is the significance behind that sentence from *Fides et Ratio*, cited at the beginning of this chapter: it is Jesus Christ who "introduces into our history a universal truth which stirs the human mind to ceaseless effort." It is coming to know certain truths which elicit our desire for the Triune Persons of the Christian God. To insist that the natural desire for God must still be elicited (*appetitus elicitus*) by, and mediated through, cultural articulations suffused with Christianity, if it is to approach its rightful object, is both to safeguard the gratuity of the *visio dei* and to stress the absolute centrality of a genuinely Christian articulation of culture. Oddly, by reapplying Bañez's doctrine of the elicited, conditional, and inefficacious natural desire to a theology of culture, the very thing that de Lubac desired is attained: a profound engagement of Catholics in the public square. It is clear from all I have said that, in my opinion, Rahner's supernatural existential is a serious impediment to even recognizing the need for an articulation of a genuinely Christian culture. We do, I think—and now to recall a more luminous Rahner—need to be "Hearers of the Word."

To rely on the *appetitus elicitus* is to affirm the privileged character of Christianity and the role it plays in cultural formation. This ecclesial privilege is a warrant for social privilege more generally, and most especially, for the inequality that stems from marriage, family, and the property holding that is a necessary corollary of the household. Affirming natural order, the idea of elicited desire also reaffirms the centrality of grace, *gratia*, with its emphases of gift, sacrifice, and gratitude. It, thus, distinguishes Christian love from humanitarian self-sufficiency; it displaces the idea of egalitarian structures as basic to order, returning persons to a responsibility for acts and achievements that respond to, and build upon, a communal inheritance of a hierarchy of value at once natural, human, and divine.[16]

The *duplex ordo* separates natural desire from an achieved,[17] graced holiness, that is, human appetite elevated by the life of virtue, natural, and divine. This separation is basic to Bonaventure's hierarchical soul.[18] In the twentieth century, Thomas was better understood by de la Taille than by his brother Jesuit de Lubac, I would say.[19] De la Taille argues that the primary object of human desire—the vision of God—can only be satisfied once a desire is created by the actuation of an already present desire by an act of God. This is to argue that the completion of human desire is found in an elevation completely beyond the human, albeit not beyond the created, order. The created actuation—the light of glory—is a medium for the vision that fixes desire on God. If Christ fully reveals man to himself it is because Christ is an ecstatic ordering of nature to glory. In Thomas, human nature is double in aspect with a sensuous propensity to sin always already moderated by an ecstatic bodily deposition elicited by the good. Contending with this propensity requires a labor of virtue, a labor incited and modeled by the wounds of Christ: *far be it from me to glory except in the cross* (Gal. 6: 14).

Notes

1. Congregation for the Doctrine of the Faith, *Dominus Iesus* (Boston: Pauline Books and Media, 2000), p. 12.
2. Various examples of these efforts are found in *I Am the Lord Your God: Christian Reflections on the Ten Commandments*, ed. C. Braatan & C. Seitz (Grand Rapids, MI: Eerdmans, 2005) and *Blackwell Companion to Political Theology*, ed. P. Scott & W. Cavanaugh (Oxford: Blackwell, 2006).
3. For an example of the philosophical grounds of the distinction, see my, "Two Case Studies in Schelerian Moral Theology: The Vatican's 2005 'Instruction' and Gay Marriage."
4. O. O'Donovan, *The Just War Revisited* (Cambridge, MA: Cambridge University Press, 2003), pp. 1-7.

5. Ibid., p. 2.
6. Please see my essay, "Rebels and Christian Princes: Camus and Augustine on Violence and Politics," *Revista Filosófica de Coimbra*, Vol. 16 (1999), pp. 253-67.
7. A special thanks is owed John Betz and Steve Weber for a memorable summer a few years back reading together de Lubac's *The Mystery of the Supernatural*. By century's close, a rash of articles suggested that the fifty-year experiment with de Lubac had perhaps given poisoned fruit. For the first time in forty years, a prominent journal published a defense of the work of the Dominican Garrigou-Lagrange, a central target of de Lubac (Jude Chua Soo Meng, "Garrigou-Lagrange on Aristotle and Aquinas," *Modern Schoolman*, Vol. 78, November 2000, pp. 71-87). Others like Peter Ryan, S. J., offered a subtle restatement of the *duplex ordo*, "Must the Acting Person Have a Single Ultimate End," *Gregorianum*, Vol. 82, 2001, pp. 325-335. Most startling of all, a three-hundred page volume of the Dominican *Revue Thomiste* took a new look at the Cajetan-de Lubac debate, with the cover art pointing towards a rehabilitation: a Renaissance printing of a page of Cajetan's theology (*Surnaturel*, a special issue of the *Revue Thomiste*, Volume 101, January-June 2001). More recently, another volume of essays appeared assessing a new defense of the pre-de Lubac tradition. This volume is a response to the rather shoddy treatment given to Lawrence Feingold's scholarship by advocates of the "revolutionary" theology of de Lubac. See the essays in *Nova et Vetera: The English Edition of the International Theological Journal*, Vol. 5: 1 (2007); cf. *idem*, Vol. 3: 1 (2005).
8. Fergus Kerr writes: "[for de Lubac] the human and the natural has always been embraced within the supernatural" (F. Kerr, *Twentieth-Century Catholic Theologians*, p. 73).
9. J. Milbank, *Truth in Aquinas* (London: Routledge, 2001), p. 38.
10. Ibid., p. 38.
11. K. Rahner, S. J. "Concerning the Relationship between Nature and Grace," *Theological Investigations* (Baltimore: Helicon Books, 1965), p. 300; hereafter = NG.
12. Cf. S.-T. Bonino, O. P., "Nature and Grace in *Deus Caritas Est*," *Nova et Vetera: The English Edition of the International Theological Journal*, Vol. 5:2 (2007), p. 234.
13. Dominicus Bañez, O.P., *Scholastica commentaria in primam partem angelici doctoris D. Thomae Aquinatis* (Venice, 1591), q. 3, a. 8.
14. Martin Stone observes that we still have no thorough history of the Baroque debates, which were long and subtle. For two introductions to the complexities: M. Stone, "Making Sense of Thomas Aquinas in the Sixteenth Century: Domingo de Soto on the Natural Desire to See God," in *Platonic Ideas and Concept Formation in Ancient and Medieval Thought* (Leuven: Leuven University Press, 2004): pp. 211-232; A. Rosenthal, "The Problem of the *Desiderium Naturale* in the Thomistic Tradition," *Verbum Analecta NeoLatina*, Vol. 6 (2004): pp. 335-44.
15. As quoted in Avery Dulles, S.J., *The Splendor of Faith* (New York: Crossroads, 1999), p. 124. Cf. S. Augustine, *Confessions* (London: Penguin, 1961), p. 21.
16. Manent sees the difference between humanitarianism and Christianity in the opposition of a general compassion and "a long labour on oneself" (P. Manent, "The Humanitarian Temptation," [*pro manuscripto*]).
17. This is not the place to enter into the question of divine predilection, though I hope to address this topic in the future.
18. S. Bonaventure, *The Journey of the Mind to God* (Indianapolis, IN: Hackett, 1993) c. 4, pp. 24-5.
19. M. de la Taille, S. J., *The Hypostatic Union and Created Actuation by Uncreated Act* (West Baden Springs, IN: West Baden College, 1952).

5

Wrongful Life Tort[1]

Whether It Is Lawful to Kill Oneself

Three state judiciaries in America—California, New York, and Washington—agree that a child can sue a doctor because the doctor harmed the child by not aborting him.[2] The child was harmed, argue the state jurists, because it is better never to have been born than to live a life with disability (W, *1037; H, *252).[3] Failing to facilitate the abortion, the doctor unjustifiably takes from the child the good of nonexistence when the alternative is a suffering existence. Taking away the good of non-being in such circumstances is the foundation for a wrongful life tort. The tort is controversial: at least eighteen American states have legislated against the tort. Crucial to appreciate is that a wrongful life tort does not rely on the idea that the doctor is responsible for the disability. This is not the harm. The disabilities involved, such as genetic deafness (H, *262), are not in the power of the doctor to change. What is in the doctor's power is nonexistence rather than existence:[4] put differently, as one commentator has it, the tort includes abortion in its definition (W, *1035). It is also important to distinguish a wrongful life tort from a related tort. A wrongful birth tort purports a harm for which a doctor can be liable if she somehow removes a woman's choice of an abortion as a solution to her child's disability (W, *1027). In this tort the harm is *the denial of a choice* to abort; in wrongful life tort the harm is *the failure* to abort.

Like many legislatures, most courts in America doubt that any coherence attaches to the basic ontological claim underlying the tort—how can life be an injury (W, *1032)?[5] One court spoke for many when noting, "the moral implications of allowing the child's claim are philosophically staggering" (W, *1036, n. 136). Indeed. At least since Plotinus (204-70) the idea that non-being is a good has made no metaphysical sense.[6] Plotinus argued that privation of being is evil.[7] Famously, Augustine made this argument a part of Christianity.[8] Thus, Aquinas can argue "the good that all things desire is being" (Sent. IV, d. 49, q. 1, a. 2, qc. 1). However, Plotinus' position is by no means self-evident to humanitarianism. Humanitarianism is an ethics that views suffering as the very meaning of evil (AL, 211) and if a person's existence is one of "terrible pain" this well warrants considering killing such a person (AL, 21). If having being is necessary for suffering, then non-being can be a solution that the doctor ought to have pursued, according to the tort and with the full support of humanitarian ethics.

In this chapter, I show that whilst humanitarianism makes the tort intelligible the tort's appeal rests on its formality of suicide. Strangely, Catholic moral theology agrees that the tort is intelligible. Granted the tort is coherent, papal moral theology must deny the tort is just. John Paul II's *Evangelium Vitae* reasserted Aquinas' philosophy of law respecting homicide. In it, suicide is again condemned by the church. Aquinas argued that suicide could only be justified if God's sovereignty were replaced by human sovereignty. Humanitarian ethics has just such an aim and so amongst Aquinas' five arguments against suicide this one is typically thought the weakest. Recently, John Paul the Great strongly reaffirmed this argument in his claim that the culture of death can be traced to the eclipse of God (EV, para. 21). In the following pages, I defend the argument of *Evangelium Vitae* and, in particular, Paragraph 20 where John Paul II argues that contemporary liberal democracy is "a form of totalitarianism," which is regarded as the most outrageous claim of the encyclical. I argue that John Paul II is right that humanitarian love is totalitarian.

Peter Singer's humanitarian ethics is a good illustration of this papal claim. The finest Catholic analyst of totalitarianism, Kolnai identified what he called identitarian or equalitarian logic as the animating principle of totalitarianism. Essential to equalitarianism is the rejection of the idea of intrinsic evil. Intrinsicalism establishes a moral hierarchy that discriminates amongst human needs. This limit to human sovereignty is rejected by humanitarian ethics and this is completely unsurprising. "Acknowledging the Lord as God is the very core, the heart of the Law," (VS, para. 11) and some of the precepts of the Law, as John Paul II argues, describe and forbid intrinsically evil acts. These precepts, I argue, are eccentric. They defend the stranger and eccentric from totality, from the urge within humanitarian love to identity and equality. They are a shield for the disabled against the humanitarian love that offers homicide as a solution to their suffering and the suffering of caregivers.

Humanitarianism is perhaps the dominant mode of valuation in the modern Western world. Certainly, Nietzsche thought this. People in the West are thoroughly familiar with ideas of humanitarian relief, humanitarian intervention, and humanitarian organizations like Doctors Without Borders. They are also very familiar with individual humanitarians like U2's Bono, who was *Time* magazine's Man of the Year in 2005. For his work in trying to secure debt relief for developing nations, Bono was dubbed "the Good Samaritan" by the magazine, this in the year that John Paul II died. It was probably Nietzsche also who first identified the phenomenon of humanitarianism. His savage criticism of the phenomenon has marked Western thought and life ever since.[9] This criticism certainly found favor with Scheler and with the later generations of the Munich School of Phenomenology, Kolnai and Wojtyla.[10] Nietzsche linked humanitarianism to a certain English sensibility that he saw most clearly exhibited by utilitarian thinkers like Bentham.[11] Suffering, Bentham argued, must guide all morals and law (AL, 7-8): even declaring that "indifference to public welfare" should be treated as crime.[12] It is no surprise that Bentham was one of the first theorists of vegetarianism, and Singer has argued that it is immoral to eat fish because the pleasures of fishing and eating what you catch could not possibly outweigh the suffering of the fish. This argument makes sense to humanitarians, and even a hard-nosed rationalist like Peter Singer discusses it without any embarrassment at all (AL, 176-78). Clearly, humanitarian ethics can make ready sense of wrongful life tort! Courts have certainly found quite persuasive the idea that a child's future suffering well warrants abortion (W, *1039). This would just be a matter of satisfying Singer's compact definition, "humanitarianism, the tendency to act humanely" (AL, 206).

The Munich School early on observed the close alliance between humanitarianism and utilitarianism (HVR, 435; 441 and R, chapter 5).[13] As is well known, utilitarianism has a strong voice in public policy discussions in the Western world, and the wrongful life tort is no exception. Philosophical defenses of the wrongful life tort tend to be variants of utilitarianism. The hope of these studies is to provide a theoretical framework to guide judges. If a sticking point for the courts has been what sense can be made of the claim that it would have been better for a child never to have existed (*Gleitman v. Cosgrove* [1967] and *Becker v.*

Schwartz [1978]), a typical response runs as follows: a child's anguished existence is a negative well-being whilst non-existence is a matter of zero well-being. A harm can thus be measured: the child has a lesser degree of well-being now than if the child had never existed at all.[14] A certain elegance attaches to this proposal but note what is missing: the alternatives are not between now existing and never having existed but rather the alternative that it is better to have been aborted than to have an anguished existence. Is it better to have been aborted—to have an aborted status, more, to suffer dismemberment or bodily dissolution—than to have been born? The proposal really needs to be cast in terms of the true alternative states. It is surely far from clear that non-existence on account of an aborted status is a matter of zero well-being and not rather a negative well-being. It is little surprise given the abstract character of utilitarianism that the reality of the alternatives is elided. Yet, this is crucial: for our intuitions are by no means so clear once we begin to wonder whether it is better for the child before us to have been dismembered than to exist even with severe disabilities.

To clarify concepts and isolate the implications of arguments is often thought the task of philosophy. But disputing the cogency of arguments offered for wrongful life tort is not yet to get at the heart of the issue. Philosophy is also concerned with strands of ideas, large shifts in the ways people think about the person and the world. Addressed at this level, wrongful life tort poses an especial problem for Catholic thinking about homicide. More than sixty years ago, Kolnai observed the peculiar conceptual threat humanitarianism posed to Catholic moral theology. Catholic ethics, he noted, is "universalistic, personalistic and moralistic" and, to a significant degree, rationalistic. It is very like humanitarian ethics, he observed, and even though humanitarianism is "a non-religious, immanentistic, secular moral orientation." Catholic ethics does agree that "God is, generally speaking, not the thematic center of natural morality" (HVR, 434; 429; 442).[15] It is unsurprising then but still disturbing that, sometimes, moral theologians share the intuitions of humanitarians. Cathleen Kaveny, without endorsing the practice, goes to great lengths to explain the plausibility of mothers choosing to kill their unborn children rather than giving them up for adoption. Noting how rare it is that a woman gives birth and puts her child up for adoption—at least in the West and where a contract for money has not been entered into—Kaveny explains that there clearly are women "who find separation worse than death."[16] These women believe that their family obligation to their children cannot be severed by the positive legal enactment of adoption but can be "completely extinguished only by death."[17] Apparently, this tells us something about "maternal instinct" and "the underlying realities of the relationships at stake"[18]—and so a "laudatory" motive might be found for abortion. "A parent may not wish the death of the child *per se*, but may privilege familial loyalty in a way that makes abandonment a fate worse than death."[19]

The underlying assumption here is that suffering is a worse evil than killing an innocent person. Humanitarianism affirms this assumption, but moral theology cannot. Christianity does not think that suffering is a moral evil whilst, for Singer, suffering is the horizon for all ethical reflection and *the* norm of ethics is to reduce suffering. Traditional Catholic moral theology distinguishes clearly an intrinsic evil, such as killing the innocent, from the evil of suffering that somehow, however, mysteriously revealed through the cross, shows "that the meaning of life is fully realized in and through suffering."[20] But humanitarianism does not identify two totally different kinds of evil here. Rather these evils are part of a sliding scale that allows them to be compared. Humanitarianism precludes identifying the qualitative difference between these evils because it cannot tolerate the restraint placed upon human judgment by the idea of intrinsic evil. Humanitarianism is a bold assertion of human sovereignty and this abolishes the sovereignty of the moral object and therewith God's sovereignty. With the "sovereignty of the object" abolished (Kolnai), a calculation amongst human needs is all there is left. This means, as Kolnai puts it, "all kinds of 'needs' and the 'needs' of all men and groups of men are equally legitimate in principle; and preconceived bias or restriction is illegitimate" (HVR, 435). Because humanitarianism recognizes an equality of needs, the "need" of a child to have been aborted to avoid suffering (wrongful life tort) is no less a need than myriad other needs to increase pleasure and avoid suffering (a mother's need for an abortion on account of the pressure of life circumstances) and one that, like them, must be recognized at law. This equalitarianism is basic to humanitarianism and contrasts sharply with the objective moral hierarchy of traditional Catholic ethics.[21] At first blush, the wrongful life tort appears to rely on an ontological oddity, but the ethical and metaphysical substructure of humanitarianism (HVR, 443) does make it readily intelligible. Ideas of suffering as a basic evil, human sovereignty, and egalitarianism, when linked, make for the contemporary mind a potent brew.

The tort sits at the very place these three ideas meet. In liberal regimes, abortion is the homicide of an innocent on the private authority of the mother, who is the equal of the state in having lethal authority. If abortion enters into the definition of wrongful life tort it is significant that it does so formally as a suicide, more specifically, an assisted suicide. Like abortion, suicide is wrong, says Thomas, because it is the killing of an innocent on private authority, in this case, on the authority of the person to be killed. The idea that a person ought to have the authority to say what he is willing and able to suffer has common appeal. [22] Wrongful life tort can be found quite compelling once its formality of assisted suicide is granted and the tort's ontological strangeness all but vanishes if its true ethical and metaphysical tissue is clearly appreciated. Consequently, it is at the level of the ethical and metaphysical substructure of humanitarianism that Catholic ethics must make its argument.

For a culture so deeply influenced by humanitarianism, least persuasive of all of Aquinas' arguments against suicide is perhaps his claim that suicide denies the sovereignty of God. Yet it is this argument that is central to *Evangelium Vitae*. As a constellation of abortion, eugenics,[23] and suicide, wrongful life tort certainly has all the marks of a paragon of the culture of death. It is a great embarrassment to Catholicism, therefore, when the tort finds its major premise in scripture. Strangely though, it is from this embarrassing similarity between scripture and humanitarianism that the glimmer of an argument against wrongful life tort emerges. Reflecting on the comment of Jesus about Judas—"It were better for him, if that man had not been born" (Mark 14: 21; cf. Job 3: 11)—medieval theologians speculated that the condition of the damned in hell certainly justifies willing non-existence over existence.[24] Not only does theology concede a crucial premise of the tort, de Vitoria's explanation for the intelligibility of the premise is a quality of life argument. Like Thomas, he argues that the damned can rightly will not to exist. Thomas' argument is exceptionally short and an argument from the authority of scripture ("Death is better than a miserable life" [Eccles. 30, 17; Aquinas also cites Apoc. 9, 6 and Eccles. 41, 3).[25] A biblical theology clearly cannot accept that all human life is sacred.[26] If this admission scrambles certain bedrock assumptions about the way Christians are supposed to conceive of life, what is the significance for humanitarianism that the tort relies upon a secularization of the idea of the damned? Is humanitarian sentiment a sufficient guide for culture if humanitarian pity resurfaces damnation? Can such incoherence be a tolerable guide for jurisprudence? For is it not odd that medieval moral theology and humanitarian pity both agree that a suffering life well warrants the desire that one should never have existed at all?

Apparently, Peter Singer once said that only two people understand the real significance of the abortion debate: John Paul II and Peter Singer himself.[27] I assume what he meant was that with him and John Paul II humanitarianism and Christianity squared off against one another. Are these two value systems really so different though? Nietzsche, of course, saw little difference, thinking of one as parent and the other offspring. Scheler accepted Nietzsche's analysis of humanitarianism as *ressentiment* but argued forcibly that Nietzsche was utterly mistaken that Christianity had anything in common with humanitarianism. Though it agrees with a certain Christian reflection about the idea of the damned, humanitarianism offers a very different meaning of damnation. The Christian idea of damnation is a punishment suffered: a retribution for unjust acts. Instead, humanitarianism offers homicide as a solution for suffering. Why this turn to homicide? What exactly is it about the mixture of human sovereignty, egalitarianism and suffering that generates the culture of death? The thinkers of the Munich School agree that there is some deep connection. Readers of *Evangelium Vitae* are typically amazed and thoroughly disturbed by John Paul II's claim that contemporary democracies are both totalitarian and tyrannical (EV, 20). Even pro-life conservative readers think John Paul II is something of a hothead at this point. Why readers should be so aghast is unclear: Singer has long-held that Western liberal democracy is a tyranny (AL, ix, 18, 192, 215) and yet he does not seem to provoke the same angry bewilderment. Elsewhere I have shown the plausibility of John Paul II's claim, but the claim was made before him, albeit a little more provisionally, by Kolnai. No one questions that Kolnai is one of the most astute observers of politics, yet, he too saw a logical movement in humanitarianism to "new phenomena of tyranny" (HVR, 430). In humanitarianism he observed "signs of shifting towards a totalitarian or "identitarian" loss of liberty and personality" (HVR, 443) and claimed that "life that has become 'its own master' is bound for suicide" (HVR, 454). Yet why should this be so? What about humanitarianism links it interiorly to killing? Singer is the foremost humanitarian philosopher writing today. It seems reasonable to test the Munich School's thesis against his work. Can one find in it an "ideological immoralism" (Kolnai)? I will show that Singer's egalitarianism underlies his ready recourse to homicide as a solution to problems of human welfare.

Traditionally understood, a tort requires that the defendant had a duty to the party bringing suit. How can a duty exist in this case? The right correlative to duty in this case is the right not to have to suffer (H,

*252)—and so a legal right not to be born (H, *252, n. 22)—whilst in wrongful birth the right is to choose an abortion secured by *Roe* (G, *1269). Until 1946 courts did not recognize a doctor's duty to an unborn child. By 1971 every American jurisdiction recognized such a duty (R, *149). By 1983 this duty, argued the Supreme Court of Washington, "may extend to persons not yet born or conceived at the time of a negligent act or omission" (R, *154). Of course, this ontologically expansive duty had already been trumped in 1973 by the duty owed first to the mother's choice whether to abort the child or not. Still, assuming certain conditions, the tort asserts a doctor has the duty to end the known future life of suffering of an unborn child. Peter Singer's work on homicide readily supplies this duty. The fourth chapter of Singer's *Practical Ethics* has for its title "What's wrong with killing?" It is now a *locus classicus* for thinking about homicide. Singer wants to change our basic laws on homicide and especially those that protect innocent children; he wants the law to enable parents and medical officials to kill children. This is putting the matter starkly, but truthfully, and Singer would not object to putting matters thus. The problem is: Are there answers to his arguments?

Like Thomas' natural law theory, Singer does not rely on rights for his theory of homicide (PE, 81-83; EC, 110-111).[28] As a leftist (PE, 36) Singer bases his thinking on an egalitarianism (ADL, 9) at the service of the essential goal of leftism, which, according to Singer, is to reduce "the vast quantity of pain and suffering."[29] Therefore, a universal assumption in ethics—which is essential to morality, we are told—is to acknowledge that "my own interests cannot, simply because they are *my* interests, count more than the interests of anyone else" (PE, 12; EC, 100, 106). This assumption requires examination because it is clearly driven not by any ordinary ethical consciousness but by a political ideology. Singer is simply wrong when he says, "we cannot, if we are to think ethically, refuse to take this step" (PE, 13). However, those of us interested in liberty and escaping the grip of totalitarian thinking certainly can refuse this first step. Without it, the power of Singer's arguments diminishes rapidly. Nowhere does this thinker famous for questioning received opinion and tradition address why one should accept that equality is basic to ethical orientation. What is known as the "order of charity"—an idea shared across centuries by authors as diverse as Aristotle (NE, 1097a24-1097b6), Vitoria (H, 199), Smith (TMS, 219-22), and Spencer,[30] to name a few—not only rejects this assumption but accords far better with our basic intuitions and behavior. The order of charity holds that family is a matter of privilege and the source of *ethical* inequality.

Let me give an example that shows Singer's claim—privileging some people's interests over those of some others is not moral—is unconvincing. I live in a city with an awful public school system. Parents that can, largely do, send their children to private schools. They seek privilege for their children. However, there is a cadre of parents committed to the local, neighborhood school. Living in a delightful, tree-lined Victorian district of an otherwise struggling, majority Black city, these parents are wealthy, and liberal in their politics. Now, the neighborhood elementary school is not all that bad: it is regarded as the city's one decent school and it even has an elite division within it where most of the white liberal parents have their children. But here's the interesting thing: not one of these parents volunteers their children to enter any other school in the entire city. If they are so egalitarian, why do they not send their children, in solidarity, to one of the exclusively black schools in the city? Why not? Because it is deeply unnatural to reject preferment for one's child.[31] It is unnatural to reject privilege and this is felt by those parents who love to read Singer! Singer, even when it comes to contemporary America and its deepest veins of liberal culture, seems to be simply wrong that a consensus has been reached that equal consideration of interests is basic to ethical judgment. Singer does acknowledge that biology imposes this preferment but he denies it any moral standing (ADL, 61). Singer accepts that there is a human nature (PE, 39) but it is irrelevant to ethics on account of the naturalistic fallacy (AL, 5; EC, 53, 73-4), that is, he recognizes that the "natural affection" of parents for children (PE, 132; EC, 31-4) is a basic feature of human nature and therefore a restraint upon reform. As part of the reform school of utilitarianism (AL, 5), Singer nevertheless accepts Burke's caution that reform must be judicious in acknowledging limits (EC, 151, 154-5); for Singer, those established by sociobiology (EC, 27; 157). Still, ordinary moral consciousness, expressed in the *ius gentium*, for example, is thoroughly rejected as a guide to moral right and wrong (PE, 78) and merely tolerated as a sign of what the reformer might best leave alone. I take my example to show that only someone with the most ideologically attenuated grasp of ordinary moral consciousness could agree with Singer. All the evidence of ordinary moral consciousness says that Singer's equality intuition—"an interest is an interest, whoever's interest it may be" (PE, 19; AL, 5) or "each life is of equal value" (PE, 88)—is no intuition at all. Sensing this himself, Singer falls back on elitism, assuring us that his position is at one with "the leading figures in contemporary moral philosophy" (AL, 5).

Scorning intuitionism as relying on "a mysterious realm of objective ethical facts" (PE, 7; EC, 107) he nevertheless, without argument, asks us to accept that "equality is a basic ethical principle" (PE, 18), a "moral idea" (AL, 5). That is, a basic ethical intuition. Singer's reliance on intuitionism is really quite extensive. He thinks, for example, that it is self-evident that any social order that provokes a sense of superiority, a feeling of hopeless inferiority or a divided society (PE, 40 & 44) stands forthwith morally condemned. Singer explicitly says, if inconsistently, that biological theories of human nature cannot provide "the ultimate premises of ethics" but they can operate negatively to make us "think again about moral intuitions which we take to be self-evident moral truths" (EC, 84). How exactly biology makes us possibly rethink moral intuition is unclear, especially as Singer is adamant that no factual knowledge can ever dislodge the core conviction of utilitarianism that suffering is an intrinsic evil (EC, 64). He tells us that the "ultimate moral reason for relieving pain is simply the undesirability of pain as such" (PE, 19; AL, 22). Thus, "if a being suffers, there can be no moral justification for refusing to take that suffering into consideration" (PE, 50; AL, 8). This is the only exceptionless moral norm (EC, 108; 165) and it is crucial; from it moral interests are derived. Interests are immediately tied to "the capacity for suffering and enjoyment" (AL, 8; PE, 27, 33). Singer denies that his ethics is a naturalism or an intuitionism. His exceptionless norm appears to be both at once. Whether Singer is coherent at this point is not decisive.[32] He could pick either and find himself in the company of moral theologians who are either intuitionists (Scheler) or naturalists (Hittinger). Nevertheless, since for Singer suffering is an intrinsic moral evil, might there not be others, such as, to kill the innocent? If it is true that the experience of pleasure is "intrinsically valuable" (PE, 100; EC, 64)—and it is worth noting that at least one intuitionist (von Hildebrand) has denied this[33]—then perhaps to safeguard innocent human life, even if that life does not experience pleasure or pain, is "intrinsically valuable." For Singer, innocence cannot be an original value and concepts essential to jurisprudence like guilt and innocence are derived from what does and does not create suffering. Singer is certainly adamant that innocence is not a matter of helplessness, poverty, brokenness, or vulnerability since we are told explicitly to "put aside feelings based on the small, helpless...infants" (PE, 123). Since innocence is not a primitive value the direct killing of the innocent cannot be an intrinsic evil. I now want to argue that the dismissal of the doctrine of intrinsic evils is decisive against Singer. Intrinsic evils diversify the moral world, discriminate amongst actions, and simultaneously limit action and conserve eccentricity. What is decisive against Singer then is not the peculiarity of his naturalistic intuitionism but his identitarianism, which exposes the totalitarian logic of his humanitarianism.

Whilst leftists and rightists have had ready recourse to totalitarian government in the past, I take it that today a thinker shown to be a totalitarian thinker is a failed thinker, although I now state a limit to my argument. Every historical instance of totalitarianism has been homicidal. Camus argued that what he called the Age of Rebellion, the history of the West since the Middle Ages, was homicidal and therefore its own refutation. Disturbingly, it is obvious to every reader of Singer that he envisages an *increase* in the number of killings of humans as part of a social project overall to reduce the number of killings of sentient creatures. And yet, clearly the homicidal character of the theory is not a refutation for many readers. I will show that Singer's theory is totalitarian but to close the argument I have to hope that refutation is found in the reader's sense that Singer's work is a formal recommendation for an increase in the number of killings of humans *and also a decrease in human liberty*. If a reader accepts that a just cost for reductions in the amount of suffering is an increase in homicides and a loss of liberty, my argument fails.

Famously, Thomas Aquinas does not rely on a rights-based theory of political order but a law-based conception. Rights are nowhere mentioned in his question on homicide. The discussion about who can be killed, by whom and when is conducted entirely free of rights talk. How can this be plausible? How does Aquinas build restraint into law itself? Strangely, but not paradoxically, he does so in part by insisting upon the privilege of public authority. In restricting to government the authority to kill intentionally, Aquinas affirms an Augustinian tradition of politics. In dividing the city into two, oftentimes hostile, cities, Augustine immediately separated Christianity from any political logic of identitarianism. The term belongs to Aurel Kolnai: identitarianism, for him, is the metaphysical heart of totalitarianism. Insisting upon the privilege of public authority to intentional homicide, Aquinas rejects a private use of lethal force—he even rejects intentional killing in self-defense—and thereby an identitarianism that would abolish political pluralism. Identitarianism finds a place inside humanitarianism because an animating principle of humanitarianism is its hatred of privilege. Self-consciously humanitarian (AL, 215), Singer's work is eloquent on this point. One of Singer's most famous egalitarian claims is that non-human animals have a moral claim upon us prior to some humans (PE,

48). Resistance to this claim is blamed on "the deep-seated Western belief in the uniqueness and special privileges of our species" (PE, 78). As Kolnai noted sixty years ago, the destruction of privilege is also the advocacy of equalitarianism and therewith the conceptual heart of totalitarianism, identitarianism. The close connection between these ideas is everywhere in Singer's work.

It is no surprise at all that Singer wonders at the fact that the idea "that human life has unique value…is enshrined in our law" (PE, 73). Singer's equalitarianism must be hostile to whatever is unique (AL, 198) or what has "special status" (PE, 117) lest it break free of being placed inside an equation (AL, 8). Discussing a court case about medical treatment given to a handicapped child, he notes the care was given "at a cost of thousands of dollars." This commodification of human life is an essential aspect of Singer's work: every life is monetary, that is, explainable in units that can be set in a calculus about worth.[34] The units establish the sameness of every life. The Old Testament comes in for especial censure, Singer lamenting that "it allots man a special position in the universe" (AL, 194). In his assessments of the kinds of human life, Singer asks repeatedly whether all the humans in a particular calculus are "normal" humans (PE, 73, 116, 131; AL, 16-17, 20, 22). This fascination with normality is a fascination with identity, the root of totalitarian thinking. Singer's utilitarianism, and most especially his attack upon the privilege of speciesism (AL, 19), absolutely requires identity for otherwise no calculus about worth can be made. "Killing them [defectives], therefore, cannot be *equated* with killing normal human beings…" (PE, 131; emphasis added). Singer's *normal* human beings have the "morally relevant characteristics, like rationality, self-consciousness, awareness, autonomy, pleasure and pain" (PE, 118) and without these characteristics a human being is best thought of as "an existence that is of no intrinsic value at all" (PE, 118; 92). Singer confirms Scheler's claim that no culture has advocated the direct killing of those who exhibit personality: "If human life does have special value, it has it in so far as most human beings are persons" (PE, 97; 107; 118). Yet, here it is well to recall Kolnai's claim that modern humanitarian love shows "signs of shifting towards a totalitarian or 'identitarian' loss of liberty and personality" (HVR, 443). Identitarianism robs the eccentric of personhood and so makes the stranger a fit object of homicide. And Singer's fascination with the normal is also an appeal to an identitarianism that destroys liberty. For, like innocence, personality is not basic and controlling. This implication is obvious given his universal moral rule: as he defines his preference utilitarianism, "an action contrary to the preference of any being is, unless this preference is outweighed by contrary preferences, wrong. Killing a person who prefers to continue living is therefore wrong, other things being equal" (PE, 80-81). Other · things being equal… Given that there is no absolute prohibition on the direct killing of persons, and no mention in this definition whatsoever of innocence as a protection against being killed, it is a matter of assessing what threat to happiness is posed by suffering (PE 131). Thus the problem with new born defectives is that they are "a threat to the happiness of the parents" (PE, 132). "But if we are preference utilitarians we must allow that a desire to go on living can be outweighed by other desires…" (PE, 83) and so a preference utilitarian takes seriously the wish of someone about to be euthanized who does not want to be killed "as an important reason against killing" but not a final reason (PE, 141). Being a person, innocent and free, is not a definitive restraint on killing if a killing can reduce suffering. Unlike Thomas' philosophy of law, people are not killed because of crime but on account of tort. Their lives harm others whose lives would be more pleasurable without them.

Equalitarianism thus drives Singer's theory of killing. The eccentric or strange resists collapse into a unit of exchange. The stranger is an exemplar of privilege, shielded by the doctrine of intrinsic evils that generates an inequality and priority amongst moral objects. Singer refuses to tolerate the moral selection proposed by this doctrine and so we look in vain to him for justice for the disabled. Singer's theory of homicide is all of a piece with his commitment to Progressive Democracy (EC, 119), Kolnai's term for humanitarianism with a dialectical relationship to communism. Singer is a statist with a fondness for the Greek law of homicide (PE, 77). This is no surprise. Greek law did not recognize the legal existence of private associations. Corporate existence was unknown and there was then nothing like the medieval *commenda,* which diversified the social sphere and limited political power.[35] Private association is always the establishment of certain privileges for some, but not all, just as every human life is an eccentricity negating identity. Singer's egalitarianism compels him to deny the sovereignty of the object, the felt primacy of a field of moral prohibitions evident in ordinary moral consciousness, and therewith God, in favor of the sovereignty of needs that must have no restraint or order placed upon them. Not even the traditional jurisprudential categories of innocence and guilt should prejudice us to which needs are to be fulfilled. The only legitimate order is that required by the imperative to decrease suffering. Homicide can be a means, a most effective means, to realizing that imperative. Wrongful life tort is an illustration of humanitarian love: the appetite to resolve "the conflict between the sanctity of human life and the goal of reducing suffering" (PE, 131) by application to homicide.

Notes

1. I would like to thank Catherine McCauliff of Seton Hall Law School who kindly read and gave suggestions on how to improve this chapter.
2. K. Wilcoxon, "Statutory Remedies for Judicial Torts: The Need for Wrongful Birth Legislation," *University of Cincinnati Law Review* [Spring 2001], *1034; henceforth, W.
3. K. Hackett, "The Fragile X Men: Scientific Advances Compel a Legislative Treatment of Wrongful Life and Wrongful Birth," *Journal of Law and Technology* (Fall, 1987), *252; henceforth, H.
4. To have a case, a child is "required to say not that he should have been born without defects but that he should not have been born at all" (*Gleitman*, 227 A. 2d at 692 as quoted in J. Granchi "The Wrongful Birth Tort: A Policy Analysis and the Right to Sue for an Inconvenient Child," *South Texas Law Review* [Fall, 2002], *1268; henceforth, G).
5. Can "the existence of human life… constitute an injury cognizable at law"? (*Azzolino*, 337 S. E. 2d 528, 533-34 [N. C. 1985] as quoted in G, *1266).
6. Earlier, Aristotle speculated that the nothingness after death made death the "most frightening" phenomenon (Nicomachean Ethics, III, l. 14, 1115a22-24).
7. Plotinus, *The Enneads,* I. 8. 3 (London: Penguin, 1991), p. 58.
8. Augustine, *Confessions*, p. 148.
9. The most self-conscious humanitarians are alive to the problem Nietzsche poses but equally quick to have it stated for the record (yet again) what a boon the man was for Nazi ideology. Typical is Glover. See the first page of his chapter on Nietzsche (J. Glover, *Humanity: A Moral History of the Twentieth Century* [New Haven, CT: Yale University Press, 2000], p. 11).
10. Neither Kolnai nor Wojtyla makes a great deal of use of *ressentiment* analysis that was so central to Scheler's ethics but they do agree about the problem humanitarianism poses. Wojtyla uses a *ressentiment* analysis when discussing chastity in *Love and Responsibility*, pp. 143-7. I know of no other places where he does so. There are a few references to *ressentiment* in Kolnai's writings. He seemingly thought it a useful tool to capture some particular moral phenomena but denied it the global explanatory power found in Nietzsche and Scheler.
11. On the close alliance between utilitarianism and humanitarianism, see the opening pages of Nietzsche's *Genealogy of Morals* and the fifth chapter of Scheler's *Ressentiment*.
12. J. Bentham, *A Fragment on Government*, p. 9.
13. For Wojtyla's strong dislike of utilitarianism, see LR, pp. 34-42.
14. M. Roberts, "Can it Ever Be Better Never to Have Existed? Person-Based Consequentialism and a New Repugnant Conclusion," *Applied Philosophy* (2003), p. 168.
15. Compare the near identical accounts of intrinsic evils in Vitoria (H, 141) and Kant (I. Kant, *Lectures on Ethics* [Indianapolis, IN: Hackett, 1963], pp. 119-120).
16. M. Cathleen Kaveny, "Conjoined Twins and Catholic Moral Analysis: Extraordinary Means and Casuistical Consistency," *Kennedy Institute of Ethics Journal*, Vol. 12 (2002), p. 126.

17. Ibid., p. 124.
18. Ibid., p. 126-127.
19. Ibid., p. 123.
20. C. Journet, *The Meaning of Evil* (New York: P. J. Kenedy & Sons, 1963), p. 236. Cf. M. Levering, *Christ's Fulfillment of Torah and Temple* (Notre Dame, IN: University of Notre Dame Press, 2002), p. 57.
21. I would argue that Charles Curran is a humanitarian theorist and not a moral theologian. He writes, *"Veritatis splendor* explicitly uses scripture to support the notion of intrinsic evil proposed by the contemporary *hierarchical* magisterium in its arguments against proportionalism and consequentialism" (C. Curran, *The Moral Theology of Pope John Paul II* [Washington, D. C.: Georgetown University Press, 2005], p. 53; emphasis added).
22. An opponent of suicide, Kant acknowledged that the argument from suffering was a powerful one (I. Kant, *Lectures on Ethics*, p. 43). Schopenhauer agreed but he too thought suicide a morally confused response to suffering (R. Marcin, *In Search of Schopenhauer's Cat: Arthur Schopenhauer's Quantum-Mystical Theory of Justice* [Washington, D. C.: The Catholic University of America Press, 2006], p. 108).
23. Positively embraced by some commentators: see K. Rhinehart, "The Debate over Wrongful Birth and Wrongful Life," *Law and Psychology Review* (Spring, 2002), *143; henceforth, R. Cf. H, *265.
24. Cf. C. Journet, *The Meaning of Evil* p. 202.
25. Thomas, IV Sent., d. 50, qu. 2, a. 1, qc. 3. The references to *Ecclesiastes* here are, in the modern Bible, parts of Sirach.
26. "And in the case before us, although not to exist is as such bad, still as a means of avoiding afflictions it can not only be thought to be good, but can actually be good. And although to exist is good in itself, nevertheless, when it is linked with some evil it can not only be thought to be, but actually can become evil" (H, 91).
27. Richard John Neuhaus, "A Curious Encounter with a Philosopher from Nowhere," *First Things*. Vol. 120 (2002), pp. 77-8.
28. Important Thomists like Maritain and Finnis argue that there is a theory of natural right or human rights in Aquinas (J. Finnis, "Natural Law: The Classical Tradition," in *The Oxford Handbook of Jurisprudence and Philosophy of Law* [Oxford: Oxford University Press, 2004], pp. 24-5). I agree with Thomists, like McIntyre, who deny this is true. As an example, Aquinas' theory of homicide nowhere mentions such things nor conceptually relies upon them, and nor does one find in the tradition of Catholic moral theory such reliance.
29. P. Singer, *A Darwinian Left: Politics, Evolution and Cooperation* (New Haven, CT: Yale University Press, 1999), p. 8; hereafter = ADL.
30. H. Spencer, *The Principles of Ethics* (New York: D. Appleton & Co., 1910), Vol. I, c. 2, pp. 17-18
31. The well-known one-time Marxist Gerry Cohen openly acknowledges this, and interestingly, on the matter of school choice. See his *If You're So Egalitarian, How Come You're So Rich?* (Cambridge: Harvard University Press, 2000), p. 179.
32. Singer would reject the option of being either a naturalist or an intuitionist and insist, I imagine, on being a rationalist. At this point Singer is like Finnis who also insists he is neither naturalist nor intuitionist. I find both Singer and Finnis completely unconvincing on this point.
33. See Kolnai's treatment of Von Hildebrand on this point in "The Concept of Hierarchy," p. 180.
34. Not, of course, worth in the original sense of dignity. For this original sense, see Kolnai's essay, "Dignity," *Philosophy*, Vol. 51 (1976), pp. 251-71

35. E. Cohen, *Ancient Athenian Maritime Courts* (Princeton, NJ: Princeton University Press, 1973), p. 120.

6

Is Carl Schmitt Right?
Is Just War Impossible?

*It appears, what was always true, that the history
of international law is a history of the notion of
war.*
                                        —*Carl Schmitt*

*The core challenge to the Security Council and to
the United Nations as a whole in the next century
[is] to forge unity behind the principle that massive
and systematic violations of human rights—wherever they take place—should not be allowed to stand.*
                    —*UN Secretary-General Kofi Annan*[1]

Whether It Is Ever Lawful to Kill the Innocent

Commenting on Thomas' sixth article I want to try to meet George
Weigel's call for a revival of "Catholic international relations theory."[2]
Weigel worries that contemporary Catholic social thought has paid little
attention to how it might contest the dominant utilitarian and Hobbesian models of international relations. The lack of Thomistic intellectual
involvement on how power is used amongst nations makes for an acute
problem, he argues.[3] Realists argue that only an amoral approach to
international affairs serves national interests whilst idealists (of various
stripes) invoke human rights as a norm by which to judge the external
and internal affairs of nations.[4] Both of these approaches ill serve the
protection of the innocent. The first encourages a no-holds-barred approach that makes the Hobbesian state of nature an instrument of policy
(PT, 9). The second serves the innocent as little as the first.[5] Carl Schmitt
has made a telling Augustinian point against the second approach. International norms are used at the behest of humanitarianism to subvert

state sovereignty,[6] he argues, a sovereignty that historically has reduced violence:[7] a reduction in violence being, for Augustine, the best peace available to the world.

To history, the idea that universal norms can subvert sovereignty is known as the *potestas indirecta*. Most famously, it is associated with those popes who tried to depose Queen Elizabeth I of England and James VI of Scotland/I of England. Linking theology and diplomacy, early modern theologians like de Vitoria and St. Robert Bellarmine argued that the popes' indirect power was, if necessary, also a deposing power. Implicit in the idea of the deposing power was a reliance on sedition and rebellion, but it was Suarez who made explicit the connection between indirect power and tyrannicide. These theologians claimed that when spiritual values are threatened, a monarch's civil authority could be suspended by the pope, and the monarch's subjects freed to depose their monarch[8] through homicide if necessary.[9]

The church no longer claims this version of the *potestas indirecta* for herself. This concept of power has shifted to the United Nations—a fine example of the secularization of a theological idea that Schmitt, following Bakunin, calls "political theology." The United Nations purports to be a moral authority with no national interest yet having a universal authority to invoke the deposing power whenever serious abuses of human rights warrant. This sort of moral valuation in international affairs, Schmitt argues, in reality threatens the innocent for it promotes private war. Schmitt is especially concerned that such a notion underwrites partisan warfare or terrorism, especially brutal forms of combat separated as they are from public norms of war.[10] During the sixteenth century, papal *breves*—not dissimilar from the *fatwas* of Muslim clerics—were sent to England urging Catholic resistance to Elizabeth. At the turn of the seventeenth, Catholic struggle broke out into terrorism with the "Gunpowder Plot" against James. Turning to terrorism, a group of Catholic gentlemen, including a Jesuit priest, attempted to blow up the English Houses of Parliament when in session with King James and his family present. James then began a war on terror, including the suppression of property rights and imprisonment without trial for those Catholics who did not swear the Oath of Allegiance. This oath, a monument of sovereigntist thinking, required Catholics to reject the *potestas indirecta* of the papacy.[11]

The difficulty with James I/VI's philosophical and theological fronts in the war on terror was the skill of his Catholic adversaries on precisely these fronts. Hobbes appreciated the struggle had to be cast in completely different terms. As Schmitt points out, the copperplate engraving belonging to the title page of the 1651 first edition of Hobbes' *Leviathan* depicts two authorities. In one column are images of military power, including cannon and lances, and in a second column are images of spiritual power, including a church, mitre, and "symbols for sharpened distinctions, syllogisms, and dilemmas." To Hobbes' mind, this second column's symbols and distinctions are "political weapons, in fact, specific weapons of wielding 'indirect' power." The first page of Hobbes' book makes clear, says Schmitt, that "the fortresses and cannons correspond to the contrivance and intellectual methods of the other side, whose fighting ability is by no means inferior."[12] Nietzsche famously made this point,[13] but it was the task of the *Leviathan* to demonstrate that these two powers are in fact identical (LST, 10-11). Pope Gelasius I distinguished between royal power and the power of the priesthood and insisted that it was these two authorities "by which this world is ruled."[14] Hobbes would not tolerate this division of powers and to show their identity, he argued, it is necessary for people to acknowledge that a miracle is whatever the state declares a miracle and, with an irony enjoyed by Schmitt, that miracles prohibited by the state are not miracles (LST, 55). The core of the state is the decision and the decision is in theology the equivalent of the miracle (PT, 36).

Schmitt is the most recent of the sovereigntists: a tradition of political thinking, with Hobbes as its greatest representative, which developed as the theoretical front of the seventeenth century war on terror. When vilifications are put to one side—and some are quite just—Carl Schmitt is widely acknowledged as the greatest legal theorist of the twentieth century. Schmitt's fame rests upon his acute criticism of liberalism and it is frequently admitted by liberals that many of his criticisms are yet to be answered.[15] Whilst there is much debate as to whether Schmitt's critique of liberalism is also a Catholic critique, he being in some sense a Catholic, it is not well appreciated that his ideas are as troubling to contemporary Catholic social thought as they are to liberalism. A hint of the trouble is found amongst the intellectuals Schmitt is fond of citing. Bodin, de Maistre, de Bonald, and Donoso Cortés are all Catholic writers, but ones that most Catholic intellectuals find a bit embarrassing and not at all representative of the contemporary church. It would be nice to be able to dismiss Schmitt for this reason alone and to think of him as a certain strain of marginalized continental Catholic thinking.

However, Schmitt's arguments possess real power and carry a certain appeal to Catholics. His arguments are Augustinian in inspiration and his sovereigntist thinking is a remote basis—and perhaps not too remote at that—of the Bush Doctrine, as well as the "global war on terror,"[16] which, along with the 2003 Iraq War, was strongly supported by leading American Catholic thinkers. Whatever the future of Iraq, Catholic thinking—dedicated to the Augustinian moderation of violence as the goal of politics—has been deeply challenged since 2001. Catholic intellectuals—and here one must include John Paul II[17]—have long supported the indirect power of the United Nations although there are few signs presently of an effective organization and its reputation is besmirched by the role of some of its managers in crafting the biggest fraud in history.[18] And, for better or worse, the role of America in the 2003 Iraq War has proven that the dynamic agents of change in the world remain *national* powers. Moreover, since 2001, a national cross-border pursuit of a war on terror continues every day with a preemptive logic that appears to have few serious detractors:[19] years earlier indeed, Elizabeth Anscombe, one of Catholicism's most significant moral theorists in the twentieth century, argued that preemption is a licit form of war.[20] For reasons like these, beginning with the run-up to the Iraq War, major American Catholic intellectuals produced many articles, oftentimes in *First Things*, arguing that the Iraq War is part of a watershed event for Catholic thinking about international relations and war. For these thinkers—Neuhaus, Novak, Turner Johnson, and Weigel—the nation state can legitimately exercise a moral deposing power.[21] Briefly put, the lineaments of the collective position of these thinkers are sovereigntist, but only quasi-Schmittean, as they clearly advocate a national deposing power linked to morality. This is a *via media* between realism (national power) and idealism (morality). It is not an indirect power that fosters sedition at the behest of spiritual values (the seventeenth-century papacy) nor an international advocacy of human rights that subverts the sovereignty of nations (the U. N.) but the application of direct ("hard") power for a national cause obedient nonetheless to objective moral standards.

Weigel, who has written most on the topic, is absolutely right, I think, to link just war statecraft with Augustine's concept of peace as the *tranquillitas ordinis*. But I also think this gives Carl Schmitt's work leverage against what might be called "the *First Things* position." Schmitt's Hobbesian Augustinianism might be a startling fusion, but it is coherent, and poses a significant challenge. These Catholic authors are committed to moral power working in tandem with strategic national interests. Is such a position coherent? There are two challenges (at least). The first, less substantial, comes from Christian internationalists who believe that no national power can act for the common good save under direction of an international authority without interest and stake in the matter at hand. The arguments of Christian internationalists do not work: they falsify the just war tradition; and what they hope will replace it is vulnerable to Schmitt's charge that humanitarian war, or exclusively moral war, is the most destructive of innocents. The second substantive criticism is whether there is a place for mixing power with morals at all. Doesn't Schmitt demonstrate that the Augustinian ideal of a moderation of violence, and thus protection of the innocent, is contradicted by any form of moral power? If so, wars of solidarity, probably first espoused by de Vitoria, will have no Christian foundation. Resources exist in Thomas, de Vitoria, and Scheler to resist Schmitt's thesis. Careful attention to de Vitoria's argument for wars of solidarity shows that intervention can reaffirm sovereignty, and arguments by Thomas and Scheler on the values invoked by such interventions show that anger and sympathy both impose limits on the scope of military action.

The position of *First Things* is a departure from the Christian internationalism of thinkers like Maritain and the Archbishop of Canterbury, Rowan Williams. Neuhaus, et al. have been especially critical of theologians who deny the nation state should be in principle the public authority able to declare war. The seminal work of Christian internationalism remains Jacques Maritain's 1950 *Man and the State*. This book, it cannot be denied, has become the foundation for much of contemporary Catholic social thought. The book begins with a critique of the founding member of the "sovereigntists," Jean Bodin, and it ends with a defense of world government—an idea clearly echoed in *Gaudium et Spes* and John XXIII's 1963 *Pacem in Terris* where, in a strong echo of Maritain, a universal public authority is thought of "as the natural evolution of human political development" (WO, 32). According to Maritain, the concept of sovereignty is "poison" (MS, 49)[22] and "evil" (MS, 193) for the "inner logic" of the concept is totalitarian (MS, 51). Though I can find no argument as to why this logic is totalitarian as opposed to despotic—Talmon, for example, insists that Hobbes' logic is despotic, not totalitarian—Maritain is clear that the concept rests on the idea of "royal privilege," a monadic sovereign power, above and separate from the people governed (MS, 37). This also means that a sovereign state is above the community of nations and therefore with the concept in place "no international law binding the States can be consistently conceived" (MS, 50). Maritain wants to replace the concept of a sovereign public authority with the idea of a highest ruling authority at the peak of a body politic and no more than a vicarious expression of the will of the people (MS, 35). Rejecting the very concept then, Maritain is open to the idea that the autonomy of nation states can be forcibly restricted should there be an organized international political community.[23] Towards the end of *Gaudium et Spes*, the Council Fathers declared it a "clear duty" to work towards the outlawing of war which would require the establishment of a "universal public authority" endowed with the necessary "power to safeguard on the behalf of all, security, regard for justice, and respect for rights" (GS, para. 81). Maritain too hoped for "*one world* politically organized" (MS, 196) and based this hope on an interesting argument.

Maritain's argument is that for Aristotle and Aquinas "self-sufficiency is the essential property of a *perfect society*," and that "the primary good ensured by a perfect society…is its own internal and external peace" (MS, 197). With this political principle in place, he observes that when a state can no longer achieve peace and self-sufficiency then it ceases to be the perfect society. Maritain argues that as a matter of historical fact this mantle in "our historical age" must pass to "the international community politically organized" (MS, 198). This is the argument that must be assessed. Is Maritain right that the innocent are now only sufficiently protected in the perfect society of a world government? Maritain envisages this government based on a "superior juridical order" (MS, 210) that will ensure "justice by law," (MS, 211) and possessed of authority and power it would be able to enforce its positive laws on member states. A community of nations, deeply diverse, will nevertheless be administered by a "World State" organized upon principles of government derived in large part from Montesquieu's division of powers model (MS, 199).

Implicit in this account is that such a world state would at least have an indirect power over the federated states (MS, 209), being able to invoke the deposing power when necessary. Such is necessary for the "future perpetual peace" (MS, 201). It is very important not to misrepresent Maritain here. He says, albeit without argument, that it is against natural law for one nation to impose its will upon another (MS, 199)—de Vitoria disagrees—and that the world state will evolve from a "moral revolution" with all nations freely standing in solidarity with one another (MS, 206-7) on account of "the will of the people… growing so powerful as to sweep away the obstacles caused by the myth of the States as sovereign persons" (MS, 210). Interestingly, Maritain tells us that member states will "surrender their *privilege* of being sovereign persons" (emphasis added) and there will be "a serious repercussion" on the "free business of a number of individuals… most attached to profit-making" (MS, 207-8). Transitioning to the political organization of the world state—and illustrating something of its final character—Maritain envisages "a new superior agency" having no power but "endowed with unquestionable *moral authority*," (MS, 213) and "completely free in the exercise of [its] spiritual responsibility" (MS, 214). In particular, says Maritain, it is this "supreme advisory council," which would pass judgment upon what stood as a just cause of war (MS, 214-5). Whilst the Council Fathers acknowledged that terrorism is a form of war (GS, para. 79), Maritain states that "the old standards with respect to which a war was to be considered just or unjust are outworn" (MS, 215) and it would fall to the members of his imagined advisory council to determine where justice might lie in war (MS, 215-6). These reflections are the very last pages of Maritain's seminal work of Catholic political philosophy. Are these reflections still viable?

Though Maritain clearly outlined a conceptual alliance between the church's universal spiritual power and the aspiration of the United Nations to world government it is very far from clear if such a conceptual link is desirable. Having Permanent Observer status at the United Nations, the church has never stopped being actively involved in international governance despite the fact that substantial battles have had to be fought, for example at the 1994 Cairo conference on population and the 1995 Beijing conference on women: conferences where the church fought vigorously to stop the attempts of various countries, including America, under the presidency of Bill Clinton, and the European Union, to have abortion declared a human right.[24] Recently (February 2005), G. W. Bush's administration demanded rewrites of some of these documents to clarify completely that there is no such human right. It is unsurprising that these conflicts have soured some Catholic intellectuals on the United Nations but it is the matter of war, as Maritain intuited in the last pages of *Man and State*, that has caused Catholic intellectuals to formulate afresh national power against internationalism. Is Maritain right that in our historical moment the nation state can no longer provide security and peace, that innocents have their best protection in norms of international law?

A more recent formulation of Christian internationalism insists this is so. Even before the 2003 Iraq War, the question of who has, or what gives, authority to fight a war had received enormous attention. Many of the nations that fought the air war over Kosovo in 1999 on the authority of humanitarian values forgot in 2003 that they had done so without authority from the United Nations. Indeed, a higher law than the authority of the United Nations was invoked—human rights. The year 2003 heard the constant refrain—with some Vatican officials joining in (WO, 36)—that only the United Nations had the moral authority necessary to fight a war. This idea (expressed in the bumper sticker "International Law Not the U. S. Senate") destroys the privilege of a national public authority to kill.[25] In response to the "global war on terror," the Archbishop of Canterbury, Rowan Williams, argued that the just war tradition is inherently internationalist because a state, as much as any individual, can act for private interest and in so doing acts on merely private authority. Only a public authority concerned with the common good can kill, he argues.[26] With a stoic gesture he assumes that the common good is self-evidently a global good—a gesture both Thomas and de Vitoria reject—and so there must be some sort of "global test" that each nation must be subject to in order to ensure that it acts as a genuine public authority.[27] Every nation must "express its accountability to the substantial concerns of international law."[28] This requires an international forum for otherwise no state will act for "a common good that is not nationally defined." As is apparent from this last comment, Williams is skeptical that nations ever act for the common good, which has good Hobbesian precedent. If Williams' implicit Hobbesianism is not troubling enough, the assumption that a nation cannot respond to the objective claims of the moral law seems desperate indeed. Williams makes the same mistake Scheler identified in Kant's work: he assumes that the "generally valid law of human volition" (Kant) must be hostile to all particularity. Williams does not seem to appreciate that his claim that the common good cannot be "nationally defined" is analogous to Kant's rejection of revelation. For revelation is an insight into, and bearing of, values peculiar to some and not held by others: that the moral law was revealed to Israel in no way prevents that law from being an objective moral law. Indeed, there is no obvious reason at all to doubt that a nation's peculiar moral sensibility, present, for example, in some Burkean tradition of the common law or legal positivism,[29] may well pay homage to the "sovereignty of the object" (Kolnai).

I would agree with Scheler that the Kantianism of some like Williams is just wrong but his position is weak for other reasons as well. A crucial element of his argument is that if a state acts on national interest it therefore acts as a private authority and forfeits its authority to kill: for there is no lethal authority to kill in the service of private interest. This reasoning is certainly not part of the political thinking of Aquinas and de Vitoria. A good ruler governs for the "advantage" of the nation, says de

Vitoria, whilst a tyrant governs "for his own advantage" (H, 161). But a tyrant who uses the authority of the state for his private interest does not thereby transform the state into a private authority; the state always remains a public authority. For this reason, Thomas and de Vitoria argue that the public authority has the power to violently depose its "legitimate lord" when he acts tyrannically. No private individual has this authority and so cannot licitly commit an act of tyrannicide against a tyrannical "legitimate lord." Under certain conditions, a "private man" can risk an act of tyrannicide against a tyrant who has usurped public authority. Even here, however, the "private man" does not act on private authority. Usurpation throws a nation into civil war and the "private man" who chances tyrannicide does so on public authority (H, 163): as Cajetan puts it, "the private man" continues a war against the tyrant begun on public authority (*In com.*, q. 64, a. 3). Thomas and de Vitoria do not accept that a public authority can ever become a private authority. In the extreme case of tyranny, the tyrant forfeits public authority but he does not corrupt it. A public authority promotes the interest, or as de Vitoria puts it, the "advantage," of *a* nation:

> ... the governor of one commonwealth is not obliged, indeed ought not, to look after the good of another commonwealth, even a greater good, if it is to the harm of his own commonwealth. Not even a private individual, indeed, is bound to undergo a loss of his own goods for the benefit of other men's common weal. (PW, 90-91)

If that advantage is pursued unjustly one has the unjust exercise of public authority (hence the need for *regime* change) *not* the collapse of public authority into private authority.

Williams also argues that it is part of the "just war tradition" that national public authority is subordinate to some international authority—presumed, I suppose, to be *for this reason* a *higher* authority—in its exercise of lethal authority. He never explains what in the tradition possessed this international authority but it is probably (and ironically?) an allusion to the papacy. Even if one assumes that the papacy has the plenitude of temporal power, as Thomas may have done, and de Vitoria certainly did (PW, 92), I think it *inconceivable* that Thomas ever held that the public authority to kill is subordinate to a universal public authority. Certainly, and famously, de Vitoria argues that princes may depose other princes, that is, orchestrate regime change without recourse to the authority of the pope (PW, 223; 288). Thomas could never have held what Williams claims is part of the tradition for his guiding assumption is worthy of Bodin, only radicalized. In developing his theory of absolute monarchy, Bodin had to find a way to reduce the *merum imperium* of regional magistrates. Medieval jurists had argued that magistrates held their powers by *right of office* and so exercised the privileges of power at their own discretion and without reliance on the king. Bodin sought to restrict the scope of this medieval *merum imperium* but even he conceded nevertheless that inside an absolute state, magistrates would hold discretionary power at least on the matter of capital punishment.[30] Williams advocates then a radicalized absolutism wherein public authorities are stripped of the privilege of lethal authority and are only to act as per the directive of some world authority. I would venture that it is an historical impossibility for Thomas to have thought anything remotely like what Williams claims is part of the "just war tradition." When Thomas spoke of public authority, he surely had in mind the *merum imperium* of regional magistrates, dukes, city states, and the like, and I know of no passage where he expresses reservations about such political order. Indeed, it is the originality of Bodin to have first done so.

Schmitt would be puzzled by contemporary commentators so at odds. The Bush Doctrine, at least in Catholic hands, relies on the idea of a moral deposing power and so too does the liberal's and Christian internationalist's humanitarian insistence on norms of international law. Both political camps share the same premise of activist international governance. The *potestas indirecta*, argues Schmitt, has for its method of war, "ostracism and moral disqualification."[31] Modern value theory (and this includes Catholic personalism derived from Scheler) is no better than older moral theories, argues Schmitt, for like them it fosters a de-valuation of the person of the enemy: this is its peculiar mode of "attack" and responsible for its peculiar savagery.[32] Moral valuation inside contemporary international law is, he argues, the source of total war for it transforms war into civil war. It is a total war because derived from the logic of the total state (FA, 43). Indirect power's moral reach relies on a universal authority that operates internationally, cutting across and neutralizing the political identities of individual states. Indirect power also intensifies violence, generating civil war, because it makes state neutrality respecting the combat impossible (FA, 45) for, juridically, the state is neutralized, that is, abolished (FA, 44). Schmitt comments:

> As a consequence, the non-discriminatory war between states changes itself into an international civil war and therewith it achieves a kind of totality that is as horrid and destructive as everything of which a facile propaganda has accused the national totality. (FA, 44-5)

Because this moral authority is held over all persons, those who reject this authority reject an identity with the world of persons and so enter into civil war with the human community. Civil war means, of course, that those rejecting the authority of the *potestas indirecta* are partisans and not the regular army of any legitimate state. Combat against partisans is always especially savage, notes Schmitt, not merely because of the ferocity of moral purpose but because inter-state war moderates combat. Liberal humanitarian criticism of American treatment of captured terrorists would again strike Schmitt as incoherent: humanitarian warfare makes the enemy not merely partisans but pirates, "the enemies of mankind." Denied the authority of the state, the partisan is nothing better than a homicidal criminal. Schmitt provides historical evidence for the peculiar savagery of civil war and partisan fighting and it is undeniable that political thinkers have been acutely aware of the horror of civil war, albeit none more so than Hobbes who had a lively appreciation that men are not good, a premise Schmitt[33] shares with Augustine and Donoso Cortés as well.

Thus, it is Schmitt's Augustinianism that makes him a realist. This is why Schmitt rejects Thomas' theory of homicide and, in *The Concept of the Political,* explains that only an existential threat can justify killing. As early as 1925-6, Schmitt began to develop the alternative of the amoralism of the friend-enemy distinction to remove moral censure from the idea of a public enemy.[34] True to his thought, Schmitt would later justify Hitler's SA purge as a friend-enemy exception necessary to defend the constitution.[35] The Vatican said that the executions without trial were murder,[36] but Schmitt almost surely relied on Bodin's discussion of tyrannicide. That discussion is a startling reversal of *late* scholastic defenses of tyrannicide. Scholastic discussions focused exclusively on what sort of tyrant can be deposed: a usurper could be deposed violently by private individuals but a legitimate prince, no matter how immoral, could not (H, 161-3). Bodin begins his analysis by treating the would-be assassin of a prince as a usurper, and thus a tyrant. He then argues, true to his method of relying on Roman law, that the Valerian law of Rome permitted government to lethally respond extra-judicially to those who sought usurpation by arms.[37] For Schmitt, government can destroy terrorists in order to forestall tyranny, and a sovereign can, quite licitly, rely on extra-judicial means.

The sovereigntist movement in contemporary American thinking whether secular or Christian develops a strain of conservatism found in Hobbes. However, Hobbes is also a principal source of liberalism and

the leftist construal of international law undoubtedly relies on his transformation of the theory of homicide. A Thomist is compelled to reject,
and every *Christian* internationalist ought to be leery of, this transformation. The privatization of lethal authority received acute intellectual
formulation in Hobbes when he cast the state of nature as *bellum omnium
contra omnes*. Aquinas would be puzzled reading this formulation, to
his mind, it ought to read *duellum omnium contra omnes*. The proper
authority of individuals to licitly kill is written into the very origin of
the natural law by Hobbes. The subtitle of Schmitt's work on Hobbes
is "Meaning and Failure of a Political Symbol." The demonstration of
The Leviathan fails because Hobbes' philosophy ultimately leads to the
neutralization of the state (LST, 33). A Thomist must completely agree
with this assessment. Once it is appreciated that *bellum* is present in the
state of nature, and not merely *duellum,* the Thomist must agree that the
state has been neutralized, for Hobbes has written into the very origin
of the Leviathan the authority of the people to licitly kill. Licit killing
is here a matter of equality not privilege. Schmitt's and the Thomist's
reservation about Hobbes are not unrelated. For Schmitt, the *ingens
potentia* of the Leviathan is not original to the state but to the people.
The neutralization of the state is confirmed in Hobbes' conception of
the state as a mechanism wherein the sovereign relates to the state as
the soul to the body in Cartesian anthropology. The state is no longer
sovereign, the territory of the nation a foreign body, as it were, and the
way is opened for later treatments of the state as pure instrument rather
than genuine public authority.[38] In later formulations of the liberal tradition, according to Schmitt, the state is reduced to the provider of welfare
and in this neutralization it loses the attribute of war powers. The failure
of Hobbes, as Schmitt shows, is that internationalism springs up on the
back of the privatization of homicide.

Catholic international relations theory must thread its way through
to a sovereigntist position that rejects indirect power as traditionally conceived *and* the radically egalitarian "sovereigntist" position
of Hobbes just described. With Schmitt, Catholic social thought must
re-affirm the privilege of a national public authority, its *sui generis*
character, including its privilege to kill. Christian internationalism must
be abandoned. The writers of *First Things* are correct about this. It is
vulnerable to Schmitt's Augustinian critique regarding innocents and it
makes common cause with a liberal humanitarianism underwritten by
the privatization of homicide. Against Schmitt, Catholic social thought
has resources to show that Schmitt's arguments are not decisive against

every interventionist doctrine nor, a slightly different issue, a foreign policy reliant on the fusion of moral categories and national power. These resources are de Vitoria's reflections on war, which can bridge the difference between "the *First Things* position" and Schmitt, himself a keen student of Vitoria's thinking. Intervention, de Vitoria shows, can serve both national and solidarity goals. Indeed, an argument from Scheler shows why this is the only morally viable form of intervention. *This* same argument answers Schmitt: Scheler being able to show how morals in foreign policy do not intensify killing. With an insight into sympathy remarkably similar to Aquinas' own about anger as basic to avenging justice, Scheler demonstrates that there are moral values, e.g., pity, that have restraint in-built.

Some argue that early modern thinkers like de Vitoria and Grotius agreed on the moral character of intervention for humanitarian reasons but that this view was eclipsed for well over 200 years by the positivist tradition of international law that strongly affirmed national sovereignty. Happily, this line of reasoning continues, the "absolutist" theory of the state assumed by this positivist tradition is surpassed now by human rights. Human rights are now "the normative fabric of international society,"[39] the basis of the indirect power of the United Nations, and an evocation of the early modern position of someone like de Vitoria. I think this view of de Vitoria wrong. There is evidence that de Vitoria took tentative steps towards a sovereigntist position that cut against his own advocacy of the *potestas indirecta* (PW, 219-21). I think de Vitoria's defense of humanitarian war is more subtle than is appreciated by those who think it an embryonic human rights argument. And this is just as well since, obviously, I suspect Schmitt is right: an international moral authority laying claim to a *potestas indirecta* is the harbinger of total war. If partisan warfare is to be avoided—and it must be if the innocent are to be protected—then war must be firmly secured in the state. This does not prevent a prince from having a deposing power, however. Actually, a deposing power can reaffirm the sovereignty of a rogue public authority subjected to the laws of war. *This* is de Vitoria's position.

The authority for a prince's deposing power, argues de Vitoria, rests on the foundation of all social order, the juristic categories of innocence and guilt. Vitoria argues that if innocents are attacked they may defend themselves, and a foreign prince can defend them also (PW, 225). A Schmittean motif can be added: intervention by the prince will regularize the warfare, diminish its partisan character, and offer the innocent the protections of public authority.

Schmitt argues that sovereignty evacuated through humanitarian or moralized intervention is a recipe for an intensification of war. Vitoria's limpid formulation, "they can defend themselves, therefore princes can defend them" (PW, 225) does not invoke any moral authority. This sparse formulation is so interesting because, of course, having no jurisdiction over a foreign sovereignty,[40] a prince has no civil power to intervene. The privilege of the public authority to kill can obviously only extend as far as its jurisdiction. Moreover, since de Vitoria is neither a natural rights nor a human rights theorist, a prince's authority to kill is not internationalized on the back of some moral imperative.

A public authority *killing the innocent* provokes resistance. "No one can give another the right to kill him," says de Vitoria. That is, a person cannot alienate personal governance. That personal governance cannot be renounced is neither Hobbesian nor Kantian. Resisting others who try to kill you is mechanistic for Hobbes, the foundation of a natural obligation to defend the self (see the role this idea plays in the court case discussed in the next chapter). Vitoria denies there is any such obligation, natural or otherwise. It is not Kantian self-determination either: this inescapable personal governance is best thought of juristically. Indeed, typical of natural law, it is a juristic idea that blends into the ontology of the person. Law (lex), as Thomas says, is derived from *ligare* "because it binds one to act" (ST I-II, q. 90, a. 1).

Thus it is not de Vitoria's position that this binding governance means that the guilty are under an obligation to try to fend off the punishments of public authority. Innocence and guilt are the basic pillars of the juristic order, not self-determination—and it is interesting that these categories are not self-evidently moral before juristic. These categories provide for a foundational social orientation. This is the premise of de Vitoria's argument. The innocent attacked by public authority resist through *duellum*, the private exercise of lethal acts. Intervention by a foreign prince is the exercise of a law of *bellum*, an act of public authority. What is the basis for this transition? On what basis can one move from "they can defend themselves" to "therefore princes can defend them"? Schmitt argued that the only licit ground of homicide was "existential threat," that is, a threat "to a way of life." (CP, 49). Vitoria's theory of resistance is not a Schmittean existential right for de Vitoria develops his ideas in the context of the suspension of a way of life. Vitoria argues that a national power can extend its privilege to kill internationally as part of a discussion on the abolition of cannibalistic religious rites. Those to be sacrificed, says de Vitoria, may welcome their having been chosen for sacrifice but since they are innocent resistance cannot be renounced. As we saw in the fifth chapter, one can certainly *will* coherently not to go on living but this is by no means to say that one can licitly forgo resistance even should one wish to be attacked. More basic still than an existential right is the juristic basis of all social orientation, innocence. Sovereignty relies upon what is most basic to the juristic order. Because the innocence of the attacked is outraged, a foreign prince may intervene. His act of war in fact re-establishes the very order on which sovereignty relies: intervention affirms the national interest of the intervening power and the territory subject to war. Humanitarian intervention may suspend sovereignty, but solidarity with the innocent is a correction of tyranny that reaffirms sovereignty, that is, right regard for innocence.

Hobbes would not be persuaded by this argument. Fully aware of an argument like de Vitoria's, Hobbes, the greatest of the sovereigntist thinkers, rejects a crucial premise. Whereas de Vitoria thinks that sovereignty degrades itself should it forsake the protection of the innocent, Hobbes argues that a sovereign power can licitly kill innocent subjects. What is basic to the juristic is avoiding civil war, not protecting the innocent. The argument does have purchase against Schmitt, at least on the face of it. Recall, Schmitt thinks that Hobbes' formulation of his civil war premise is in fact contradictory: *bellum* in the state of nature neutralizes the state. To find an alternative to Hobbes' failed politics, Schmitt had recourse to Scotism. A better formulation of the civil war premise (for, like Hobbes, Schmitt also wants to curtail revolutionary violence) is unbounded voluntarism.

Scotus defends the idea that the will is indifferent, that is, a free power in relation to inclination, unmoved by impulses of natural desire, and a free power even in relation to the good.[41] He certainly disagrees with Thomas that God because "by essence goodness, cannot be displeasing to any will" (C, 355) and claims that it is possible to love and take pleasure in hate (C, 331).[42] The awesome, dramatic quality of Schmitt's decisionism, its absolutism, is actually a function of his Scotism: "Every concrete juristic decision contains a moment of indifference from the perspective of content, because the juristic deduction is not traceable in the last detail to its premises" (PT, 30).[43] Elsewhere I show that Scotus defends these claims because he thinks that Aquinas' naturalism destroys the love of God.[44] That is, he thinks Aquinas' theology is not genuine theology but a philosophical support of humanitarianism. This criticism is also found in Scheler (R, 89-91 & 139, nn. 28 & 25). In Schmitt's hands it becomes the devastating charge, if sustainable, that state action obedient to the good—whether that be a "thin" good of Hobbes' natural obligation, humanitarianism, or Thomism—destroys innocents. Even if de Vitoria's natural law argument for wars of solidarity only relies on the elemental juristic values of innocence and guilt, he is still vulnerable to Schmitt's critique of values.

Whether one is Maritain or an anarchist it is a commonplace to regard the state as "a mere impersonal mechanism of abstract laws and concrete power" (MS, 192). Schmitt argues that this commonplace is a superficial phenomenology of the state. Careful attention to politics shows that the state is a decision, an act of generating order. The sovereign is whoever makes this decision. Far from an abstract, impersonal, machine-like bureaucracy, every state is a personal decision since the state of exception, an always possible reality in domestic and international politics, relies on persons and their decisions (PT, 6). Decisionism, in Schmitt's Augustinian personalism, is an elemental norm-creation. A Thomist can respond that some values encourage restraint. The values that have restraint built into them are all values rejected by humanitarianism. They are values ultimately rooted in love. I think Benedict is absolutely right when he argues, "whoever wants to eliminate love is preparing to eliminate man as such."[45] Schmitt's argument is successful against the humanitarian but not the Thomist, I argue. Thomas, of course, agrees with Scheler who writes: "The important thing is not the amount of welfare, it is that there should be a *maximum of love* among men" (R, 62). With this statement, Scheler puts in relief the basic conflict between Christianity and humanitarianism, and, yes, Christian advocates of social justice as well.

Schmitt is wrong, I think, that values always possess the quality of "attack." Consider the wonderful passage from *The Lord of the Rings*:

> [Frodo] What a pity that Bilbo did not stab that vile creature, when he had a chance!

> [Gandalf] Pity? It was Pity that stayed his hand. Pity, and Mercy: not to strike without need. And he has been well rewarded, Frodo. Be sure that he took so little hurt from the evil, and escaped in the end, because he began his ownership of the Ring so. With Pity.[46]

Some values restrain and ennoble. Part of Scheler's value hierarchy is that holy and spiritual values are restraining. It is at these levels one finds values like pity, mercy, forgiveness, gentleness, and so on. It is an essential part of Kolnai's analysis of privilege that each privilege is a locus of generosity, that is, every site of privilege generates values, some admittedly higher than others. Humanitarianism is a danger to the innocent precisely because it replaces the "height" of love with welfare and thus erodes restraint.

Scheler thought a key thesis of the Scottish Enlightenment was basically correct. Adam Smith gave final form to a manner of social explanation that had gripped the Scottish imagination, namely, that social order is explainable in terms of sympathy. Scheler thinks this is certainly true up to a point. In fact, sympathy is underwritten by love and love has an upward trajectory beyond the social bonds of sympathy to persons' radically individual acts of love, often best explained in theological terms. Love is not really sympathy at all since it is not a feeling but an act; it is not a reaction but an active engagement of persons with the world around them. Scheler, following Augustine, argues that underwriting an individual's entire affective life is a certain loving engagement with the world. But careful attention to the phenomenology of sympathy reveals, interior to the highest acts of pity and love, are lower, but constitutive, movements of sympathy. These are what Scheler calls "laws of dependence" and his insight here is telling against Schmitt.

Phenomenology, says Scheler, discerns five distinct affective levels to sympathy standing in a strict hierarchy. These are identification, vicarious feeling, fellow feeling, benevolence, and love. Identification is distinct from vicarious feeling or fellow feeling because in the last two a separation from the feeling of the other person is actually felt and structurally present in the interior of the vicarious or fellow feeling. Scheler insists that brutality, for example, is completely misunderstood if it is regarded as a primitive phenomenon. Identification is a primitive phenomenon: it is a unity of feeling with no felt distinctions among the people involved. This is the kind of feeling often present in a nation's unity of feeling in time of war. However, brutality and cruelty only make sense if the difference between recipient and giver is experienced. Brutality is an experience made possible by fellow feeling where the suffering of another is perceived as different and enjoyed. Scheler adds a very dark tone to this analysis. Vicarious feeling and fellow feeling are the same in that there is a felt distinction between sufferer and the companionate experience of that suffering but they differ significantly. Vicarious feeling does not have as one of its qualities the experience of the worth of the sufferer. Vicarious feeling is best thought of as a cognitive feeling, an apprehending of the fact of what a neighbor feels. Such a feeling carries within it no valuation, for, as Scheler points out, the knowledge of someone's suffering can leave us thoroughly indifferent. It is only fellow feeling in which first appears a valuation of the sufferer. It is the very sensitivity of such a feeling that makes brutality possible, however. As Scheler observes, one cannot brutalize a stone or a tree. Brutality is only possible on the back of an experience that includes the suffering of the other and the knowledge that his worth is outraged by one's act.

Despite this dark turn, atop what Scheler calls the "order of functional dependence" amongst the varieties of sympathetic feeling sits benevolence and love. The *experience* of another in an emotion shared need not happen. It is not present in certain mass experiences of the transfusion of emotion, for example. Nonetheless, vicarious feeling, a shared experience, obviously depends on identification and on the fact that emotion can transfer or be communicated. But vicarious feeling does have its own peculiar formal structure upon which rests the very possibility of moral experience at all: a felt insight into another's experience. In turn, fellow feeling—the first emotional experience to *discern* value in another's experience—relies on vicarious feeling opening up *the field of possible moral experience*: awareness of another's emotion.

Scheler identifies humanitarianism with feelings of benevolence. The highest affective relationship, love, is an affirmation of the unique value of an individual person. Acts of love, Scheler argues, are impossible without a more general love of humanity. Humanitarianism is a value; it has a role to play! It is in benevolent feelings that love of humanity is expressed. This general positive valuation of *human* worth is only possible in turn on the back of fellow-feeling, an experience whose cognitive content includes the intuition that the one suffering is a person, equivalent in status (though not necessarily moral worth) to the person with companionate feeling. Feelings of benevolence intensify that intuition of equal status and actually introduce a valuation that selects out that status as of a higher worth than other objects of the world. Love, however, makes yet a further selection, and out of the general class of most valuable objects, persons, elevates some particular persons to be privileged objects of unique loving acts of peculiar persons (e.g., marriage). Whilst humanitarianism has an invaluable role to play in creating broad communities that transcend tribal loyalties with their values and disvalues, its limitations must not be ignored.

As it rests on benevolent feelings, humanitarianism is not the expression of our highest affective life. When a humanitarian like Singer argues that humanitarianism warrants the killing of the disabled because of how much they suffer he ignores that acts of love trump benevolent feeling.

Love relates to individual persons and so rejects the idea that persons can be lumped together as items within a calculus of the "greatest happiness for the greatest number." Public policy that lists persons as items in a utility calculation has inverted the value hierarchy and turned away from what has highest value—love and persons. Humanitarianism again misunderstands itself when it espouses an international policy that transcends the national state. This is a case of benevolent feeling for peoples of other nations ignoring its dependence on the affective attachments that are made possible by identification, vicarious, and fellow feeling. These feelings express, and are the expression of, community and cultural values that do not, and cannot, attain the generality of benevolent feeling.[47] Benevolent feeling separated from the more elementary soil of identification, vicarious, and fellow feeling, will be emptied of genuine sympathy and become indifference.

Scheler's analysis is eerily accurate: in my opinion, the analysis is very like Aquinas' (De malo, q. 12, a. 4, ad 3; ST II-II, q. 108). Take the trajectory of humanitarian intervention: benevolent feeling demands action be taken about some outrage (Somalia, say). But when the national militaries involved suffer, domestic public opinion demands "our boys" come home; the people whose suffering so excited benevolence are then left to their own devices, now with the consequences of war added to their burden. The NATO intervention in Kosovo showed the accuracy of Scheler's analysis even more acutely. Horrified by the Serbian treatment of the Kosovars, NATO populations demanded war but with zero casualties for NATO forces. Balancing benevolence with the more tribal reality of identification and vicarious feeling, NATO devised an air war policy wherein pilots flew high—so surface to air missiles were no threat—and "bombed" the enemy. Flying high, their armaments were released above doctrinal height and were inaccurate, tending to miss the enemy and arbitrarily killing those on the ground, including the population to be saved by intervention. Benevolent feeling was seen to be utterly dependent on identification, vicarious, and fellow feeling, and policy made in ignorance of this reality became indifference. Wars of solidarity rooted in love and national power are likely to be rarer than wars expressing benevolent agitation. Sometimes the sense "something must be done" or the anxiety "not on our watch" will be left unmet but, assuming prudent statesmanship, domestic populations are likely to stand longer behind a war of solidarity that defers to identification and yet be more alert to the particularities of the conflict if love (and not benevolence) animates national action. Furthermore, if higher values of pity and love animate the action a generosity of spirit will help prevent the distortions of sacrifice (see the eighth chapter) that plagued the Kosovo intervention.

Notes

1. 1999 Annual Report to the General Assembly as quoted by M. Cook, "'Immaculate War': Constraints on Humanitarian Intervention," *Ethics and International Affairs*, Vol. 14: 1, p. 58.
2. G. Weigel, "World Order: What Catholics Forgot," *First Things* (May, 2004), pp. 31-38; hereafter WO.
3. Catholic practice in international relations—the papacy of John Paul the Great—has outstripped Catholic thinking on this matter (see G. Weigel, "Papacy and Power," *First Things* [February 2001], pp. 18-25). Perhaps John Paul the Great's practice even outstripped his own thinking: see the comments of Jeffreys in his *Defending Human Dignity: John Paul II and Political Realism* (Grand Rapids, MI: Brazos Press, 2004) and WO, 37.
4. This is true of liberal humanitarians, neo-conservatives, and Christian churches, including the Catholic Church. Of course, diverse groups have very different ideas about what human rights are and what sort of preferences and actions might be covered by human rights.
5. During the war in Kosovo, the first humanitarian intervention by liberal democratic powers, more innocents were killed than military personnel. See my detailed discussion of Kosovo in the eighth chapter.
6. C. Schmitt, *War/Non-War?*, trans., S. Draghici (Corvallis, OR: Plutarch Press, 2004), p. 2. Cf. "A Young Lawyer Helps Chart Shift in Foreign Policy," WSJ, September 12, 2005 [A1 & A12] on the conservative American lawyers known as "sovereigntists" who were influential during the Bush years. One of their number, John Yoo, makes points very similar to Schmitt and Hobbes (J. Yoo, *War by Other Means* [New York: Atlantic Monthly Press, 2006], especially p. 16).
7. C. Schmitt, *The Theory of the Partisan: A Commentary/Remark on the Concept of the Political* (www.msupress.msu.edu/journals/cr/schmitt), p. 7; R. Scruton, "The Dangers of Internationalism," *The Intercollegiate Review* (Fall/Winter, 2005), pp. 29-35; M. Cook, "Moral Foundations of Military Service," *Parameters: US Army War College*, Vol. 30 (Spring 2000), pp. 117-30. Unfortunately, Weigel does not mention whether he thinks this is true or false though he does acknowledge that the nation state is here to stay (WO, 34).
8. PW, 90-4; Saint Robert Bellarmine, S. J., *De potestate papae in rebus temporalibus*, c. 3 & 13 as cited in J. Rager, *Democracy and Bellarmine* (Shelbyville, IN: Qualityprint, 1926), pp. 73-4.
9. Höpfl Harro, *Jesuit Political Thought*, c. 14 on the papal indirect power.
10. An obvious example was the Iraqi insurgency with its beheadings, mutilations, and open warfare on innocents that scarred greater Baghdad and destroyed American confidence.
11. It is printed in King James I/VI, *Political Writings* (Cambridge: Cambridge University Press, 1994), pp. 85-131. Here, James also provides a commentary on how the text is to be understood.
12. C. Schmitt, *The Leviathan in the State Theory of Thomas Hobbes: Meaning and Failure of a Political Symbol* (Westport, CT: Greenwood Press, 1996), p. 18; hereafter LST.
13. F. Nietzsche, *Genealogy of Morals* (Oxford: Oxford University Press, 1996), III Essay, c. 15.

14. G. Weigel, "Papacy and Power," *First Things* (February 2001), pp. 18-25.

15. See, for example, W. Scheurmann, *Carl Schmitt: The End of Law* (Lanham, MD: Rowan & Littlefield, 1999).

16. See John Yoo's theory of the role of a monarchical decisionism in the war powers clause of the U. S. Constitution (J. Yoo, *The Powers of War and Peace: The Constitution and Foreign Affairs after 9/11* [Chicago: The University of Chicago Press, 2005], especially chapters 2 & 5).

17. Cf. D. Jeffreys, *Defending Human Dignity*. Substantial strain in all the international organizations established after the Second World War is now plain, George Melloan, "World War II's Do-Good Offspring are Flagging," WSJ, September 20, 2005.

18. For the shocking failures of the organization under the tenure of Kofi Annan, see "Kofi and U.N. Ideals," WSJ, December 14, 2006; though nothing can rival Annan's revolting role in facilitating the Srebrenica massacre (see the UN's own report on the matter [November 1999]). Cf. N. Ferguson, *Colossus: The Rise and Fall of the American Empire* (London: Penguin, 2005). For the enormous hopes placed on transnational organizations by liberal political theorists, see summaries in J. Fonte, "Liberal Democracy vs. Transnational Progressivism: The Future of the Ideological Civil war Within the West," (Hudson Institute, 2002) and M. Plattner, "Sovereignty and Democracy," *Policy Review*, Vol. 122 (December 2003).

19. Robert D. Kagan, *Imperial Grunts* (New York: Random House, 2005).

20. G. Anscombe, "War and Murder," in *The Collected Philosophical papers of G. E. M. Anscombe, Vol. III: Ethics, Religion and Politics* (Minneapolis, MN: University of Minnesota Press, 1981), p. 52.

21. G. Weigel, "Moral Clarity in a Time of War," *First Things* (January 2003), pp. 20-7; hereafter MC.

22. J. Maritain, *Man and the State* (Washington, D. C.: The Catholic University of America Press, 1998); henceforth = MS.

23. "The full *external* autonomy of the body politic means that it enjoys comparatively supreme independence with regard to the international community, that is, an independence which the international community—as long as it remains merely moral and does not exist as political society, therefore has no political independence of its own—has no right and no power forcibly to make lesser with respect to itself" (MS, 40-41).

24. G. Weigel, *A Witness to Hope* (New York: Cliff Street Books, 1999), pp. 715-27 & 766-71; cf. G. Weigel, "Papacy and Power," *First Things* (February 2001), pp. 18-25.

25. For a certain European horror of this privilege, see G. Weigel, "Europe's Problem—and Ours," *First Things* (February 2004), pp. 18-25.

26. Rowan Williams & George Weigel, "War and Statecraft: An Exchange," *First Things* (March 2004), pp. 14-21. Williams' position is a staple of the international governance literature, e.g., *Private Actors and Security Governance*, ed. A. Bryden & M. Caparini (Zurich: LIT, 2006).

27. Williams thinks that it is Thomas' position that the use of the state's lethal authority "will always need publicly available justification in terms of the common good." This is not true. The idea of a "publicly available justification" is an equivocation of Thomas' use of "public." Vitoria explicitly denies that soldiers or the population must understand the reason for a war—indeed their ignorance grants them immunities from punishment should their side lose (PW, 321; H, 228-9)—and Thomas explains that unless there is "manifest injustice" in a judgment of public authority the person commissioned with acting on that authority is to do so for "he has no right to discuss the judgment of his superior" (a. 6, ad 3). Indeed, Thomas and de Vitoria both grant a tyrant who is a "legitimate lord" as opposed to a usurper enormous, if not total, latitude in the exercise of his authority.

28. Catholics should be extremely concerned that international law is currently being cast as a *ius cogens*—the moral sensibility of international organizations and universities—and not the *ius gentium*, the moral sensibility of peoples across the world. For the application of the content of the *ius cogens* to business practices (and one does not need to be Adam Smith to have concerns) see T. Donaldson & T. Dunfee, *The Ties That Bind* (Cambridge, MA: Harvard Business School Press, 1999).
29. Consider Burke's comments on America, for example, in his parliamentary speech, "Conciliation with America," *Pre-Revoluntionary Writings* (Cambridge: Cambridge university Press, 1993).
30. J. Franklin, "Introduction," to Bodin, *On Sovereignty* (Cambridge: Cambridge University Press, 2004), p. XIV; cf. PR, 290.
31. C. Schmitt, *Four Articles*, (Washington, D. C.: Plutarch Press, 1999), p. 45; hereafter = FA.
32. C. Schmitt, *The Tyranny of Values*, trans., S. Draghici (Corvallis, OR: Plutarch Press, 1996), p. 22; 26-7.
33. J. Bendersky, *Carl Schmitt: Theorist for the Reich* (Princeton, NJ: Princeton University Press, 1983), p. 87. Is this an intensification of "the permanent allurement of sin" (GS, para. 58) perhaps?
34. Ibid., pp. 87-9
35. Ibid., pp. 215-216
36. Ibid., pp. 215-16.
37. J. Bodin, *On Sovereignty* (Cambridge: Cambridge University Press, 2004), pp. 110-11. Herman cites John of Salisbury on this issue (PR, 282). As I read the cited passage, John uses the Valerian law and is no advocate of the (highly constrained) right of resistance found in the Thomistic analysis of tyrannicide.
38. C. Schmitt, *Three Types of Juristic Thought* (Westport, CT: Praeger, 2004); cf. PT, 48-9.
39. A. Coll, "Kosovo and the Moral Burden of Power," in *War Over Kosovo*, ed. A. Bacevich and E. A. Cohen (New York: Columbia University Press, 2001), p. 134.
40. For the close relationship between jurisdiction and territory, see St. Anthony of Florence [1389-1459], O. P., *Summae Sacrae Theologiae, iuris pontificii et Caesarei* (Venice, 1571), Part II, Book 7, c. 8, f. 274vb.
41. J. Capreolus, *On Virtue*, pp. 256-7; hereafter = C.
42. Respecting the damned, Scotus claims: "they simply speaking hate God with pleasure and without remorse of conscience. It is clear, therefore, from these points that the right dictate can be simply speaking present in the intellect without the right choice of that dictate being present in the will."
43. This theory of inclination is also basic to the anarchist Max Stirner's work on the obduracy of the will.
44. "Pleasure: A Reflection on Benedict XVI's *Deus Caritas Est*," *Nova et Vetera: The English Edition of the International Theological Journal* , Vol. 5: 2 (2007), pp. 315-24.
45. Benedict XVI, *Deus Caritas Est*, para. 28.
46. J. R. R. Tolkien, *The Fellowship of the Ring* (Boston: Houghton Mifflin Company, 1994), p. 58.
47. Cf. Scruton on membership, *The West and the Rest* (Wilmington, DE: ISI, 2002); cf. PR, 528.

7

Why the Case of the Maltese Twins
Was Wrongly Decided

Whether It Is Lawful to Kill a Man in Self-Defense

Court cases frequently cause media storms. Typically, this happens when there is something sensational about the case; far more rarely, it happens when something philosophical is at issue. In Autumn 2000, England was gripped by the latter variety. The case of "Jodie and Mary," Siamese twins, is well known.[1] At the heart of the controversy were the Lord Justices who argued that Mary could be intentionally and deliberately killed by the doctors charged with her care. The court, to its credit, was explicit that at issue was an operation that involved the direct, intentional killing of an innocent child and this raised the question how to assess the "murderous intent" of the surgeons (*773 & 791). In a ninety-page judgment, the Lord Justices found ways to justify the killing so that the doctors could not be prosecuted for homicide when they separated the twins. The commentary on the case by moral theologians and philosophers has divided on the issue, with a substantial part of Catholic commentary denying that Mary was in fact murdered.

There are dozens of issues at play in the judgment of the court. To give a sense of its intricacies, consider the role double effect theory played. Two Lord Justices dismissed a possible defense for the doctors through application of double effect. Suspicious of the theory, these judges argued that in English law any fatal foreseen consequence is part of the primary intention of the act. The doctors must be judged to have the intention to deliberately kill an innocent child, they argued.[2] The parents of the twins, devout Roman Catholics, refused consent for the operation and the church supported the parents in the courts. The Lord Justices had *certain* sympathies with the church. Two of the Lord Justices had attended prestigious, private Catholic schools, had nine children between them, and the other Lord Justice had four children and was the brother of a Conservative Member of Parliament. On the face of it, one could not claim that the church had judges ranged against her who were rank anti-natalist secularists. Concluding, I'll return to darker elements of the judges' preconceptions in the case, identified by a number of commentators. Howsoever lay the loyalties or sympathies of the judges, one of the two judges with a Catholic education, Lord Justice Walker, implicitly argued that the court had no authority to order a direct, intentional killing of an innocent (*836). For this reason, he invoked double effect theory (*836). Lord Justice Walker thanked the Catholic Archbishop of England for his carefully crafted legal submission. He observed that the principles invoked by the Archbishop were in near complete continuity with English law but he wondered how the Archbishop could have missed mentioning double effect theory. Clearly puzzled, he commented about the arguments put forward by the Archbishop, "they do not explain or even touch on what Roman Catholic moral theory teaches about the doctrine of double effect, despite its importance in the Thomist tradition" (*834). Indeed, the Lord Justice went on to note that in a somewhat similar case in Philadelphia in 1977 it was reported that Catholic nurses who were to take part in the operation had been reassured by this doctrine (*834).

Catholic commentary on the application of this doctrine to the case is divided but there is broad agreement about one thing: whilst the judges were concerned with criminal causation, theologians and philosophers have wondered whether or not the operation was moral. Relatively little attention anywhere has been paid as to whether the operation was legal, that is, did the judges find convincing ways to describe Mary's homicide as justifiable or excusable? I have enormous admiration for the judges. Their judgments are thorough and profound; certainly, no shame attaches to the English judiciary in this matter. Still, I think all three justifications offered by the court fail. The other Catholic educated judge, Lord Justice Ward, argued that the operation could proceed as a matter of "quasi self-defense," and Lord Justice Brooke relied on a necessity defense. Brooke's judgment is regarded, quite rightly, as intellectually fascinating and rigorous. I do not think it works, however. But the analogy used by Ward is especially powerful. This analogy also fails to bear the weight placed upon it: nonetheless, anyone who thinks the operation was illegal, and I believe Thomas and de Vitoria both would, must cope with Ward's "quasi self-defense" analysis.

The stages of the argument are (1) discussion of journalistic reaction to the judges' decision, which was harsh; (2) noting the peculiarity that Catholic commentary on the case eschews the theological, I introduce relevant theological motifs; (3) consideration of Lord Justice Ward's judgment, with my argument that his lone analogy bearing the weight of his decision relies upon a radical, and false, subjectivization of crime; (4) examination of Lord Justice Brooke's judgment, especially his analogy to the sea and his reliance upon the concept of "designated for death;" finding both analogy and concept wanting; and in summation (5) consideration of the role of humanitarianism in the case. The problems each judge's analysis faces certainly warrant the conclusion that future such operations ought not go ahead, and more, that this operation was a state mandated murder. My thesis is that the judges did not find cogent reasons for justifying *or excusing* the surgeons' act of homicide.

The reaction in England (1) to the Lord Justices was hardly muted. Daniel Johnson of *The Telegraph* wrote, "the court ordered her death and the doctors became, in effect, her executioners."[3] Getting to the nub of the issue, Johnson asks: "Was the death penalty Mary's punishment for assault?" That is, the court recognized that Mary was doing nothing criminal but she was to be killed for tortuously harming her sister. Actually, the court's reasoning might have been subtler and stranger both. Katie Grant of *The Scotsman* reacted with real anger when, after the operation, hospital authorities declared: "Unfortunately, despite the best efforts of the medical team, Mary sadly died." Grant is right to identify something sinister here. Whilst a number of commentators think the separation was a matter of saving one twin "while leaving the other to die,"[4] the Lord Justices were explicit that the medical presentation of the character of the operation to the court meant nothing less than that Mary was to be killed: as the *Hastings Center Report* puts it, the doctors "were certain…that separation would therefore directly cause her immediate death."[5] Grant does not draw upon Arendt, but Arendt's comments regarding the falsification of language when evil is being covered up are quite appropriate.[6] From the first, the hospital and surgeons were anxious. After all, it was they who asked the Solicitor General to make clear that if they killed Mary they would not be charged with murder. Anxiety was also expressed by the court lest anyone think there was a "rush to judgement" about the killing of Mary (*729; 725; 746).

Rush to judgment there certainly was in some quarters. Grant makes an extremely telling point.[7] The medical team of the hospital, according to some reports, and seemingly confirmed by Ward at the appeal, first advised a late-term abortion. As Grant points out, had the parents made that choice there would have been no incident and not a demur in the house. Lord Justice Ward himself points to the same "irony" (*743). When the parents chose not to kill their children, and later refused to kill one child for the sake of the other, how was that choice viewed? Then, a mother's choice and parental liberty mattered not at all. They would be told by the doctors and the judges what choice was being made for them.[8] The court acknowledges the parents continue to struggle to understand this switch (*745). One also has to wonder why the hospital authorities initially suggested killing both through abortion and then rose up as the champions of Jodie lest she die because of Mary. Ward mentions twice that the hospital was entitled to agree to the parents' wishes. There was no obligation on the part of the hospital to seek legal permission for the operation. The hospital, as part of England's National Health Service and so an agency of government, had at its "discretion" the power to seek this permission, and the hospital did so (*746). One has to wonder about this: the hospital had previously encouraged late-term abortion of the twins and now rejected the parents' judgment. The court acknowledged that the parents' position was quite reasonable and so could certainly have been followed by the hospital. We have seen the germane point before in Arkes: liberty is not the issue in contemporary jurisprudence. What is at issue? Johnson of *The Telegraph* thought the motivation at work in the case of Mary was state sanctioning of eugenics.[9] When considering Singer's ethics in the fifth chapter, I argued that cases of homicide regarding the unborn and the newborn often reveal a totalitarian logic. Insistence on normality and identity pervades Singer's work. This betrays a monism typical of totalitarian utopias and the medical evidence presented to the court is heavy with such language. Only consider Lord Justice Brooke's notorious question at the appeal: "What is this creature in the eyes of the law?" Of course, coarsening of the court's sensibility had precedent in *Bland* (1993): Tony Bland, one judge said, is "grotesquely alive."[10]

Interestingly, in contrast to the journalists' skepticism, the philosophical literature (2) has tended to see the operation as moral. Actually, a review of the Catholic literature shows that the church has more to fear from its own moralists than judges.[11] Someone who tells us that she "want[s] to defend the vulnerable against the powerful" thought performing the operation to save Jodie moral because, after all, "as God wills healing, flourishing, and life for Jodie, we are called to do likewise."[12] This is pretty thin as theology and really bespeaks a humanitarian benevolence that demands the crookedness of the world be resolved into justice. Still, it is at least theological, whereas large tracts of Catholic commentary have no theological character at all. What might theology add? Are not Jodie and Mary a symbol of the church? Is not the pilgrim church vulnerable, living only because of the blood of Jesus? At the core of reality is "the Lamb slain before time" (Apoc. 13: 8) and all of created reality is ontologically weak, vulnerable, and lifeless, unless it continually touches the bleeding Lamb (this, the core demonstration of Bonaventure's *Itinerarium*).

The church lives because of the *viscera caritatis* of Christ. The church reveals something about our bodies, which are both particular and shared—like all of nature, they possess an instinct of sympathy. As Scheler puts it, "every living being has a natural instinct of sympathy for other living beings...*we have an urge to sacrifice* before we ever know why, for what, and for whom" (RS, 59). This point is basic to Aquinas and Levinas, as well. Only when the body is deposed in the "groaning of its entrails" (Levinas) is the body's propensity to cancel out the other's "place in the sun" (Pascal) overcome. This same point is made by the church in its claim that sensuality has an inclination to sin: for the particularity of the body insists on its "place in the sun" and it is only through the viscera becoming the *viscera caritatis*, through a wound opening up in the body, that the other may live (EM, c. 5). Judges and commentators are unanimous that the case of Jodie and Mary was tragic (for one of many invocations of tragedy, see *836). Theology, which rejects the category of tragedy, can see in Jodie and Mary something very hard to bear: the *mysterium tremendum* of a divine embrace to which we are all called even *usque ad sanguinem*.

There is something missing from this symbol of the church, and it is perhaps the most difficult part of all theology: the relationship between election and liberty. The church is not a willed contract amongst individuals but nor must it be claimed that the conjoined life of Mary and Jodie is a perfect imaging of the church. Whilst the people of God are a chosen people and Jesus was *sent* by the Father, Jesus nevertheless accepted the cup just as we must freely imitate Him. The *viscera caritatis* of Jodie is imperfect for charity is a willed act (yet, even here, the election of some by divine predilection cannot be ignored). But, an imperfect image is still an image. The parents and their priests were quite right to see something divine in their midst. Their response was theological: we can rightly expect them to have held this position with a mixture of anxiety, ambivalence, and love, for in what other way can one experience the *mysterium tremendum* of the life of the church? They sensed something divine that evacuated the tragic, something, sadly, ignored by all the Catholic commentary.

Typical is a very long article by Cathleen Kaveny which, though having no theological content at all, appeared in *Theological Studies*.[13] She assumes that Jodie and Mary are the legal actors in the case and not the state. I do not think this plausible but at times the judgment is unclear about who exactly is the agent at the heart of the case. The court does insist that it is acting as a true public authority (*751) without any reference whatsoever to any implied consent on the part of the girls, the parents, or even the hospital (*821). Journalists, doctors, judges, and the church, all were alive to the fact that the problem concerned criminal liability: Should the doctors perform the operation, could they be tried for homicide?[14] But, of course, the real question before the court is: Can the state *acquiesce* in the killing of an innocent child on private authority? After all, the judges were expected to provide legal justifications or excuses for the surgeons killing Mary. The "court was invited to sanction a defense (or justification) of necessity," observed Lord Justice Brooke (*801) and he added that the necessity defense need not only be a private defense, that is, it can also be the rationale for state action, nor need it be a matter of emergency (*816) but can be a response to "objective dangers" (*809).

Kaveny's essay asks (3) whether Mary was a "materially unjust aggressor." If so, Jodie had a right to self-defense and the court was right to defend Jodie. Kaveny's approach appears closer to Lord Justice Ward's "quasi self-defense" analysis than is in fact the case; his position ("in self-defense of others" [*778]) is closer to that of de Vitoria on the idea of rescue. At one point in his judgment, he writes that if Jodie could speak she would surely shout "Stop it, Mary! You are killing me" (*771-2). An initial problem with this approach is obvious: Would Jodie want to save her life? There is a case in which one conjoined twin refused to be separated from her sister dying of cancer, preferring to die shortly after her.[15] The court, however, explicitly follows Hobbes and others, claiming that persons are under an obligation to save themselves (*796-7). Vitoria argues it is certainly lawful to save oneself when attacked but there is no obligation (H, 95-105).

But trying to find a justification for the operation at some deep level in self-defense is really a non-starter. Killing in self-defense is only legitimate when the state cannot be present to provide protection. Jodie's right to self-defense[16] could never emerge in respect of Mary *once* the surgeons' had asked for the protection of the state: the act of separation would necessarily then have to take place in the presence of the state. I can kill my attacker when there is no police officer there to do so, should such be necessary. If a police officer is present and able to protect me, my right to self-defense does not even emerge. I defer to "law enforcement privilege" (Moore). With the court's involvement, Jodie's need for protection is never going to be a matter of self-defense but a matter of the state's privilege[17] to violently protect its subjects from harm.

Lord Justice Ward seeks justification for the operation as "quasi self-defense," and by this he means a rescue attempt using lethal force.[18] For Aquinas and de Vitoria killing the innocent is an intrinsic evil. Ward acknowledges that Mary is innocent, and insists she must not be thought of as an "unjust aggressor." However, imagine a six-year-old boy, asks Ward, shooting schoolmates on the playground. It would be a justifiable homicide to kill the boy even though he is innocent of crime, or, as he rather cleverly adds, innocent of sin (*778-9). Following the analogy, Mary is like the boy innocently killing another child and so it is a justifiable homicide to kill Mary. The analogy clearly works at one level: we recognize that although quite horrible, the boy does need to be stopped and by lethal force if necessary. Here, our intuitions are at one with Lord Justice Ward.

At another level, however, something is wrong with the analogy. For the problem the case now poses to philosophical reflection is that our intuitions are united about the boy in the schoolyard, yet sharply divided about Mary and Jodie. Recall that journalists tended to think that judicial murder had occurred. The purported analogy is clearly not obvious. Before trying to clarify what exactly is amiss, note what else is implied by the analogy. Ward does not imagine that some other six-year olds in the schoolyard will kill the boy; he assumes a teacher will. It is not a matter of self-defense but "quasi" self-defense: Rescuing someone under lethal threat by the private exercise of lethal force and it is imagined, in this case, that the surgeons are the rescuers (*779; *842).[19]

When Ward speaks of "quasi self-defense" is it not really that his analogy leads us to imagine that the police will kill the boy? Given current gun ownership restrictions and the reality of what happens in school shootings, this really is the only analogy with much truthfulness. The analogy surely is that public authority in the guise of an armed response unit will exercise its privilege to kill just as the court now exercises this same privilege by deputizing the surgeons with lethal authority. After all, the court insists that the operation will happen, if at all, on account of its authority and no one else's (*821 & 751). And this explains the dismay of journalists that the court issued a death sentence for an act that was not criminal. If there is some confusion as to who the actors really are in the analogy, there is perhaps a still more crucial issue to be resolved: Why do our intuitions stand united with Ward about the boy but not Mary?

One would think if the analogy is tight, no division amongst intuitions will likely be felt. Medically, Ward is right that Mary is killing Jodie. So far so good as far as Ward's analogy is concerned—and I point out that no supplementary reasoning is offered besides the appeal to the analogy. Of course, this is not unusual in common law reasoning; the use of analogy is one of the things Bentham most disliked about common law.[20] But about the boy he says: "the six-year-old boy indiscriminately shooting all and sundry in the school playground is not acting unlawfully because he is too young for his acts so to be classified" (*842). And here an equivocation sets in. There is no act (following Aquinas's distinction between *actus humanus* and *actus hominis*) and so the boy is "not acting unlawfully" but something unlawful is being done: shooting children is criminal and known by everyone to be an offence. But being born attached to someone's aorta is not merely "not acting unlawfully" it is not even an offence, something unlawful. The boy might not *commit* an offence but an offence there still surely is. Ward himself even hints at a dis-analogy: "This unique happening cannot be said to be unlawful." If being born attached to someone else's aorta is a "unique happening" then there is no offence on the books, nor could there be. Mary and the boy are alike in subjectively being innocent and they are objectively alike in both killing others. But still, objectively, there remains an enormous difference. The intuitive dissonance between the boy and Mary rests on this remaining objective difference. The boy, however innocently, accomplishes something well recognized as criminal. If an adult did this same act, he would presumably be said to be criminally insane and put into confinement. Indeed, I imagine this boy (if stopped alive) would be monitored psychologically with a certain eye to further criminal intent. That the category "criminally insane" exists means that crime is not reducible to *mens rea*. There can be an excuse for having done something criminal: one is not then branded a criminal despite having done something criminal. Lord Justice Ward radically subjectivizes crime here in order to give his analogy purchase on the case of Jodie and Mary. In so doing he forfeits our intuitions and this alerts us that some equivocation has crept in.

It might be that Ward is trying to get at something exceptionally deep, the piacular. Recalled in modern times by Adam Smith, this Roman element of law tells more against Ward than for. Smith, one time lecturer on jurisprudence, recounts the ancient pagan phenomenon of the piacular. Touched upon in the second chapter the idea is—and Tolkien makes use of it in the *Lord of the Rings*—that even if one steps on sacred ground completely unaware (say, on account of being a stranger to town) one's life is forfeit. Smith relies on the idea to show that even in the absence of *mens rea* desert, of a particular kind, piacularity, exists. In modern register, the ground not to be trodden on is each and every individual. A worthy idea, says Smith, for we learn to dread being an object of "animal resentment." Piacular in mind, do we glimpse here a difference between Mary and the boy? Strange though it may sound, the boy unwittingly does a harm that means he *deserves* to be killed: indeed, any but a cool professional probably does kill the boy only through animal resentment. I do not think we can say the same of Mary. There is no reactive anger in her case which points, I think, to an encounter with a contingency stranger and more profound than the contingency attaching to the piacular even.

For these reasons, Lord Justice Ward does not provide coherent justification for the surgeons' act of homicide. The operation was thus illegal, especially as Ward did not find a coherent explanation for why the surgeons were not bound by Article 2 (2) of the *European Convention on Human Rights*. The ECHR states that life may only be intentionally taken after due process and with respect to crime or [Article 2.2 (a)] "in defence of any persons from unlawful violence" (*833). Ward's analogy appears to fall foul of this provision for he insists that Mary is not an "unjust aggressor," and even if he concedes (and I think he must) that the schoolboy is an "agent" of "unlawful violence," Mary is no such "agent." Our intuitions rebel against the idea that Mary does anything "unlawful" yet they grant this is true of the boy. The analogy fails.

In his judgment, (4) Lord Justice Brooke chose a necessity defense. This allows him, in my opinion, to elide the question of who exactly is the agent of the act of homicide. However, the analogies he relies on, again suggest the court itself is the agent. Lord Justice Brooke crafts his argument by drawing on a set of analogies drawn from cases that happened at sea. Brooke at one point cites a book, *Cannibalism and the Common Law* by A. W. B. Simpson.[21] Largely a social history of the *Mignonette* case, Simpson's book in odd places expresses strongly utilitarian views about the famous case.[22] The judges are clearly nervous that they may be thought to be doing the same: again and again they stress that at issue is not a departure from "the absolute sanctity of human life" in favor of some balancing of the worth of one human life over another. Lord Justice Brooke thinks he escapes the temptation by applying to the necessity defense for homicide. Kugler observes that the court sometimes argued for necessity as excuse: this is not possible for an *ex ante* judgment. The necessity defense as excuse is meant to cope with cases of "strong fear and mental pressure."[23] He notes that Brooke himself shows hesitations and wonders if the judgment should be read not as excuse, but justification, by necessity. I think this is right.

Immediately, one wonders whether an analogy from cases at sea to those on land is possible. After all the law of the sea is a *sui generis* strain of jurisprudence and this is surely recognition that the sea imposes itself on people in ways different from land. It is clear that laws governing conduct at sea are remarkable. Admiralty law is the one area of law that can claim Hellenic influence as opposed to the primarily Roman basis of other law.[24] Simpson cites a Victorian English barrister, Sir George Sherston Baker, who at the time of the *Mignonette* trial observed a connection between Admiralty law, based, in part, on the Sea Law of Rhodes, and the Bible. Baker observes that in the story of Jonah there is a casting of lots for the sake of survival, and Jonah is travelling from Joppa, which is close to Rhodes. Baker concludes that sacrificing some for the sake of others appears to be very old maritime custom and has perhaps a certain biblical warrant.

The phrase "the law of the land" is not without significance. Certainly, Carl Schmitt believed that sea and land belong to two quite different juridical orders. Blackstone agrees.[25] Indeed, for Bakunin, land and sea contrast as government and anarchy.[26] For Schmitt, these two orders were akin to two principles of political order: the sea power of English politics and the land power of continental states; with an enmity towards one another that at moments in his thinking are something like Augustine's two cities driving history forward.[27] Putting this aspect of Schmitt's thinking to one side, his identification of the sea with the leviathan (LST, 7) and its radical violence (*there is no power on earth to compare to its* [Job 41:24]) is quite germane. The point is not that the sea is sheer violence—for the sea also offers protection (LST, 10) and sea powers have, as Schmitt points out, been bearers of civilization.[28] The point is rather that the containment of the sea by law is also a radical accommodation to the reality of human life at sea. Perhaps the particular origin of Admiralty law pays deference to "the elemental opposition between land and sea...acknowledged throughout history" (LS, 6). A sort of phenomenological reduction of the point is found in the differences between law governing land and sea warfare. These bodies of law express "two distinct worlds, and two antithetical, juridical convictions" (LS, 47). So far as this case is concerned, and the importing of analogies from the sea, Schmitt revealingly points out that land warfare observed non-combatant immunity whereas the trade nature of sea warfare equals total war against entire populations (abolishing the distinction between guilt and innocence) (LS, 47-48).

The defense of necessity is permitted in Admiralty law, Baker argued (in 1884). He notes it is not permitted at common law, and indeed, it seems it was only acknowledged in common law in 2000 in this very case (which Kluger, for one, welcomes). Also of some interest, Baker argues that the sailors of the *Mignonette* ought to have been tried at civil law, not common; for Chief Justice Mansfield ruled in 1807 (*Regina v. Depardo*) that the Admiralty applies civil law and maritime custom.[29] The 2000 court sees the operation as a criminal matter at common law; pointing to the fact that the role of the sea is inappropriate? Of course, if civil law is apropos, then a battery/tort model seems more fitting to help settle the matter. I return to the question of battery shortly. Which is to say, an analogy between law at sea and law on land does not sit easily and for deep reasons, metaphysical and social.[30]

Just as one can expect property law to capture something of extreme metaphysical and social significance about the law of the land, so too one might expect laws governing life at sea to speak in some special way to the nature of the sea. To have rule of law at all without the stability and order brought to the social world by property law is hard to conceive (N, 74-5). Indeed, the evidence is that developments in Roman property law helped create the idea of the person.[31] The fixity of property tracks the fixity of land and life on land, whilst the opposite is true of the sea (N, 42-3). The laws of the sea guarantee navigation and free passage, commerce, and communication with the stranger. An axiom of Greek law—that only a member of the *polis* could be heard before the judges of the *polis*—was suspended in Greek sea law.[32] The sea passage of people, ideas, goods, and culture tracks the fluidity, openness and, yes, turmoil of the sea. Indeed, so important is the idea of open passage, the

Greeks held all suits in abeyance until the winter months (when no one was travelling on the sea) and only then would the sea courts hold session.[33] At a very real level, whilst on land there is always somewhere else one could go from danger, on board ship there is not. This is why we expect the captain's orders to have the significance of law: at sea, the rule of law is replaced at least to some important degree by the rule of man. Thus, between fixity and fluidity can an analogy take hold, as the Lord Justice supposes? The court itself was aware of many of these elements. Brooke noted that murder is a common law offence with a jurisdiction "within any county of the realm," as the phrase goes (*784). Note was made of a sea captain's complete authority in conditions of necessity (*803).

The argument of Brooke relies on an incident relayed at the inquest into the Zeebrugge disaster of 1987.[34] Use of the incident is problematic for its moral intelligibility relies on the law of the sea and involves military rank. A young man became petrified on the escape rope leading from the ship, perhaps frozen, speculated an army corporal, through a combination of cold and fear. Waiting and remonstrating for ten minutes, the corporal (a passenger) gave "instructions" for the young man to be pushed off the rope into the sea (he was never seen again) so that others could use the escape rope. Brooke's use of this incident as a basis for his reflection suffers: from the undertow of a quality of life argument through association with the *Mignonette*; from the role of the sea; and from the hint that someone with rank gave orders (suggesting a return to the privilege of public authority to intentionally kill). Would the judge be as persuaded if the story was merely about another passenger kicking a young man off the ladder into the sea? Would he make that story the premise of his argument? If so, what would that premise be? In what follows I argue the premise must either be (a) combat or (b) privilege. I will argue there are obvious reasons Brooke could countenance (b) but not (a), and following the lead of an example de Vitoria gives, I show that Brooke's reasoning gave the nod to either murder or tyranny.

The judge offers this story from the inquest as an example of a homicide justified or excused through necessity. At the same time not just any example will do. Brooke mentions the classic legal textbook example of necessity, the case of two seamen fighting after a shipwreck to see who shall have the plank. He identifies Cicero as the originator of this classic example of homicide through necessity, but does not dwell on this example or make it basic to his argument. He mentions, but does not dwell on, Blackstone's fascinating treatment—which is largely the same as that of Adam Smith's written at the same time (early 1760s)—for Blackstone explicitly views the matter as one of combat and a return to a Hobbesian state of nature.[35] Smith sees the Cicero case as a matter of justifiable killing, but Blackstone does not. Both view it as primal combat, however, since, in Smith's words, the one had "no better right to push the other off than the other had to push him."[36]

However psychologically realistic Blackstone might be and, however true it might be that the law is effectively suspended in that situation, Brooke cannot follow Blackstone. For even if Lord Justice Brooke wants to argue that the surgeons would have the necessity defense on hand to justify their act of homicide on private authority, he cannot allow a Schmittean acknowledgement that legal order is sometimes suspended *by the public authority*. The latter is obviously completely unsuitable for a court of law whose eminent Lord Justices are trying to find legal grounds for the public authority to give the go-ahead for the separation of the twins. Actually, the judgment shows that not only is Lord Justice Brooke trying to find a way to acknowledge that the direct killing of Mary is legal but to find a justification that is morally suitable. He must avoid Blackstone's recourse to Hobbes for in the state of war there are no *moral* rights at all (as Smith points out) only the kinetic violence of struggle. He twice notes that English courts have consistently maintained that the *Mignonette* case shows that the necessity plea implies a complete divorce between law and morality which is intolerable (*843). Some might find his anxiety about this a little precious since, as the Lord Justices point out (*787; 807; 815; 837) judgment in matters like these has been clarified by the statutes on abortion: in particular, the British statute that abortion of a baby up to the point of birth, and long after the baby is "viable," is lawful (*832). Of course, Mary is born so that statute does not apply, and now she is protected by ancient formulations of English law (*755). Nevertheless, because there must be some moral constraints upon law, Brooke is especially anxious not to have introduced into common law intentional killing on private authority whenever someone finds himself in a bit of a jam.

The Hobbesian suspension is an entry into combat—as Blackstone makes clear—and such would be implicit if the necessity defense as justification was accepted at common law; and therewith, following Hobbes, the private authority to intentionally kill the innocent. This, at all costs, is what must be avoided and so there must be no dwelling upon Blackstone. Of course, Blackstone and Smith are unsuitable for another reason. The judges want a justification to kill Mary so as to save

Jodie. This preference is obvious to all because Jodie could very well live once separated; her major organs are viable. In combat, of course, the necessity that brings it on is utterly indifferent to whether one is more wounded than the other; both may struggle the best they can for the plank. If we follow Blackstone, what it very much looks like is the court ganging up with Jodie against Mary. The mob quality of this is completely intolerable, thus the deepest origin of Brooke's defense is elided, and the classic sources not dwelt upon.

We are back to the crucial reliance in the analogy on public authority and its privilege to intentionally kill. Yet, this reliance shows the dis-analogy between the action of the corporal and the surgeons—they hold no public office whilst the corporal does. Brooke cannot have it both ways: anxious to avoid the Hobbesian suspension of law as bare combat between individuals, which does appear to be part of the custom of the sea, he is forced to make the necessity defense one invoked by public authority. But, in turn, this smacks of dictatorship. Brooke, although he elides this issue in my opinion, is seemingly forced to claim that the surgeons become public officials, ranking officers of the law, as it were. This is confirmed because he says that were there some future need then surgeons must seek permission again from the court (*816). And yet, this only points up an incoherence in the argument: for the corporal never asked permission before giving his order, it came with rank. Presumably, if such authority was applied again, an inquest would not demur. Brooke wants to avoid the harsh combat language that seems proper to the necessity plea for it runs counter to the humanitarian aspects of the case, and the image of combat between the twins with the surgeons ganging up on one baby simply departs from the analogy of the sailors' struggle too, too far. This is why the image of rank is so important, but it also fails. Lord Justice Brooke insists that because the doctors would need to return to court again for judgment in some future case of the same kind, no homicide on private authority has been bestowed by the court. This will not do though. For that possible future judgment would be perfunctory if even sought: for could the surgeons not rightly think they now basically had permission? Haven't they been made rankers, after some fashion?

The incoherence goes even deeper though. The Zeebrugge incident also had a structural aspect that Lord Justice Brooke found crucially important. The young man was "designated to die" for had he not been cast off the ladder into the sea he would still have died anyway—for, like the others, he would have been killed by cold and sea. The phrase comes from a rabbinic decision in an American case involving Siamese twins. The logic of the rabbinic decision, as Annas points out, has been much criticized, not least by eminent Jewish religious authorities.[37] Imagine a traveler with a caravan party, a rabbi suggested. Attackers are willing to refrain from killing all if the party either kills the traveler or hands him over to be killed. Adding to this example, the court imagined a skydiver latching onto a colleague when his parachute fails to open. Does the colleague murder when kicking off the skydiver? Like the rabbi, Brooke thinks not, because the "victim" is "designated to die" either way (Ward also finds this concept compelling *770-1). This point is so important because it allows Brooke to show that the case of Mary and Jodie is structurally dissimilar from the *Mignonette* case. English courts consistently point out, says Brooke, that what is so disreputable about that case is that the captain chose the boy rather than some other surviving member of the crew to be killed and eaten (*805). Though do remember that public opinion at the time, and this is why Queen Victoria was grudgingly made to offer a pardon, did think that the captain's decision was his to make. As Carl Schmitt might put it, this seagoing nation intuited the role of the captain at sea and recognized his absolutist near king-like status. In this case, Brooke points out Mary has "self-designated herself" as the one to be killed (*815) and so the English court's well-placed scruple does not apply (*805; 815).

Bemoaning the fact that the court chose to ignore the legal and moral commentary upon the original rabbinic decision, Annas points out the dis-analogy. The original example, and the others supporting, are risky ventures (acknowledged by the court *828) voluntarily entered by adults. Indeed, they are examples of activities where adults normally sign waivers that risk is taken of their own free will; further, in one of the examples at least, an adult by his *action* puts another in danger (the skydiver). The same cannot be said of Mary.[38] Annas is, of course, right, but the problems go far, far deeper. I think de Vitoria offers a *reductio* of the reliance on this idea of "designated for death." If this is true, then once again, and quite apart from earlier stated suggestions of incoherence in Brooke's analysis, the court will not have shown that the operation is legal and the killing of an innocent able to be excused or justified.

Recalling that the judges take it as their primary task to show that the separation is an act of homicide, but one justifiable at law, consider this example from de Vitoria. The Turks have besieged a city. They ask for the life of a preacher who has spoken ill of Islam. If he is killed or handed over to be killed, the city is spared. Vitoria argues that if a private individual kills the preacher it is murder, if the city, tyranny. Designated for death he may be, but his innocence makes any action either murder or tyranny. Worse, much worse, the individual or city that acts is a collaborator, aiding and abetting the enemy (H, 183-5). What de Vitoria convincingly shows is that being "designated for death" is not "a get out from jail free card" regarding moral complexity: once the designated for death status is settled *then* moral claims start to get a purchase. If this last point is not true, then collaboration does not even arise, but it does. The Rabbinic decision certainly decides the example differently but only at the cost of collaboration. Given that here we are talking about a state without an enemy (save the will to justice), what we really have is a case of tyranny.

Vitoria's argument is far more in line with Blackstone's assertion that common law recognizes a class of acts that are intrinsically evil (*mala in se*).[39] Brooke gives no consideration to this class of acts, revealing, I suggest, the subtle but pervasive influence of Bentham's dismissal of such acts (*802). To my mind, the Rabbinic decision returns us to Moore's balancing of evils text (third chapter) which justifies torture. The *Mignonette* court rejected the necessity defense (*797) noting the role it has played in tyranny (*800). The 2000 court nonetheless insisted that the *Mignonette* court was not decisive in the matter (*815) and performed a "balancing act" (*837). I imagine de Vitoria has in mind the *Decretum's* position that a person may not do an evil so as to stop another person from doing a greater evil.[40] This is different from the case where the doing of one or another of two intrinsic evils (proscriptions) is unavoidable; then one must pick the lesser of the two evils.[41] The court believes itself in the latter position (*766) but only on account of ignoring the role of emphasis. The court thinks it has an *equal* obligation not to kill one innocent for the sake of another innocent and to preserve the life of an innocent when this is feasible (*774; 777). In its legal submission the church argued the latter can never be done at the cost of the former (*834). In my opinion, this church's challenge was never adequately addressed by the court. When the challenge was met, interestingly, but unsurprisingly, it was met with abortion law. Abortion cases show, argued the court, that the obligation to help "the enjoyment of the right to life" warrants "the intentional deprivation of life" (*837). A great deal of moral latitude seems to be encouraged by these phrases. Vitoria provides a number of fine examples and arguments that we are not always under an obligation to save lives that we could in fact save, including our own (H, 95-105). I discuss this problem at length in the eighth chapter. The common thread of his arguments is that the role of emphasis needs to be considered, and, of course, not killing the innocent is an exceptionless norm; it has hard emphasis. In fact, the judges stress some dismay that the idea of the intrinsic evil would curtail "sacrificial separation operations" (*794). The *Decretum* acknowledges a biblical darkness (Jn. 1: 5), opaque to human acts of justice. To ignore this darkness and the limit it poses to human action is to try to wring justice from doing evil. This is the problem graphically posed by Tolkien's Ring of Power wrought in the Darkness of Mount Doom.

I think de Vitoria's example is extremely damaging to Brooke's reasoning, about as close as one gets to a knockout blow in philosophy, and yet there are still other problems. One commentator has rightly noted that since Mary cannot live without touching Jodie there could be no assault since she too has a necessity defense. If one is allowed to kill to preserve life, Mary can kill Jodie.[42] This is certainly an implication of the plank example. Moreover, Brooke's reasoning works against Ward's and one is left wondering like one commentator whether coherence is only gained when it is admitted that "behind" the legal arguments the judges were making "judgements about the relative quality and worth of Mary's and Jodie's life."[43] Certainly, Lord Justice Ward seemed to show his slip when he spoke of Mary's "parasitic living" (*771). Meanwhile, Walker thinks both Brooke and Ward wrong, since he argues the state cannot tolerate killing the innocent, hence, his application to double effect.

His general wariness is fully justified. The terms of the analogies built at the appeal are tenuously linked. Justice Ward's analogy is built from an imaginary case of assault and the idea of the "designated for death" comes from the rabbinic consideration of an attack upon a caravan. The assault theme is not present, however, either in the *Mignonette* or Zeebrugge case. It is not present, as I argued considering Justice Ward's analogy, in the case of Mary either. I argued there that Mary cannot be said to assault in the way this is said of the schoolboy because she does nothing unlawful, although he does. If there is no assault then Lord Justice Ward's effort to cast the operation as one of lethal rescue has no basis, nor Brooke's. Blackstone and Smith insist the necessity defense falls under the genus of homicide *se defendendo*. They cast it as straightforward combat where any crime or tort for assault is suspended by brute necessity. What Lord Justice Brooke appears to be doing—and innovative it truly is—is creating a new *genus*, not species, of homicide. For Blackstone and Smith the genus is attack-defense, but Brooke wants to argue a genus no-attack-defense exists. With a mind to the *failed* necessity defense from the *Mignonette* case, in which the boy killed had committed no assault, Lord Justice Brooke preferred to argue that what was crucial is that Mary, like the young man on the ladder at the Zeebrugge disaster, was "marked for death." One wonders why, in Brooke's eyes, the captain of the *Mignonette* would have no recourse here since he picked the boy because he was the weakest and closest to death. Perhaps he does think the captain would have had a case since he says the *Mignonette* court is not decisive. After all, at the appeal some of the doctors revised their original prognosis of an early death for Mary and admitted that the twins (unseparated) might live for up to three years.[44] But is there any coherence at all—especially out of the water—to the idea of a genus no-attack-defense justification for homicide? The no-attack aspect tracks the sense that Mary is an innocent, but the defense aspect seems to fail. The point is especially clear if we change words a little. If we drop "attack" or "assault," is there any sense in which Mary exercises *force* against Jodie? Does 'force' have any purchase here? "Defense" seems the wrong name for the act. Surely, the act is one of attack precisely on the defenseless and vulnerable. It is obvious what the *Mignonette* and Zeebrugge cases have in common: the one killed was in no position to fight back. Strange to say, but Blackstone's eighteenth century Hobbesian struggle of the strong has more humanity to it than this humanitarian innovation of 2000.

In concluding, it is well to note the following: speaking about fetal reduction in IVF as a matter of "tragic circumstances," one commentator says fetal reduction stems from "the basic instinct that it is better to save one life than to stand by and let both die."[45] To stand by this is what is intolerable! It is perhaps for this reason that all three judges agreed the operation should happen despite being at odds about why and, as Annas laments, not one of them appeared to come up with a principled decision.[46] Certainly, the English justices show far more compassion and intellectual nerve than Catholic moralists who flippantly apply to double effect anytime a remotely tricky case offers itself. Yet, when Singer claims that Christianity has for too long "prevented any fundamental reassessment" of killing (PE, 125), I wonder if the justices do not in fact agree. Wasserman is correct to point out that the judges, despite insisting that they were treating Jodie and Mary as moral and legal equals, saw Mary as an inferior (Annas concludes likewise). Moreover, is it not strange that the three opinions of the judges all agree? How is it that such an unusual case provoked no disagreement unless Wasserman's contention is correct and there is something in the way of *ad hoc* reasoning afoot?[47] We can be suspicious, lament the decision, and simultaneously acknowledge the seriousness of the judges' reasoning. It is still something that the killing of an innocent out of the womb requires elaborate reasoning. Brooke's reasoning elides necessity's complete indifference to who should prevail amidst necessity and his claim that the defense from necessity permits the state to intentionally and directly kill a child relies upon a defense that the stronger party's interest prevails. A hidden vitalism operates that is at least congruent with Singer's basic claim: "true scales favour the side where the interest is stronger...they take no account of whose interest they are weighing" (PE, 19).

Failings aside, the Lord Justices are to be commended: their reasoning is more attractive than that of some of the philosophers. Some philosophers have little compunction in encouraging judicial killing, or rather, what is worse in my opinion, granting sanction to individuals to decide on the killings. Without explaining what Jodie's putative "right against a lethal imposition," against "lethal aggression" on the part of Mary, an "innocent aggressor," might be, Wasserman tells us that he accepts the utilitarian logic of killing one to save the other.[48] Better that such a decision is left to private choice rather than the state when decisions balancing interest and claims to quality of life are made. Wasserman is concerned lest court decisions "take a small but significant step towards establishing the priority of anatomically and cognitively normal lives in our health care policy, and perhaps towards state-sponsored eugenics."[49] This comment blithely assumes homicide on private authority, and seemingly with no self-consciousness at all attempts a distinction between state-sponsored eugenics and the state sanctioning private choice in eugenics. Eugenics is not the problem, just the agency.

Notes

1. I will not review the medical evidence since my arguments dispute nothing in the record. Interested readers can go to the case itself for full information or a host of Internet entries on the case. I will simply note that the twins shared an aorta and that Mary, on account of her very weak heart, was living because Jodie's heart worked for herself and her sister. In the operation, this aorta would be cut causing the immediate death of Mary.
2. Cf. L. Gormally, "The Maltese Conjoined Twins," *Second Opinion*, Vol. 8 (October 2001), p. 38.
3. D. Johnson, *The Daily Telegraph*, November 7, 2000. The editorial comment of the paper is somewhat different.
4. D. Sulmasy, O. F. M., "Heart and Soul: The Case of the Conjoined Twins," *America*, December 2, 2000; W. May, "Jodie and Mary: Separating the Maltese Twins," *National Catholic Bioethics Quarterly*, Vol. 1: 3 (2001), pp. 407-16.

5. Alex John London, "The Maltese Conjoined Twins," *Hastings Center Report*, Vol. 31 (January/February 2001).
6. H. Arendt, *Eichmann in Jerusalem*, pp. 69 & 217. The same point is found in Cicero. See Augustine's use of Cicero in *City of God* (London: Penguin, 1984), XIV, c. 18, p. 580.
7. K. Grant, "False Tears of the Doctors Who Dealt Sentence of Death," *The Scotsman*, November 12, 2000. Like Johnson, Grant also thinks that Mary was executed.
8. There were alternatives: *The Lancet* reported that Cardinal Tonini of Ravenna offered the family "indefinite and completely free medical services and hospitality" (S. Ramsay, "Landmark Ruling on Siamese Twins in U. K.," *The Lancet*, September 2, 2000).
9. This point is also made by D. Wasserman, "Killing Mary to Save Jodie: Conjoined Twins and Individual Rights," *Philosophy and Public Policy Quarterly*, Vol. 21 (2001), p. 14.
10. *The Catholic Times*, Sunday, Nov. 19, 2000, p. 5; for Peter Singer's valorization of the *Bland* judgment, see the long discussion in RLD, 65-80.
11. The commentary on the case by Daniel Sulmasy, a Franciscan monk who is a medical doctor and both the holder of a chair in ethics at a Catholic hospital and the head of a bioethics institute at another hospital, is, in my opinion, *irresponsibly* confused. Sulmasy's article appeared after the events took place and he could have read the court case. The article reveals no knowledge of the case nor the intricacies of the medical issues. He consistently casts the problem at issue as stopping a course of treatment, reverting to the image of cutting off the means of life support, an image the Appellate judges rejected and which had been the basis of the lower court's judgment. Thus, we learn that "Jodie could let go of Mary without committing sin." This is a preposterous comment. The Appellate court was clear that it was being asked to consider whether the doctors could actively intervene in Mary's life in order to end it.
12. M. T. Lysaught, "Is it Killing? Jodie, Mary and God," *Commonweal*, October 20, 2000.
13. K. Kaveny, "The Case of Conjoined Twins: Embodiment, Individuality, and Dependence," *Theological Studies*, Vol. 62:4 (2001): n. 13 on how double effect resolves the moral issues; and her, "Conjoined Twins and Catholic Moral Analysis: Extraordinary Means and Casuistical Consistency," *Kennedy Institute of Ethics Journal*, Vol. 12: 2 (2002): p. 120 on double effect to the rescue, again.
14. Crime concerns "the loss which the state sustains" (W. Blackstone, *Commentaries*, Book Four, c. 1, *6).
15. See M. Barilan, "One or Two: An Examination of the Recent Case of the Conjoined Twins from Malta," *Journal of Medicine and Philosophy*, Vol. 28 (2003), p. 40.
16. I speak loosely here. I in no way mean to imply that Thomas accepts there is a *right* to self-defense.
17. For the Crown's understanding that privilege is derived from the state, see *767. Cf. R. Scruton, *The Meaning of Conservatism* (South Bend, IN: St. Augustine's Press, 2002), c. 8.
18. Cf. W. Blackstone, *Commentaries*, Book Four, c. 14, pp. 180-1 & 184.
19. Aquinas in his short eight articles never addresses the question of lethal intervention on private authority to rescue an innocent. Not addressed at length by de Vitoria, the idea is nonetheless present. Rescue has its own *sui generis* obligatory character, albeit requiring attention to emphasis (H, 95).
20. J. Bentham, *A Fragment on Government*, pp. 3, 16 & 24-5. Cf. R. Posner, "Blackstone and Bentham," *Journal of Law and Economics,* Vol. 19: 3 (1976), p. 599.
21. A. Simpson, *Cannibalism and the Common Law* (Chicago: The University of Chicago Press, 1984).

22. Ibid., 238.
23. I. Kugler, "Necessity as a Justification in Re A (Children)," *Journal of Criminal Law*, Vol. 68 (2004), p. 443.
24. E. Cohen, *Ancient Athenian Maritime Courts* (Princeton, NJ: Princeton University Press, 1973), pp. 4-5; PR, 340.
25. W. Blackstone, *Commentaries*, Book Four, c. 5, *69; *71.
26. M. Bakunin, *Statism and Anarchy*, pp. 89-91.
27. C. Schmitt, *Land and Sea* (Washington, D. C.: Plutarch Press, 1997), p. 5; hereafter = LS; cf. C. Schmitt, *The Leviathan in the State Theory of Thomas Hobbes*, p. 35; hereafter = LST.
28. Schmitt identifies Ancient Greece as a nation of sailors in the first instance and points out that it was the Byzantine empire's fleet that continually saved Christian civilization from Islam during the Middle Ages. Islam was finally thrown onto the defensive by the power of Venice and its historic naval victory at Lepanto. It is worth noting that in Tolkein's *The Lord of the Rings,* the king who returns and restores order is descended from sea folk although his return is only accomplished in fellowship with the most essentially terrestrial people, the hobbits.
29. Cf. W. Blackstone, *Commentaries*, Book Four, c. 5, *71.
30. For example, in Sparta the council of elders concerned itself with all homicides and high crimes against the state, whilst the sole judges in matters connected with the highways and free passage were the kings (Cf. Herodotus, *The History*, trans., D. Grene [Chicago: The University of Chicago Press, 1987], VI, c. 57, p. 430). Cf. G. Calhoun, *The Growth of Criminal Law in Ancient Greece* (Westport, CT: Greenwood Press, 1973), pp. 112-113. Echoing Sparta perhaps, on the old sailing ships the Captain's writ ran far indeed. He was, as it were, a king under the King.
31. P. Nemo, *What Is the West?*, c. 2.
32. E. Cohen, *Ancient Athenian Maritime Courts* (Princeton, NJ: Princeton University Press, 1973), pp. 8 & 59.
33. Ibid., p. 45.
34. For Lord Justice Walker's heavy reliance on events at sea, see *828-31.
35. W. Blackstone, *Commentaries*, Book Four, c. 14, *186.
36. A. Smith, *Lectures on Jurisprudence* (Report of 1762-3), p. 115.
37. G. Annas, "Conjoined Twins—The Limits of Law at the Limits of Life," *New England Journal of Medicine*, Vol. 344: 14 (2001), p. 1107.
38. G. Annas, "Conjoined Twins—The Limits of Law at the Limits of Life," *New England Journal of Medicine*, p. 1107; cf. G. Annas, "Siamese Twins: Killing One to Save the Other," *Hastings Center Report* (April, 1987), p. 28.
39. W. Blackstone, *Commentaries*, Book Four, c. 1, *8-9.
40. Gratian, *The Treatise on Laws* (*Decretum*, Distinctions 1-20) (Washington, DC: Catholic University Press of America, 1993), p. 52.
41. Ibid., p. 48-9.
42. M. Barilan, "One or Two: An Examination of the Recent Case of the Conjoined Twins from Malta," *Journal of Medicine and Philosophy*, Vol. 28 (2003), pp. 27-44.
43. Lori Knowles, "Hubris in the Court," *Hastings Center Report*, Vol. 31 (January/February 2001).
44. *Idem.*
45. D. Thomasma, "The Ethics of Caring for Conjoined Twins: The Lakeberg Twins," *The Hastings Center Report* (July-August, 1999), p. 9.
46. G. Annas, "Conjoined Twins—The Limits of Law at the Limits of Life," *New England Journal of Medicine*, p. 1106, 1108.

47. D. Wasserman, "Killing Mary to Save Jodie: Conjoined Twins and Individual Rights," *Philosophy and Public Policy Quarterly*, Vol. 21 (2001), pp. 10-11.
48. Ibid., p. 13.
49. Ibid., p. 14.

8

Kosovo Air War and Why Malthus Was Really a Wise Man

Whether One Is Guilty of Murder through Killing Someone by Chance

Many scholars have commented upon whether humanitarian intervention meets the traditional *ius ad bellum* conditions for war.[1] Fewer have discussed the *ius in bello* conditions of humanitarian warfare and, in particular, whether there might not be *special* combat responsibilities involved. The Kosovo crisis of 1999 is the initial concern of this chapter though it ends looking at an aspect of population ethics. Together these concerns demonstrate the basic thesis of the book: humanitarianism's critique of privilege condones the killing of the innocent and totalitarianism. The Kosovo crisis prompted the first humanitarian intervention by "Western liberal powers"[2] and it is thought likely that its model of "distance" or "zero-casualty" warfare will be the only such model used in future interventions.[3] The intervention, as infamous as it is famous, is styled "distance warfare" because NATO planes flew very high in the sky in order to avoid loss of aircraft and the death of NATO pilots. The air campaign was a "unique" event in the history of warfare for NATO suffered no combat losses at all.[4] A cost came with this uniqueness, however. At higher altitudes, weapon accuracy fell off and sometimes stray munitions killed innocent members of the population, and, of course, sometimes targets were mistaken. What is the precise moral problem here?

In this article Aquinas asks: Is someone who kills by chance guilty of murder? Assuming the *ius ad bellum* conditions are met and intervention justified, the part of Aquinas's answer that interests us is if a man during a lawful task kills because there was no "due care" to avoid accidental killing then the man is guilty of murder. This category of homicide is philosophically interesting because the agent does not intend to kill the person(s) killed. Might not double effect theory dissolve the moral issue? Cannot one simply argue that the pilots intended to kill the enemy and that the killing of the innocent was "beside the intention"? Vitoria's gloss on Thomas's article explains why double effect is not at issue here: "if anyone gives cause for a homicide, which he could have removed, and which he is obliged to remove, and he did not, for him such a homicide is voluntary and consequently a sin" (H, 205).[5] In the case of innocent Kosovars and Serbians killed by NATO bombs the cause of homicide could have been removed by flying lower and thereby gaining near pinpoint accuracy in targeting.[6] This category of homicide can be thought of as a control on applications of double effect for it reveals that there is an objective responsibility or liability to acts. As was seen in the previous chapter when discussing Lord Justice Ward's crucial analogy there is a tendency to over intellectualize what exactly is a crime or what it means to be culpable. Many Catholic commentators on Aquinas have taken his theory of double-effect to very much intellectualize what stands as culpable action. It is quite clear from this category of homicide that moral responsibility does attach to what might be thought of as the immediate history of an act, a history that tracks out causation. Aquinas gives the example of a man hunting who mistakenly kills a man, confusing him for a wild animal. Here there is no intention to kill a man, yet the man lawfully engaged in hunting is held liable for the evil of murder (De malo, q. 2, a. 2). As Vitoria puts it, "irregularity" can attach to someone for putting "in place a cause of homicide" (*quis ponat causam homicidii*) (H, 205).

Applying Aquinas, I argue that for NATO combat in Kosovo to have been moral NATO governments had a moral responsibility to order the pilots to fly low. Only in this way is Aquinas's "due care" requirement met: such an order would have removed a cause of homicide and one that NATO was obliged to remove. This obligation is founded on the prohibition against intentionally taking innocent human life. Agents must not kill the innocent in direct, voluntary, and intentional homicide nor, Aquinas insists, may they when the homicide is "voluntary and intended accidentally." It can happen, says Aquinas, "that what is not actually and directly voluntary and intended, is voluntary and intended accidentally." This latter kind of homicide could only be excluded during the Kosovo war by flying low and risking the lives of NATO pilots. Only in flying low could the Serbian murderers be killed and the innocent population saved from the "directly voluntary and intended" homicides the Serbs plotted, and I shall presently argue that there is a special obligation to kill the plotters. From a Thomistic perspective, only in flying low could that same innocent population be saved from homicides wrought by NATO that were "voluntary and intended accidentally."[7]

I also defend another thesis and, although it might seem strange, in part I shall do so through the thought of Albert Camus. At the time of Kosovo there was a great deal of talk about Serbian barbarism, that once again a European nation was reverting to a barbaric militarism that had not been seen since Nazi Germany. Conveniently forgotten by much of the media was that barbaric militarism in Europe only ended in 1989 with the fall of the Soviet Union.[8] Even further from sight, however, was the question whether a contribution to barbarism was being made by the Western "liberal democracies" through their strategy of air war. Throughout this commentary on Aquinas, I have argued that the humanitarianism, which is now a valuation basic to Western "liberal democracies," is structurally part of the culture of death. Negligent homicide of the Kosovo air war is a fruit of this culture. We saw in the fifth chapter that humanitarianism condones homicide because it rejects intrinsicalism, that is, moral hierarchy. There, I explained how humanitarianism rejects any superior moral authority. Here, the homicidal aspect of humanitarianism is best explained by its refusal to acknowledge an origin in sentiments it regards as unworthy, beneath the grandeur of its benevolence. Recall from the sixth chapter Scheler's law of dependence and consider the trajectory of humanitarian intervention: benevolent feeling demands action be taken about some outrage (Somalia, say) but when the national militaries involved suffer, domestic public opinion demands "our boys" come home; the people whose suffering so excited benevolence are then left to their own devices, now with the consequences of war added to their burden. The NATO intervention in Kosovo showed the accuracy of Scheler's analysis even more acutely. Horrified by the Serbian treatment of the Kosovars, NATO populations demanded war but with zero casualties for NATO forces. Balancing benevolence with the tribal reality of identification and vicarious feeling, NATO devised the air war policy. Benevolent feeling was seen to be utterly dependent on identification, vicarious emotion, and fellow feeling, and policy made in ignorance of this reality became indifference. Scheler's law of dependence is another way of speaking about emphasis. The weak emphasis of global benevolence must foster corruption if the privileged emphasis of identification is contemned.

It is an implication of Aquinas's eighth article that humanitarian intervention includes a special moral responsibility to save the innocent through direct and intimate combat with the enemy. While it is an absolute moral law that the innocent are not to be intentionally and directly killed in any kind of warfare it is not sufficient when considering humanitarian intervention to merely speak of noncombatant immunity. In war normally understood, the enemy's noncombatant population is not to be targeted but in war driven by humanitarian intervention a population, of course, is meant to be saved. This requires an intensification of killing effort on the part of their rescuers. Since "zero-casualty" warfare is excluded by the main holding of Thomas's eighth article the only moral alternative is intimate combat with its risks and increased ferocity[9] but also its greater potential for rescue. Martin Cook has recently argued that no such obligation could exist, at least not for an army in a liberal democracy. He argues that a volunteer army is based on a contract with an assumption made on the part of the servicemen that they defend their nation's interests. Humanitarian intervention cannot pretend to be in a nation's interest and therefore the force protection built into "distance warfare" is an obligation of government. However, since force protection kills innocents humanitarian intervention itself is inescapably immoral for liberal democracies. Obviously, Aquinas rejects Cook's starting assumption: a soldier does not gain authority to kill on account of some contract made in self-interest with the state but on account of the mantle of privilege he *derives* from public authority. Nonetheless, Scheler's ethical warning that benevolence cannot forget its origin in the less finer feelings of tribalism confirms Cook's basic point. Humanitarianism separated from national interest is immoral. Denying any role as a mere contrarian, this is why I argued in the sixth chapter that the 2003 Iraq War was moral, and here, why I argue the Iraq war is more moral than the Kosovo humanitarian intervention.

Camus's late work, *The Rebel*, thought by Camus to be his best work,[10] broke new ground. Not merely was it a departure for Camus's *corpus*, but it reintroduced into modern political and moral philosophy a long forgotten genre: the tract on homicide. Yet, why should Catholics be interested in Camus's thoughts on the subject of homicide and their application to Kosovo?[11] Camus was hardly a Catholic thinker,[12] and are there not resources enough in the Catholic tradition? There are at least two reasons to go to an "outside source," as it were. Sadly, few Catholic intellectuals have yet addressed the issue of the lessons to be learnt from the Kosovo war,[13] and this is perhaps because some confusion appears to have entered the church's thoughts about war. *Gaudium et Spes* (para. 80) called for a "completely fresh reappraisal of war," but it is unclear that this has happened. In an otherwise laudatory biography, George Weigel has noted that amongst all the intellectual triumphs of John Paul the Great's papacy the only singular failure has been in the realm of thought about war. A second reason to use Camus, and despite the fact that I will claim that Camus's theory of homicide restates Aquinas's use of proportionality, is that Camus provides a brilliant, and unique, *theological* insight into the true nature of so-called "zero-casualty" warfare: Romanticism's rebellion against God, and its cult of Lucifer.

Scheler thought Romanticism a counter-movement against humanitarianism (NS, 94-5). I think they are related. Certainly, the anarchist Bakunin channels both. Schmitt observes that Bakunin hoped to "disseminate Satan" and thought this basic to true revolution (PT, 64). As Schmitt reads Bakunin, he is a devotee of nature convinced of "the natural and intrinsic truth and beauty of human life" (PT, 64). Typical of Romanticism, Bakunin views nature as elemental, chaotic, and authentic. He identified the natural with the working class. Recalling the Greek model of education, Bakunin argued that this passionate nature must be complemented by the principles of human truth, justice, equality, and universal brotherhood. These principles, of course, are defining of humanitarianism. He thought revolutionary activists amongst students who had turned their backs on bourgeois life would bring the necessary discipline and abstract thoughtfulness to the elemental workers to hone the right weapon, a "conscious fighting force," for successful revolution. Advocating a politics of hate so that love might rule, Bakunin constantly attacks privilege as the enemy and identifies its redoubts: God, aristocracy, the military, banking, property, the family, Jews, and the entirety of bourgeois civilization.[14] Contemporary humanitarianism is firmly lodged as the ideology of Western leftism and Bakunin's themes make up much of the syllabus in the contemporary university.

In sum, the argument of this part of the commentary on Aquinas's eighth article (1) demonstrates that the air campaign over Kosovo was immoral for reasons stated above and (2) shows the structural similarity between "zero-casualty" air war and Romanticism. Using Camus' reflections on Romanticism (3) it is argued further that the claim of Michael Ignatieff,[15] that this "distance" innovation in warfare will be less destructive of life than more traditional means, is likely false. On the face of it, Ignatieff's claim is plausible. The Kosovo intervention had been preceded by an American humanitarian intervention in Somalia. In the now famous firefight that pitted American soldiers against gunmen in Mogadishu about five hundred civilians were killed in twenty-four hours. About this many innocents died in the many weeks of the NATO air war over Kosovo. Across the globe populations are moving into cities and the number of large cities is growing enormously, so conventional combat *in* cities would be well to avoid given the difficult conditions of urban warfare that make high civilian casualties very likely.[16] Virtual war may contain its own relentlessness, however. Intimate combat, and its attendant ferocity, is not necessarily the same as inhumanity. John Keegan points out that amongst troops in the field, a surrender is a very delicate matter in the heat of battle. Oftentimes a surrender is not accepted, but to accept a surrender is "something difficult to do when friend and enemy met so rarely face-to-face."[17] Might not the faceless quality of virtual war spawn its own inhumanities? I think this very likely, for "zero-casualty" humanitarian intervention, or what one commentator has dubbed "immaculate war" (Cook), lends itself to utopianism. The Clinton Administration adamantly refused to use the word "war" for NATO attacks,[18] and NATO and national briefings constantly evoked the image of the "nearly perfect" and "bloodless" war.[19] Convinced that technology permitted a near perfect war, NATO briefings during the war claimed that out of 20,000 bombs dropped 99.6 percent hit their targets. This was not true.[20] The argument concludes (4) that such warfare is part and parcel of the culture of death. A significant indication of the cultural dimension of such warfare, I will argue, is that action films, like air war, are suffused with Romantic motifs.

"Zero-casualty" air war (1) is, for some commentators, simply a reflection of the zero-tolerance for casualties that Western populations have for the consequences of warfare.[21] As Ignatieff points out in his *Virtual War*, this view relies on a very particular "moral" calculus on the part of Western society. About Kosovo, he comments, "preserving the lives of their all-volunteer service professionals was a higher priority than saving innocent foreign civilians" (VW, 62; 104-105). Of course, this understanding of the sensibilities of the West, and thus the *political* suitability of "zero-casualty" warfare, has its detractors in the military.[22] There is serious debate within military circles concerning just how future wars should be fought, whether on land or by air.[23] Those who favor air war approvingly tout what appears to be its very least moral aspect: you can kill the enemy before you send in soldiers on the ground. As these proponents put it, paradoxically, you kill your opponent before combat.[24] Others, including General Wesley Clark, the Supreme Allied Commander during Kosovo, distance themselves from any such model of warfare. In Ignatieff's words, Clark came to the conclusion during the war that "the air campaign alone could neither halt ethnic cleansing nor avoid mounting civilian casualties" (VW, 62). Clark's unease stems from the logic of "zero-casualty" air war: "To target effectively you have to fly low. If you fly low, you lose pilots. Fly high and you get civilians" (VW, 62).[25]

In the Kosovo war rooms, lawyers were used to judge whether the targets selected by the Western military for possible attack were compatible with the Geneva Conventions on war (VW, 100; 197). Nevertheless, this patina of legality cannot mask the reality that the very means of attack meant that intentionally the lethal risk to combatants was given a priority over the lethal risk to the innocent: "zero-casualty" air war is a simple inversion of natural law doctrine concerning just war. Indeed, the most telling blow of the war was based on just such a calculation of risks. The central power grid of Belgrade was a target of undoubted military importance but of even greater civilian importance. Instead of directly attacking combatants, the West's intent for this bombing was to immobilize Serbian troop movements by disabling the command systems of the Serbian military. Destroying the power grid, however, also "meant taking out the power to the hospitals, babies' incubators, water-pumping stations" (VW, 108). Whether any civilians in fact died as a consequence of this strike (and first hand accounts say this was so) does not alter the fact that as a matter of policy the lethal risk to innocents was given a lower priority than the lethal risk to combatants and, perversely in this case, even lower priority than the enemy combatants. Bacevich wonders whether the moral tradition of war was not turned on its head when "combatants rather than noncombatants [were] provided immunity from the effects of fighting."[26] However vile and murderous was the conduct of Milosevic and his forces and however rightly condemned, his actions must not hide from view the intentional, and multiple, homicides of the Western powers. Our leaders and our troops are *in some sense* guilty of (and are we complicit in?) war crimes.[27] Aquinas notes that homicides resulting from a lack of "due care" make the agent "in a sense guilty of voluntary homicide." Reading Camus, we can reach the conclusion that such a perverse political and military doctrine does not reflect a risk-averse culture but rather is part of the West's contemporary theological character: Diabolism.

In Ignatieff's opinion (2) the Kosovo war was the first post-modern war.[28] "We live our lives in language and thus in representation," (VW, 214) and the war was no different. Ignatieff explains that the war was conducted on television and computer screens, bombing instrument panels, or video playbacks of bomb strikes. Thus, Kosovo was a virtual war for all concerned except, as Ignatieff points out, those on the ground being struck by munitions. Certainly, so far as the West and its military were concerned, the war was virtual. Camus would not disagree with this analysis, I think, save to point out that if Kosovo was the first post-modern war, the script at least was thoroughly modern: Kosovo was the first fully Romantic war. Echoing Schmitt's analysis of political theology, Camus helps us see that the war was not premised on the West's "high-tech" character but on Romanticism's appropriation of theology.

Camus' treatment of Romanticism, theology, and homicide is part of a general cultural theory about Western history. In this history, the French Revolution is the beginning of a violent cultural struggle between justice and grace.[29] It marks the age of rebellion in which various intellectual movements, all in their deepest theological essence, have set themselves in opposition to God and the church[30]—thus de Sade, the revolutionaries themselves, Nietzsche, Fascism, Surrealism, Marxism, and more. Curiously, as Camus points out, while these movements have all sought to replace God and the church as the custodians of human salvation, each and every one of them has developed a logic which exalts violence against humans. Horrified by a church whose God dispensed grace to some and not to others, the theorists of rebellion sought to deliver justice for all. All have seen the need to disincarnate God (and therewith grace) as a precondition to their delivering universal justice. With de Sade, Camus tells us, the attempt to remove God is made by denying the natural law, and thus murdering the innocent, torture, and sodomy become "licit" (R, 36-47). Saint-Just seeks to disincarnate God not by dismissing the moral law but by denying original sin. As humans are naturally good, and since there is no original sin, there is no need for grace. This logic in place, once confronted with refractory citizens, those who failed (for whatever reason) to conform to the moral law, resort to the terror was the only logical response of the revolutionaries, argues Camus; mercy, in Saint-Just's eyes, was immoral *because rooted in grace.* Unable to forgive, the revolutionaries, in their own "immaculate war," were led by the logic of their own position to execute all who did not realize human impeccability (R, 112-132).

Though Camus only devotes about eight pages to Romanticism, his analysis is amongst the most trenchant of the book. Neither rejecting the law as in de Sade nor denying human moral ineptitude as with Saint-Just, the Romantic rebels against God by seeking to possess His role as the master of life and death (H, 93; 214, n. 76). The church, ever-mindful of Satan's wish to possess such a role, has always insisted upon the authority of the natural law, the law that refuses any such role for man, angel, or state. The Romantic, however, will exercise the moral law since God, through His grace, has seen fit to allow some of the infractions against the law to go unpunished. Now, the rule of law will be insisted upon in all of its universality, purity, and force. In Romanticism, writes Camus, "hatred of death and of injustice will lead, therefore, if not to the exercise, at least to the vindication, of evil and murder" (R, 47).

Writing in the 1950s, Camus saw Romanticism solely as a literary rebellion, "useful for adventures of the imagination" (R, 47). The pages of classic Romantic texts (Sir Walter Scott's, for example) are filled with "the romantic hero," who, writes Camus, "considers himself compelled to do evil by his nostalgia for an unrealizable good" (R, 48). Certainly, viewing air war as in some sense literary, as Camus would encourage us, is strengthened by recent military estimates that throughout the Kosovo war perhaps only between eight and ten Serbian tanks were actually destroyed.[31] It is far from clear that the ineffectiveness of air war in Kosovo has in any way dented the prestige of zero-casualty "combat" in Western eyes.[32] And nor is its continued ineffectiveness likely to do so. For, in Camus' analysis, Romantic rebellion is a dominant form of the West's self-understanding, and, I would argue, "zero-casualty" air war demonstrates that Romanticism is now a primary structure of our action, as well.

Romanticism is typified, says Camus, by "the criminal with the heart of gold, and the kind brigand," whose "works are bathed in blood" (R, 50). On our behalf, the West's airmen were asked to pursue a good intention but through an objectively evil means, and so under the guise of doing good, murder became legitimate. What more perverse inversion could Lucifer desire: to be a bringer of death cloaked in God's own mantle? Moreover, murder is made legitimate here in a manner of "combat" in which one kills without offering oneself to the other to kill. Scripture has Lucifer killing by proxy (1 John, 3, 11-12) and, of course, stresses his immortality ("He was a murderer from the beginning..." [John 8, 44-45]). For this reason, Camus favors a return to an historical rebel like Spartacus (R, 105-111) who wished to fight his Roman masters and thus "to die, but in absolute equality" (R, 110). Hence, of the rebel, he says, "If he finally kills himself, he will accept death" (R, 286). Camus's theoretical alternative to the Romantic hero can be viewed as an interesting re-formulation of the law of proportionality that is at the root of all just war theory.

Crucial to the use of force for Thomas is a certain restraint and applying to legal tradition, he writes, "jurists [have noted] it is lawful to repel force by force, provided one does not exceed the limits of a blameless defence" (ST II-II, q. 64, a. 7). What combat has traditionally meant—but which the logic of "zero-casualty" air war does not respect—is "a basic equality of moral risk: kill or be killed" (VW, 161). Camus wants to add to the idea of "blameless" combat a proportionality of moral risk that is simply abandoned in "zero-casualty" warfare. It is structurally part of "distance" warfare that innocents die for without the intimacy of combat, killing necessarily becomes to some degree indiscriminate.[33] Strangely, the savagery of close-quarters combat is a consequence of proportionality, and thus a mark of justice. The alternative proffered by "zero-casualty" air war bears within it a deeper savagery, perhaps. Von Balthasar has argued that to be a person requires "a form of sympathy or at least natural inclination and involvement" with another person (Keegan has spoken of the place of "empathy" in traditional combat).[34] Citing Ratzinger, von Balthasar notes that Diabolism is marked by a fostering of "the decomposition, the disintegration of being a person."[35] Does the very deepest level of savagery during the Kosovo war emerge in a means of combat, promoted by the West, in which involvement with the other is severed and therewith the personhood of all concerned?

The "zero-casualty" style of air war (3) over Kosovo is already known as "spectacle warfare,"[36] a style of warfare that does "not demand blood and sacrifice" (VW, 111). And once more, a stunning parallel with Camus' analysis of Romanticism emerges. Horrified by the injustice of death, the Romantic rejects death but in a contradictory fashion. Laying claim to a new, more intense life, the Romantic cultivates magnificence (R, 51) which requires that the hero must be seen. Thus, Camus' comment: "[the Romantic hero] can only be sure of his own existence by finding it in the expression of other' faces. Other people are his mirror" (R, 51). With aerial combat, of course, the mirror is the multiple systems that represent the image of the combat: the recordings, playbacks, news footage, etc. Camus lets us understand then why the post-modern conditions of representation (well documented by Ignatieff) are not accidental to the possibility of "zero-casualty" warfare, but constitutive. Recognizing this deals a terrible blow to a commentator like Ignatieff. Ignatieff sees the recording of the combat as a means of accountability. The killing with impunity that typifies "zero-casualty" air war is controlled and reduced, thinks Ignatieff, through the means of representation; they establish a record of combat, able to be judged. It is for this reason that Ignatieff favors such combat, for at the end of the day, he thinks, the sum total of homicide will be less (VW, 161-162): the West cannot be seen to be, his word, "murderous."[37] Yet, if Camus is correct, the imaging of the "combat" does not moderate air war but exacerbates it: the Romantic's desire for magnificence is stimulated and satisfied. On Camus' analysis, we can expect more killing—all rebel logics which ignore proportionality inevitably lead to such—not less. Indeed, most of the commentators on the war are far less sanguine than Ignatieff. Virtual war increases the likelihood of the return of early modern cabinet wars, only now "distance" warfare stands as a convenience, which will permit politicians to avoid "responsible [military] leadership and the moral courage it requires."[38] Thus, since this warfare "divest[s] war of the very gamble in human sacrifice" we can expect the use of war to become more casual.[39] Moreover, Cordesman argues that the drive for the "perfect" war has led to a "moral and analytic corruption" in NATO reporting of "collateral damage."[40] A suggestion I find fascinating, and one from a highly regard commentator, is that the abolition of real war in favor of virtual war is also the abolition of "officership as a profession."[41] Which is also the abolition of a class of high privilege,[42] the trappings of officer life, of course, founded upon the deeper privilege of commanding the exercise of the public authority's privilege to intentionally kill.

"Spectacle warfare" is (4) hardly a surprise, therefore. Behind it lies a dominant theological attitude, the rejection of God, the cult of Satan and of death, and one of its species is a pervasive motif in modern Western consciousness, the hero who enforces the moral law as "Lethal Weapon." It is surely no coincidence that our culture's film presentations of police-enforcement are, like the Kosovo police enforcement of the moral law, saturated with Romantic motifs. A central theme in Romanticism, according to Camus, is that "bloodshed is on its way to being acceptable" (R, 49) and do not the action heroes of today's Hollywood films pursue this theme? The heroes of such films are all enforcers of the law who are nevertheless unrestrained by the law[43] and in so doing claim for themselves the role of master of life and death. All such heroes are judge, jury, witness, and executioner (for they never seek to apprehend their victims)[44] and, in Diabolical fashion, they create more bloodshed than originally found. Thus, their names: *Lethal Weapon*; *Die Hard*; *Enforcer*; and, of course, the one who is *Licensed to Kill*, James Bond. They are all, as Wesley Clark noted of the airmen over Kosovo, put in an "impossible position," that is, "to wage a war that was clean yet lethal" (VW, 111). Impossible, indeed, for they are lethal and criminal. These characters are identical to the airmen: never dying (hence the sequels) they kill with impunity at the very moment that they enforce the moral law.

Once the similarities between Romanticism, "spectacle warfare," and action films have been identified, it becomes quite plausible to see the presence of the same culture of death in all three. Acknowledging such makes it easier to understand how an informed commentator, like Ignatieff, can dismiss in a paragraph the moral issues involved in such air war and reduce the matter so: "The real question is whether risk-free warfare can work." He takes it as a matter of course that "no commander worth his stars will do anything other than seek victory with minimum loss to his own troops" (VW, 162). Or, as he puts it mockingly, do "we have to lay down our lives in order to prove our moral seriousness" (VW, 162)? Well, yes, we do. Natural law insists that no commander can seek to minimize his soldiers' lives by the voluntary homicide of the innocent (recall Thomas's use of the jurists' dictum, "it is lawful to repel force by force, *provided one does not exceed the limits of a blameless defence*").[45] Thus, indeed, to prove our moral seriousness, more, to be just, it is incumbent upon the West to lay down the lives of its soldiers,[46] and for its culture to transform the sensibilities of its citizenry so as to be able to sustain sacrifice.

That the distinction between combatant and innocent has been utterly obscured in Ignatieff's mind ("Interventions which minimize casualties to both sides must be the better strategy" [VW, 162; 170])[47] is, in Camus' analysis, the deepest, most troubling aspect of Romanticism. "The romantic hero," Camus writes, "first of all brings about the profound and, so to speak, religious blending of good and evil. This type of hero is 'fatal' because fate confounds good and evil without man being able to prevent it" (R, 48).[48] Thus it is that Ignatieff, at the end of the day, is less concerned with morality and more with "what works." But also Ignatieff reveals, in a luminous manner, what was of such concern to John Paul the Great: the contemporary Western confusion in conscience between good and evil, innocence and guilt. Certainly, Ignatieff does not believe any moral Rubicon was crossed in Kosovo (VW, 184),[49] though he does think Kosovo may have made such a crossing more likely in the future (tellingly, it will be the Americans who do this, and not, to his mind at least, the more sophisticated Europeans).

By way of concluding the first part of this chapter's arguments, the lessons of Kosovo will, of course, be learnt slowly, or, God forbid, not at all. The idea remains, even amidst critical discussions of Kosovo, that, for example, the United States is the only country that could fight a war for a long period of time. Kosovo surely showed, however, that war is a "low-tech" and precisely not a "high-tech" affair. Some do appreciate this.[50] There are implications here for justice, morale, and culture. The implications of justice have been discussed: such air war is unjust and it leads to multiple homicides of the innocent that cannot be defended by the application of double-effect theory. Such air war, therefore, makes criminals of the West's pilots and their political masters. Though seldom mentioned—in the collections of personal perspectives of the war I could find no entries by the airmen—one can only guess at the problems for morale in the air forces of the Western powers. Not merely are the pilots refused the status of warrior but they are ordered to conduct themselves in a manner contrary to the natural law *and this they do intuit*. As the church has always maintained, the natural law is present to conscience, and such does appear to be the case here. Wesley Clark is reported as saying of his aircrews that they were unhappy with the conduct of the war in Kosovo: "it was a sort of an *unnatural act* for airmen to fight a ground war without a ground component" (VW, 98; my italics).

Interestingly, Ignatieff points out that development of "zero-casualty" warfare, in which the concept of the warrior that has dominated Western society is gutted of all its significance and resonance, tracks closely sociological evidence that the culture of the soldier is increasingly incomprehensible to Western societies (VW, 186-188). And yet, if Huizinga is correct, not merely does "zero-casualty" warfare mean the end of the warrior, and therefore the end of justice in war, but it also signifies the end of mercy. In his classic analysis of the dissolution of the Middle Ages, Huizinga argued that the knight as a cultural form promoted an ideal—often not lived up to—but an ideal that nevertheless civilized the Western world. Huizinga identifies pride as the leading characteristic of the medieval warrior. Such pride,[51] of course, ensured that only other combatants were worthy opponents and that killing the innocent was *beneath* the knight. Thus, argues Huizinga, principles of honor, loyalty, self-respect, and rules of virtue, blended with the developing laws of war and the two reinforced one another. The result was the savagery of war *and* ideals of justice, protection for the oppressed, right conduct and mercy for the innocent.[52] "Zero-casualty" air war is neither just nor merciful to the innocent: Kosovo was, as Bacevich puts it, "at once pusillanimous and needlessly brutal."[53] Its diabolical inspiration, in Camus' analysis, seamlessly adds to John Paul the Great's analysis of a growing culture of death[54] in which the innocent are destroyed through the *libido dominandi*. "Zero-casualty" warfare is a manifestation of the city of man, dominated by the lust to dominate, and its victims are justice and mercy. Strange to say, and yet perhaps not so strange, if there is to be war, then for war to contribute to a culture of life, airmen and soldiers must be ready to be killed as well as to kill.

Humanitarianism exhibits an indifference to murder (Kosovo) and advocates killing as social policy (discussed in the fifth chapter in connection with Peter Singer). Population ethics acts like what the phenomenologists call a "reduction": it offers basic insight into the phenomenon of humanitarianism and shows an abiding link between humane feeling, killing, and totalitarianism. In the last decade of his pontificate, John Paul the Great spearheaded some very public clashes with the city of man over population ethics. It is well that he did so. The city of man tends to see population ethics as a matter of promoting what the church identifies as intrinsic evils—contraception and abortion. This is bad enough, of course, but proponents of such ethics forget the basic insight of Thomas Malthus: population ethics is intimately tied to the problem of dictatorship. The second part of this commentary on Aquinas's eighth article does not concern the tight relationship between population policy and abortion but how population ethics links to totalitarianism. Malthus is a fascinating thinker, in fact, but it seems to be his fate that no one is willing to read him closely enough. This is a great pity for as the first theorist to systematically think through the relationship between population and dictatorship his thought stands as a fine model of careful and cautious consideration of the issues. And such a model is very much needed for population ethics tends to generate bizarre inversions, omissions, and failures of thought.

Vittorio Hösle, who claims to be a natural law theorist, reveals the temptation to dictatorship in this area. He tells us that demographic growth (but not demographic decline?)[55] "is undoubtedly one of the fatal questions of the twenty-first century."[56] Malthus may have got the mathematical nature of the population principle wrong, says Hösle, but he is not wrong that such a principle exists and that human fecundity does outstrip the earth's fecundity to feed (WPP, 157). He promptly then ignores seemingly everything else Malthus had to say. Thus, Malthus's elegant pages on the vicious consequences of turning to vice (contraception)[57] as a solution to the population principle are ignored (WPP, 163). Paul VI could usefully have inserted Malthus's pages into *Humanae Vitae* for he makes the same argument but Hösle, without any argument, proposes that the West's contraceptive control of population is a model for the world (WPP, 158). Departing completely from Malthus's axiom that government is no part of the solution to the population principle (PP, 57), Hösle insists that Western governments must restrict aid to only those countries whose governments give incentives to curb population or who penalize financially large families and whose state education systems promote contraceptive thinking (WPP, 163-4). Should penal government and education reduced to propaganda and social control not work, then it is licit for governments to forcibly sterilize parents who already have two children assuming "it is done justly, i.e., if it is informed by the principle of equality" (WPP, 164). "Eunuchs for Equality" anyone? Despite it being a part of traditional legal philosophy that there is a "general right to bring as many children into the world as one wants," and this ought to read, "a privilege accorded family life," this legal tradition has assumed this "without much reflection" (WPP, 164). So there you have it: Let's reject a moral consensus stretching back thousands of years and affirmed constantly by thousands of judges over the ages in a host of countries.

And yet, does the alternative to the universal legal tradition show "much reflection?" Hardly. We are told that exceptions to government forcibly sterilizing its fecund citizens could be made "for cultural minorities"—for "rights exist not only at the individual level but cultures, too, are endowed with rights" (WPP, 164). Cultural majorities like Catholics and Muslims seemingly do not have such rights and nor does the family. If minority cultures can have rights, why does the family not? What strange theory of rights is this that jumps from individuals having rights to minority cultures whilst skipping over the family and stopping before reaching the rights of cultural majorities? Incoherence and the failure to *argue* against Malthus to one side, the underlying logic of Hösle's position ought not to escape notice: the essence of the welfare state is solidarity—that is, equality—and the financing of population policy will usher in "global welfare." Of course, this necessitates "monitoring and control" of countries receiving aid but "the era of sovereign countries is about to close" anyway (WPP, 166). Not only does Hösle not read Malthus closely, he does not read Schmitt closely enough either. Hösle is sympathetic to Schmitt's theory of the state[58] and yet, as was seen in the sixth chapter, it is absolutely basic to Schmitt's theory of the state that the state not be a welfare state: the exchange inherent in economic values is anarchical;[59] and basic to political order is the orientation that comes of a state bounded to land, which an international welfare state certainly must fail to be. I think Malthus would view Hösle's contentions as symptomatic of what government involvement in population control will look like anarchy oscillating with dictatorship.

Liberal political theorists likewise start saying strange things when matters turn to population. One often hears that the problem of poverty and violence in certain countries is the problem of overcrowding: that humans are bound to get violent if they've little room to live in. This strange evocation of Hitler's *Lebensraum* thesis seems to go unnoticed by these commentators. This common overcrowding theory does not fit all the facts. As Robert Kaplan has pointed out, Islamic Africa with population and environmental conditions rather similar to those of Christian Africa is far more stable and well organized.[60] Nor are all shantytowns the same. The densely populated shantytowns of Turkey are remarkably crime free whilst those of West Africa are sites of anarchy and its attendant shocking violence.[61] Fukuyama is quick to tell audiences that he is pro-choice and yet he identifies as the primary source of potential instability in the world such countries as South Korea and India. The problem there is that elective abortion favoring boys has radically altered sex ratios. In South Korea, there are now roughly 121 boys to 100 girls. Fukuyama posits that if young men do not have young women to marry there is likely to be violence. Put crudely, his thesis is a reprise of the British pub dictum, "It's Friday night: time to f _ _ _ or fight." Made with more refinement, the thesis is perhaps the claim that women have a pacifying and civilizing effect on men. Still, it is unclear how Fukuyama can bring coherence to his politics and his anxieties.

Robert Kaplan, who is probably best thought of as a Hobbesian conservative, has a similar point to make. Following an observation found in Gaetano Mosca's 1939 *The Ruling Class,* Kaplan argues that a long duration of peace will inevitably result in tyranny. Mosca argued that every society has an important percentage of males with inclinations to physical actions. War, and military life, is a good outlet for such inclinations. This point made into policy can be found as far back as Urban II and his proclamation of the First Crusade. Peace closes off this outlet and one can then expect rising crime rates and an attendant culture of surveillance, segregation, and prisons. Kaplan concludes, "true peace, of the kind many imagine, is obtainable only through a form of tyranny, however subtle and mild."[62] We could also add, oftentimes a form subtle and harsh, as well. Commentary on the positive effects of abortion on crime rates is already available. Thoughts about population typically drift to international situations in Africa and India but population control internal to nations is also operative. No one suggests that there is an explicit policy of abortion population control for the American black population, but social scientists with their typical bluntness have speculated that the 50 percent abortion rate of black pregnancies has helped diminish crime in the United States.[63]

Yet even a commentator as astute as Kaplan gets himself into potential intellectual troubles. Regarding population in the world's poorest countries, Kaplan thinks that the Catholic moral theology of proportionalism has a theory adequate to the problem. As he puts it, it is basically a theory "about doing or accepting a certain amount of 'evil' to make possible a proportionately greater amount of good." Applied to aid policy this would include the promotion of contraception as a means of reducing both birth and abortion rates, say, or supporting authoritarian regimes that provide stability so that women's literacy programs can be set up: increased literacy among women, studies show, reduces birth rates, and brings other social benefits to women themselves, their children, and the environment. Catholic proportionalism, Kaplan states, "is about beating a retreat in order to preserve what is most important."[64] Malthus argues that this "retreat" is a capitulation and that the adoption of vice in the family is the adoption of a vicious social order (PP, 23). The social order that Kaplan envisages for the Third World might not be so dissimilar from the subtle and mild (and not so mild) tyranny he observes creeping into the First World. Why this might be so has very deep sources indeed.

Kaplan is a Hobbesian. It is Schmitt, of course, who clarified the role the exception plays in counter-revolutionary thought from Hobbes to Donoso Cortés. Kaplan, rightly, I think, senses that proportionalism, at root, is a theory of the exception. Kaplan might not be spooked by moral theology as such but he may be by the shifting sands of exceptionalism. Schmitt's ambiguous legacy to political theory is to show the relationship between the exception and dictatorship. Troublingly, Schmitt shows that rule of law is not possible apart from personal decision, apart from power the innermost essence of which is not law but will. The rule of men is not perhaps in direct conflict with constitutionalism (Schmitt thought it saved constitutionalism) but it is more tenuously related than someone like Kaplan might like. If, as I suspect, proportionalism is a false friend to Kaplan, who I imagine is mortified by its dictatorial logic, then Peter Singer is such to moral theology.

It might seem strange to think him an ally in any fashion but Singer, like the church, has a concern for the poor: he develops a humanitarian argument for international aid that relies cleverly on a theory of negligent homicide. This chapter will close with the argument that Thomas's theory of negligent homicide does not have the application which someone like Singer might want to make. Though it might seem implausible, I conclude this chapter with the argument that Malthus is a true friend of moral theology.

Singer begins to build his case by first denying that there is any significant moral difference between direct killing and killing by omission (PE, 158). Aquinas and de Vitoria think just the opposite (De malo, q. 2, a. 1; H, 103). Perhaps the most famous passage Malthus ever wrote relies heavily upon this very moral difference, also. Singer knows this full well, of course. For although both thinkers have a great interest in population control, and both are utilitarians, they nevertheless disagree over fundamentals. Singer has become famous as an eloquent defender of what Malthus called a "positive check" to population, namely, vice, that is, contraception and abortion. Malthus thought vice a check to population all right but also a harbinger of social disorder and despotism both, and therefore not a solution at all. But if Malthus would find Singer's ethics no ethics, Singer is equally disgusted by Malthus—for Malthus argues against welfare provision or international aid (PE, 230). The only genuinely moral "positive check" to population growth is sexual restraint on the part of the poor and middle classes. The rich need no restraint for they can afford their offspring. On the surface, Malthus's position seems to rest on self-reliance and thus some version of individualism. Singer thinks individualism as a philosophical theory "inexplicable" (PE, 166), for it contradicts what can be learnt about human social organization from anthropology, and even more importantly, sociobiology (EC, c. 5; LD, cc. 3 & 4). He is unpersuaded that there are rights against interference (PE, 166) for these sit ill with his statist aspirations. Individual self-reliance is not, in fact, the premise of Malthus's crucial argument as to why we are under no obligation to save anyone from starvation. We will return shortly to this argument, and Malthus's certain charge against Singer is that he does not look closely enough at consequences and the inevitable despotism of his position. For Singer's part, he does not think we are obligated to save everyone we possibly could but he does think there is a middle position between this and Malthus, an obligation to save some (PE, 167).

Singer asks us to imagine his walking to lecture past a child that has fallen into a pond and he wonders: Does anyone doubt that he ought to pull the child out even though it will be something of a nuisance to do so, what with getting his clothes wet, arriving to lecture late, etc. (PE, 168)? The reason why we all agree that Singer ought to act, and that an omission would be gravely reprehensible, he argues, is that we intuit the following crucial principle: "If we can prevent something bad without sacrificing anything of comparable significance, we ought to do it" (PE, 169). I suspect this is not the principle we sense, but even if it is, Malthus denies the consequences Singer draws from this, and he is right to do so. The point of the example and principle is to lock us all into the obligation of international aid: if I fail to give money to organizations that funnel aid overseas to people who would otherwise die then I am like the man who walks by the child struggling for life in the pond. There clearly are competing reasons for why Singer must act, for example, that we are proximate to the child in a way we are not to the people of Africa, but such a reason is not relevant for Singer and can make no "crucial difference to our obligations" (PE, 171). Adam Smith would argue here that Singer is engaging in "artificial commiseration" (TMS, 140) and the crucial difference is that the impartial spectator that judges moral action and whom we all obey, being the moral consensus of those living around us, is, precisely because a living judge, orientated locally (TMS, 219-20). Put simply, the spectator expects us to act in the case of the child and does not expect anything similar from us in respect of people in Africa.

Singer does acknowledge that his ideas here "run up against" human nature and the "near-universal" partiality we show family and friends (RLD, 196). But, of course, Singer's impartial spectator is not living but the rational principle of utilitarianism: a mathematization of moral life rooted to Bentham's famous egalitarian principle each to count for one. Smith would reject outright Singer's premise. Scheler would be equally dismissive. The category of neighbor is a very real moral category (earlier we saw how it cripples humanitarian intervention divorced from national attachments) and only the *ressentiment* of humanitarianism would have one think differently.[65] Kolnai would not be persuaded either. There are two very different moral emphases in play here. It is easy to obey the rule against killing people, says Singer, and hard to be morally alert to saving all those one can through various sacrifices of consumer goods, etc. So, for Singer, the difference between directly killing people and allowing them to die is a matter of difficulty (PE, 163; RLD, 195-6) and has nothing to do with the "imperative pressure" of two very different moral emphases. Kolnai would certainly insist that an ordinary moral consciousness recognizes a difference between helping the child in the pond and feeding starving people in Africa and, of course, Singer's intuitive appeal to us *about the child in the pond* is in fact riding on this very ordinary moral consciousness. The sleight of hand here is the same pulled on us by Dworkin when he relies on our intuitive grasp of tyranny only to then deny ordinary moral consciousness. Thus, Singer's premise is not convincing to important traditions of ethical thinking and it is not convincing to his fellow utilitarian, Malthus. But in Thomistic terms, might Singer be right?

Singer can easily remove a cause of homicide by pulling the child from the pond. By analogy, in failing to act so as to feed the poor can a "voluntary and intended accidentally" homicide be imputed to us? Through indifference or lack of solidarity with the poor, do we simply refuse to remove a cause of homicide?

Were Singer to make use of Thomas's theory of negligent homicide I actually think he would be on stronger ground than that afforded him by his own argument. For, as a consequentialist, his argument is open to the criticism Malthus brings against it (for it is not a new argument). I also think though that Malthus's argument reveals something very important about natural law arguments, that they depend on a certain moral surrounding or ordinary valuational consciousness, as Kolnai would put it, as well as certain insights into social order, insights shared by Vitoria, Kolnai, and Malthus. Singer argues that the child in the pond is to be helped unless some other greater loss would follow from intervention, and by analogy the same holds for each and every one of us in relationship to international aid. Malthus argues that welfare provision does have such a greater loss attached to it, namely, the loss of liberty that follows dictatorship.

Malthus's famous banquet passage is too long to quote here but the underlying logic of the passage can quickly be stated (PP, 249; 243-4; 251). The passage is an evocation of Plato's passage in the *Symposium* where Poverty stands outside the garden of the gods (the world of the forms) uninvited to the banquet. Poverty is never invited in but surreptitiously gains her place amongst the gods by having sex with a drunken and unconscious god, Resource. Malthus has us imagine a child whose parents are too poor to feed the child coming upon Nature's feast at which mouths aplenty are being fed. Some of the guests have pity on the child and make room at the table. However, other poor people seeing this start to insist that everyone be treated equally and that government act on this equality by providing welfare so that all may eat at the table. It is at this point that the population principle kicks in, thinks Malthus, and the consequences are untenable. Malthus holds that government cannot long sustain welfare provision because the initial population cared for will, of course, increase by procreation.[66] As soon as government fails to continue to contribute to the welfare of all claimants, and with equality assumed the claims *are* just, righteous anger will start to destabilize government. At this point, government will have no choice but to act dictatorially to shore up social order.

Malthus argues that it is an implication of utilitarianism that social order is fostered by privilege, the result of marriage and property. In arguments against William Godwin, someone Singer is rather fond of (EC, 148-52), Malthus argues that marriage, property, and family are inescapable aspects of human life and that these institutions introduce inequality (PP, 65-6). Singer acknowledges that sociobiology confirms this (LD, c. 2) although he rejects the notion that the natural order includes any inherent moral value as such. Malthus, however, does not argue from natural order but rather asks what social arrangement promotes the greatest happiness for the greatest good. He holds that the institutions of marriage and property, and the privilege they generate, preserve social order and liberty. The starting point of Malthus's feasting passage is privilege (which is always communal [PL, 21-2]) rather than individualism or self-reliance. It is also the starting point of this famous passage that government must acknowledge the foundational role of inequality to social order or, and this is how the passage ends, ultimately acknowledge this when forced to violently reassert order and abandon equality as an organizing principle of social order. Given the reality of the population principle—which Singer and Hösle both accept—liberty is guaranteed by privilege, dictatorship by equality, concludes Malthus.

Malthus's argument against Singer is a consequentialist one and is the argument that liberty and limited government are essential to the meaning of the happiness of the greatest happiness principle. Malthus thus argues that helping the child from the pond is morally correct just as making room at the banquet table for the child of poor parents. However, were these acts to abolish privilege then, to speak in terms of Singer's principle, something of "comparable significance" has been sacrificed and the greatest happiness principle fouled. The moral difference between an act of commission and an act of omission is annulled in principle for Singer by equality—a value of absolute and original

moral significance for Singer (PE, c. 2). Consequentialism must affirm
the moral significance of the distinction, believes Malthus, for the greatest happiness principle is incompatible with dictatorship. I have argued
that natural law thinking senses the moral positivity of privilege and
that Thomas assumes it throughout his analysis of homicide. Although
Malthus's argument is consequentialist, I think the position it affirms can
be adopted by Thomism for it accords very well with an ordinary valuational consciousness. To put this in more explicitly Thomist language,
Thomas's Question 64 is an analysis of homicides and, thus, crimes.
There can be criminal prosecution for negligent homicide but, clearly,
no such prosecution is possible for a global failing to feed the starving.
It might be a political error, a lack of charity, or failing in solidarity, but
it is not a crime. Thomas's "due care" clause is, in fact, part of a description of an action: it is a question of how one must go about an action.
In the case discussed earlier, how one must go about an air war. Peter
Singer's effort to claim that there is an obligation to international aid, for
otherwise negligent homicide is imputable, is not a part of a description
of an action; rather it is an attempt to develop a moral motivation for
starting an action one otherwise would not do.

Notes

1. As previously seen, de Vitoria thought such interventions in principle justified (H, 227, n. 193). Whether the Kosovo intervention was itself justified is unclear. For a Catholic commentary that doubts a just end was pursued, see Richard John Neuhaus, "The Clinton Era, At Home and Abroad," *First Things*, May 1999, pp. 77-78. For the role abortion now plays in the United Nations management of Kosovo, see *idem*, "While We're At It," *First Things*, December 1999.
2. A. Coll, "Kosovo and the Moral Burdens of Power," in *War Over Kosovo*, ed. A. Bacevich and E. A. Cohen (New York: Columbia University Press, 2001), p. 128.
3. C. Bell, "Force, Diplomacy, and Norms," in *Kosovo and the Challenge of Humanitarian Intervention*, ed. A. Schnabel and R. Thakur (Tokyo: United Nations University Press, 2000), p. 459.
4. *The Kosovo Report: The Independent International Commission on Kosovo* (Oxford: Oxford University Press, 2000), p. 98.
5. Anscombe expands a position like de Vitoria's when she claims that "unscrupu-lousness in considering the possibilities" is straightforward murder (G. Anscombe, "Mr. Truman's Degree," in *Ethics, Religion and Politics*, p. 66).
6. All commentators observe that the most effective NATO weapon for the situation was the helicopter gunship. Although sent to the area, these weapons were never used because of their likelihood of being downed by enemy fire.
7. Coral Bell makes an interesting observation. There was much criticism at the time that no land engagement was planned and President Clinton very publicly declared at the outset there never would be a land invasion; his comments are roundly criticized in the literature as terrible, bad leadership and a gift to the enemy both. However, Bell argues that a land war would have killed far more Kosovars than

did the air campaign (C. Bell, "Force, Diplomacy, and Norms," in *Kosovo and the Challenge of Humanitarian Intervention*, ed. A. Schnabel and R. Thakur [Tokyo: United Nations University Press, 2000], p. 454). The utilitarianism assumed by Bell is at odds with the Thomist tradition. Vitoria's rich example of the priest and the Turks shows that sometimes being just can have the consequence that more innocents will die. This is not the situation in the current argument though. My point is that the air campaign should have been conducted in a moral fashion and being moral would also have had the consequence that fewer innocents would have been killed.

8. Typical of commentary at the time is "War without Risk," *Times Higher Education Supplement*, December 2000, Millennium Magazine, p. 35; hereafter cited as THES.

9. In the sixth chapter I defended the idea of humanitarian intervention from Schmitt's criticisms.

10. Although not a much-discussed work, Camus said of the text, "It's the book of mine which I value the most." Cited in Olivier Todd, *Albert Camus: A Life*, trans. B. Ivry (New York: Alfred A. Knopf, 1997), p. 315.

11. On Camus' recent re-emergence as an intellectual presence in France after years of obscurity, see "Le triomphe de Camus," *Le nouvel Observateur*, June 1994, pp. 5-13.

12. Yet, Camus' thinking is at times quite close to Christian thought, and certainly closer than he himself realized.

13. An exception is Derek Jeffreys is his *Defending Human Dignity*. He argues that national sovereignty is subordinate to the norm of the person in John Paul the Great's thought. Evidence for this claim is garnered from speeches made by the pope at the time of the Kosovo war.

14. M. Bakunin, *Statism and Anarchy* (Cambridge: Cambridge University Press, 2005), pp. 6, 7, 20, 28, 78-9, 135.

15. Michael Ignatieff, *Virtual War: Kosovo and Beyond* (London: Chatto & Windus, 2000), p. 118; hereafter cited as VW.

16. A. Lieven, "Hubris and Nemesis," in *War Over Kosovo*, ed. A. Bacevich and E. A. Cohen (New York: Columbia University Press, 2001), pp. 103 & 111. American and Iraqi efforts to quell insurgents in Baghdad from 2003 on is a case in point.

17. J. Keegan, *The Illustrated Face of Battle* (New York: Viking, 1989), p. 246.

18. A. Bacevich, "Neglected Trinity," in *War Over Kosovo*, ed. A. Bacevich and E. A. Cohen (New York: Columbia University Press, 2001), pp. 155-6.

19. A. Cordesman, *The Lessons and Non-Lessons of the Air and Missile Campaign in Kosovo* (Westport, CT: Praeger, 2001), p. 95.

20. After the war, NATO reported (September 16, 1999) that 23,000 weapons had been used in the air war of which two-thirds were *unguided* weapons. At this time, NATO said they could only confirm half of the 1,955 target hits that pilots had reported. Cordesman notes that 50 percent confirmation is an outstanding military performance (A. Cordesman, *The Lessons and Non-Lessons of the Air and Missile Campaign in Kosovo* [Westport, CT: Praeger, 2001], p. 97). It has also been observed that given the altitude the planes flew at there were in fact only fifteen of the seventy-two days of the air campaign clear enough when pilots could reliably differentiate between civilian and military targets (C. Cavanagh Hodge, "Casual War: NATO's Intervention in Kosovo," *Ethics and International Affairs*, Vol. 14 [2000], p. 48).

21. B. Rooney, "The PlayStation Theory of War," review of M. Ignatieff's *Virtual War, The Daily Telegraph*, February 19, 2001. At least in America, this is a new phenom-

enon. The history of American warfare has seen presidents and public alike willing to tolerate very high casualties. Lincoln famously wondered where he would find a general willing to "face the arithmetic," that is, the necessary high casualties to prosecute war successfully (see E. Cohen, "Kosovo and the New American Way of War," in *War Over Kosovo*, ed. A. Bacevich and E. Cohen [New York: Columbia University Press, 2001], pp. 38-42).

22. Opinion polls at the time showed that the American public had a high toleration of casualties if political leadership was shown (A. Cordesman, *The Lessons and Non-Lessons of the Air and Missile Campaign in Kosovo* [Westport, CT: Praeger, 2001], p. 100).

23. "Land Warfare," *The Economist*, November 18, 2000, pp. 29-33; hereafter cited as EC.

24. David Ochmanek of RAND comments: "The enemy's army should be already destroyed before we get on to the ground" (EC, 33). For Michael Walzer's conerns about such a logic, see M. Walzer, "Kosovo," in *Kosovo: Contending Voices on Balkan Interventions*, ed. W. Buckley (Grand Rapids, MI: Eerdmans, 2000), p. 334.

25. Clark implies here that civilian deaths occurred because of stray munitions. The truth about the number of casual killings as opposed to killings from mistaken targets will probably never be known. *The Kosovo Report* claims 495 civilians were killed by NATO bombing, with 820 wounded. Only 300 Serb soldiers were killed but most civilian deaths occurred through mistaken targeting (*The Kosovo Report: The Independent International Commission on Kosovo* [Oxford: Oxford University Press, 2000], p. 94).

26. A. Bacevich, "Neglected Trinity," in *War Over Kosovo*, ed. A. Bacevich and E. A. Cohen (New York: Columbia University Press, 2001), p. 155.

27. For the different judicial standards applied to an enemy of the West in respect of its war crimes and those of our own soldiers and political leaders, see VW, 128.

28. VW, 110; cf. B. Rooney, "The PlayStation Theory of War," *The Daily Telegraph*, Saturday, February 19, 2001.

29. For a comparable analysis by a contemporary of Camus, see Gaston Fessard, S. J., *Par-delà le fascisme et le communisme*, (Paris: FNAC, 1945).

30. Scheler makes the same argument and does so when trying to explain the origins and character of the First World War. See his, "Christian Love and the Twentieth Century," *On the Eternal in Man* (New Brunswick, NJ: Transaction, 2010), especially pp. 267-72.

31. THES, p. 35. For the aircrews' knowledge that at the time they were having next to no impact on the situation on the ground, see some of their comments in VW, 105. At the war's end the Serb army left the field in good order with huge amounts of military hardware and 45,000 soldiers (A. Lieven, "Hubris and Nemesis," in *War Over Kosovo*, ed. A. Bacevich and E. A. Cohen [New York: Columbia University Press, 2001], p. 100).

32. Some view the whole escapade as no better than "farce" and "devoutly" wish that the air campaign sets no precedent (C. Cavanagh Hodge, "Casual War: NATO's Intervention in Kosovo," *Ethics and International Affairs*, Vol. 14 [2000], p. 54). Others, as has been seen, do think a precedent has been set for the style of humanitarian intervention. The anti-terrorist wars of the Bush Administration have been very different in character.

33. As noted earlier, I am mindful of the indiscriminate shootings that happened at Mogadishu. Nor do I want to deny that given the pressures of combat such killings are often likely. Still, John Keegan has spoken of "an aristocracy of combat"—that it is impossible to know before the fighting who will rise to the challenge of being

a warrior (*The Illustrated Face of Battle* [New York: Viking, 1989], p. 10)—and this is structurally absent from "distance warfare."

34. J. Keegan, *The Illustrated Face of Battle* (New York: Viking, 1989), p. 277.

35. Hans Urs von Balthasar, *Dare We Hope "That All Men be Saved"?* trans. D. Kipp & L. Krauth (San Francisco: Ignatius Press, 1988), p. 145.

36. THES, p. 34; cf. VW, 191.

37. Commenting that Milosevic's strategy to beat the NATO air war was not to fight the aircraft but to ensure that the consequences to the civilian population of the air war were made readily available to the Western media, Ignatieff writes, "he gambled his regime… on the assumption that the Western public would not allow an air campaign to become murderous" (VW, 52).

38. C. Cavanagh Hodge, "Casual War: NATO's Intervention in Kosovo," *Ethics and International Affairs*, Vol. 14 (2000), p. 53.

39. Ibid., pp. 39-40.

40. A. Cordesman, *The Lessons and Non-Lessons of the Air and Missle Campaign in Kosovo* (Westport, CT: Praeger, 2001), p. 121.

41. A. Bacevich, "Neglected Trinity," in *War Over Kosovo*, ed. A. Bacevich and E. A. Cohen (New York: Columbia University Press, 2001), pp. 183-4.

42. For Bakunin's analysis of officer privilege, see *Statism and Anarchy*, pp. 77-9.

43. Think here of Clint Eastwood's character, "Dirty Harry," or Mel Gibson's, "Martin Ricks."

44. It is contrary to natural law for one person to perform all these roles (H, 157).

45. The troops were told that the "first mission" in Kosovo was "force protection." See E. Cohen, "Kosovo and the New American Way of War," in *War Over Kosovo*, ed. A. Bacevich and E. Cohen (New York: Columbia University Press, 2001), p. 55.

46. De Gaulle's words now appear prophetic: "International law would be worthless without soldiers to back it."

47. This is a variant of the equalitarianism I discuss in the fourth chapter.

48. For this religious blending of good and evil consider the preternatural dimension of films starring Clint Eastwood, *Pale Rider* and *High Plains Drifter*.

49. Although, please note his final words at VW, pp. 214-215: "We see war as a surgical scalpel and not a bloodstained sword. In so doing we mis-describe ourselves as we mis-describe the instruments of death." A bit like the aircrews themselves, Ignatieff seems to *intuit* that something is seriously amiss in zero-casualty warfare.

50. For example, General Ronald Griffiths writes, quoting approvingly an historian of the Korean War, that at the end of the day, for effective combat you must do what "the Roman legions did, by putting your young men in the mud." (EC, 29) By contrast, Ignatieff does not grasp this: see his hard-to-believe pages, VW, 169-170. After the Iraq War, and especially the insurgency there, Griffiths' point is, hopefully, now thoroughly appreciated.

51. I do not see any conflict between this pride—*gloire* is perhaps the better word—and Catholicism. For Thomas on pride, see his nuanced pages at *De malo*, q. 8, a. 2. Cardinal Richelieu and De Gaulle were devout Catholics, as well as statesmen and soldiers who were animated by the desire for *gloire*. On the culture of *gloire* in France in the seventeenth century—and the role St. Francis de Sales played in generating it—see, Anthony Levi, *Cardinal Richelieu and the Making of France* (New York: Carroll & Graf, 2000), pp. 152-155. For a Catholic who thinks there is a conflict, see Pierre Manent, *The City of Man* (Princeton, NJ: Princeton University Press, 1997).

52. Johan Huizinga, *The Waning of the Middle Ages*, (New York: Dover Publications, 1999), pp. 91-94.

53. A. Bacevich, "Neglected Trinity," in *War Over Kosovo*, ed. A. Bacevich and E. A. Cohen (New York: Columbia University Press, 2001), p. 185.

54. It also supports the contention of Neuhaus that liberal democracies pervert themselves when they take no account of the intellectual and moral heritage of orthodox Christianity. See Richard John Neuhaus, *The Naked Public Square: Religion and Democracy in America* (Grand Rapids, MI: Eerdmans, 1984).
55. "The West Ignores Low Birthrates at Its Peril," *International Herald Tribune* (October 23, 2004); "Empty Maternity Wards Imperil a Dwindling Germany," *New York Times* (November 18, 2004); Richard John Neuhaus, "Where Have All the Children Gone?" *First Things* (May 2005), pp. 58-60. For a funny but profound example of issues connected to population decline, see Mark Steyn, *America Alone: The End of the World as We Know It* (New York: Regnery, 2006).
56. V. Hösle, "Moral Ends and Means of World Population Policy," *Objective Idealism, Ehics, and Politics* (South Bend, IN: St. Augustine's Press, 1998), p. 152.
57. T. Malthus, *An Essay on the Principle of Population* (Cambridge: Cambridge University Press, 1992); henceforth, PP.
58. V. Hösle, *Morals and Politics* (Notre Dame, IN: University of Notre Dame Press, 2004).
59. C. Schmitt, *Tyranny of Values* (Corvallis, OR: Plutarch Press, 1996), p. 3; henceforth = TV.
60. R. Kaplan, *The Coming Anarchy* (New York: Vintage, 2001), p. 6.
61. Ibid., pp. 30-4.
62. Ibid., pp. 175-6.
63. See Richard John Neuhaus commenting on Levitt & Donohue's *Legalized Abortion and Crime*: "While We're At It," *First Things*, December, 1999, and October, 2001.
64. R. Kaplan, *The Coming Anarchy*, pp. 122-123.
65. For Scheler's argument, see the fifth chapter of his *Ressentiment*. I discuss this argument in relationship to gay marriage at, "Two Case Studies in Schelerian Moral Theology: The Vatican's 2005 "Instruction" and Gay Marriage."
66. One could cite dozens upon dozens of news articles about the economic and demographic problems facing state socialism in Europe. It is worth recalling that the European welfare state is only about forty years old. Even the far more minimal social security system of the United States is famously in turmoil and requires fundamental revision. Of course, if Europe suffers a fundamental trauma it will not be directly on account of the population principle but what Malthus termed "positive checks." On all of these issues, see N. Ferguson, *Colossus: the Rise and Fall of the American Empire* (London: Penguin, 2005).

Conclusion

Natural Law as Political Theology

*Well, Prince, Genoa and Lucca are now nothing
more than estates taken over by the Buonaparte
family. No, I give you fair warning. If you won't
say this means war, if you will allow yourself to
condone all the ghastly atrocities perpetrated by
that Antichrist—yes, that's what I think he is—I
shall disown you.*
—Opening lines of War and Peace

It is odd that the greatest novel begins with an idea that most in the West today find either preposterous or frightening. We've all heard of Jihad and grasp the basics of the idea but talk of a Christian holy war is largely incomprehensible. The incomprehension goes very deep. Recently, at a meeting of Catholic intellectuals gathered to speak about war, I heard a priest argue that what justice means is to be in right order to God; he denied there is such a thing as natural rights. Condemnation was immediate: More than one participant at the meeting threw at him "You sound like an ayatollah," and no other "argument" had to be given. Participants were spooked by the idea that if just wars are possible, but justice is right order to God, then just wars are also holy wars. Far preferable, for these Catholic intellectuals, was a notion of justice derived from some natural law of reason. Such a notion of rationality keeps the ayatollahs (and priests?) marginalized and encourages broadminded conversation about ethics where all, irrespective of faith and allegiances, can contribute.

There is something old-fashioned about this condemnation, however. Its vigor assumes the obviousness of the strength and availability of a natural normative foundation contrasting with the flimsy opportunism of religion. Yet for decades now intense skepticism about the natural

187

has dominated the world of ideas. Certainly, natural law thinking is in an unenviable position these days. It is squeezed theologically and philosophically. Moral theological reflection and the church's self-understanding now revolves around, in a very explicit way, the life of Christ; for many theologians, assuming a stable natural order to which Christ is added as a baroque decorative item is untenable. Philosophy, at least since Hume, has been awash with skepticism about the natural. In the contemporary academy, any form of moral realism is besieged by hermeneutics, moral fictionalism, projectivism, some strains of feminism, and Foucauldian historicism, to name only some forms of contemporary anti-foundationalism.

Of course, my book is old-fashioned for its thesis is that Aquinas's natural law theory of homicide is the best available to us. I, too, rely on the idea of the natural but, unlike the participants at the meeting, I side with the priest. Natural law rightly understood is to stand in right order to God. And in a strong sense—not merely in the sense that to follow conscience or to act rationally is to imitate the rationality of God but only acts that are eucharistic, acts that are Christological, stand in right order to God. To paraphrase the participants, to rightly understand law we need to look not to the ayatollahs but to the popes. The conference participants are under the impression that there is some natural normative rationality accessible separate from the "sectarian" life of Christ. This is a mistake.

Catholic intellectuals all too frequently rely, seemingly unaware, on Kant's search for purity, an account of rationality independent of the body.[1] Rationality is constitutively animal and the naturalism that looks to biology has already proven its explanatory power and will likely continue to do so. Moreover, Schmitt is right to point out that the legal tradition stemming from Kant, so aptly captured by Kelsen's pure theory of law, struggles to explain the intimate relationship between law and protection. Whether Kant, Kelsen, or Habermas, this tradition elides the problem of the body and vulnerability. Far more concerned with the body are those theologians who take the life of Christ as basic to any account of natural law. This is correct but I understand matters rather differently than people like Rowland, Ward, and Milbank. Their position tends to collapse natural law into divine positive law. Rightly, they celebrate the revolutionary newness of redemption but rather over play the *novum* at the expense of the *ovum*. These theologians misconstrue the Incarnation because they have not adequately assessed the body and its deep history. They never dwell on the natural history of the body, nor completely enough, the metaphysics and theology of the body, in my opinion. To acknowledge the natural history of the *ovum* is not to concede that Darwinian naturalism is straightforwardly correct. The appetitive structure of animal inclination is ecstatic, that is, self and other directed simultaneously. In EM I argued that the Cross is metaphysical, the Cross is the very starting structure of embodied inclination and communication. The *ovum* is a piece of the true Cross. This is why natural law is sectarian: Christ is the life of the Cross lived rightly. Life is eccentricity, always already communicative, ecstatic. It is guided communication, always already a response to an order of value; completed in the Incarnation, the *ovum* is now accelerated towards a deposing ecstasy, not now only the alpha of solidarity but the omega of a love that wounds.

Many of the arguments in this book already make these points but let me conclude by making the broader argument about natural law more explicit.

Treating a good number of contemporary legal issues ranging from international trade law to criminal procedure, I contrasted Thomas with leading traditions of jurisprudence headed by the likes of Carl Schmitt and Peter Singer. My arguments, I believe, show the enduring power of Thomas's thought as a foundation for law. This foundation is "sectarian," and law can have none other. By showing that Thomas gives the best account of homicide the point was not to eke out some place for Catholic thought in contemporary political discussion but to offer an argument for John Paul II's claim that law without God collapses into a homicidal humanitarianism. Political theology is not merely a necessary part of thinking about law it is the privileged site for jurisprudence.

Against the contemporary conventionalist mood, my commentary relies on an ethical realism reliant on an objective value hierarchy, evidence for which is found in moral consensus. In a forthcoming book, I defend David Hume's celebration of refinement as the rampart of liberty. Isn't it a problem that the claims of this book are so out-of-step with today's refined opinions? It is an implication of the thesis defended in this book that Christian holy war is conceivable. My local gun shop in Baltimore is called *Christian Soldier*—at least the people who go there are not baffled by the opening lines of *War and Peace*. But they are not the right sort, are they? Nor is the priest who denies natural right.

In fact, aren't all the associations wrong? Distinguishing between utopia and myth, Anarchist Georges Sorel argued that the workers' revolution could only be instigated if workers were inhabited by a myth. Sorel identified as motivating myths the Napoleonic and the church militant.

A myth is an image of battle and struggle. Action, thought Sorel, could not be motivated by the refined scientific mentality inquiring into constitutive parts (e.g., genetics), subtly navigating the relations between centers of agency, but only by pictures. I doubt that in modern France the Napoleonic is still a myth and I'm positive his second example isn't. Sorel writes, "Catholics have never been discouraged even in the hardest trials, because they have pictured the history of the Church as a series of battles between Satan and the hierarchy supported by Christ."[2] This myth of the church militant is thoroughly depleted. More evacuated still is any image of Christians marching to war with the cross of Jesus before them. But doesn't my reliance on ordinary moral sensibility at least give the nod to Sorel, poster boy of the Phalange? Hardly worse, but utterly embarrassing, doesn't this all sound a bit like George W. Bush?

In his book *The President of Good and Evil*, Peter Singer expresses much horror for George Bush, and partly on account of his forming public policy by Christian lights. Famous for his humanitarianism, Singer allows that Christians can of course take part in politics but he insists no political claim they make can be confessional. Politics requires that reasons and arguments be given. Singer writes:

> The Islamic militant who believes he is doing the will of God when he flies a plane full of passengers into the World trade center is just as much a person of faith as the Christian who believes she is doing the will of God when she spends her days picketing a clinic that offers abortions. Faith cannot tell us who is right and who is wrong, because each will simply assert that his or her faith is the true one. In the absence of a willingness to offer reasons, evidence, or arguments for why it is better to do one thing rather than another, there is no progress to be made.[3]

It really is Singer's position that any proposition inflected by confessional belief is not a *bona fide* reason and more, it is also anti-democratic. Agreeing with Carl Schmitt that the essence of democratic pluralism is conversation and intellectual outreach to those who think differently,[4] Singer writes:

> When we take part in this conversation, we seek to justify our views to others, and in so doing we should acknowledge the fact of political and religious pluralism. We should show that we recognize that we live in a community with a diversity of political and religious views. Hence we should offer reasons that can appeal to all, not only to other members of our own community of belief. Otherwise there can be no public conversation that embraces the entire society; we are implicitly dividing society into separate communities that do not seek to persuade each other. That is a recipe for increasing antagonism and mutual hostility...[5]

There is much that is ludicrous in Singer's portrayal of Christian belief—which is not to say that Singer isn't super smart, because he is—but Singer's position is quite conventional. Disagreeing with Singer about what he has called "liberal eugenics," Habermas would nonetheless agree with Singer about the role of secularism. Habermas might now think religion is important to secure solidarity but he remains convinced that public law issues exclusively from pure reason. In the interesting volume he published with Cardinal Ratzinger, the *Dialectics of Secularization*, Habermas writes: "systems of law can be legitimated only in a self-referential manner, that is, on the basis of legal procedures." These procedures have "a nonreligious and postmetaphysical justification," and stem from a "rational law that renounces the 'strong' cosmological or salvation-historical assumptions of the classical and religious theories of the natural law."[6] To go to war for reasons of religious confession would be, for Habermas, the vanquishing of the Enlightenment.

What would it mean for a Christian to take Peter Singer as a guide on this matter? Yet Catholics hardly need to since by other routes Singer's position seems assured. If you were to ask a fifty-five-year old in the US who had been an excellent student as an undergrad at a good Jesuit or Dominican college about natural law, this is what he'd say: "Natural law is how the Catholic church engages a pluralistic nation like America on matters of public policy. It is the claim that a basic set of rational norms are known to all human beings. Public law must acknowledge these norms and there is no reason for it not to: these rational norms are discerned through natural reason but they are not specifically Catholic nor even Christian norms; they are rather the common heritage of mankind." If you posed the "What Would Jesus Do?" question about war, this good student would deftly respond: "Though there is no killing in the New Law, indeed, in the Gospels Jesus neither spills blood nor seeks that it be spilt, the natural law says otherwise. Its norms do include war—famously explained by Thomas Aquinas—and the particular revelation that Christ throws on the moral life doesn't affect these natural rational norms." Growing up in the Catholic church of Maritain and JFK, this student learned well. Moreover, a brisk reading of de Vitoria would apparently bear this view out. In his *Relection on Homicide*, de Vitoria writes:

> Fourth, I say and conclude that by that commandment [Do not kill] there is prohibited every homicide which, *by the law of nature alone*, is evil and irrational. And it is *only* to this that we must look, and not to exceptions or permissions given in divine law. For all of these are only judicial, and have ceased to obtain, or if they are moral are explanatory of the natural law. Accordingly, when it is lawful to kill and when

it is not must be *ultimately* referred to this. However, it does help to *consult* the Scriptures. (OH, 83; emphasis added)

Contemporary theology doesn't recognize the theory of natural law offered by our erstwhile student. Tracey Rowland is well known for the argument that this version of natural law is a strategic failure. Natural law stripped of the theological, she writes, "leads to a situation in which Catholics talk to Catholics in an idiom which was devised for dialogue with unbelievers, while unbelievers are either not persuaded or so poorly educated as to be unfamiliar with the idiom."[7] Rowland's point is well taken: A survey of the leading lights of contemporary Anglo-American moral theory, books by the likes of Doris, Velleman, Nichols, shows all manner of disagreements but each author is equally silent about natural law. There is complete indifference.

Quite apart from the strategic issue, powerful currents in contemporary Catholic thought have generated competing versions of natural law.[8] Benedict XVI's fascinating thesis about the pathologies of reason[9] does not perhaps collapse into Luther's horror of a *Deus glorious* theology but it strikes a chilling tone for anyone who would write with de Vitoria's confidence:

That which is essentially good and laudable is not forbidden by Divine law. But, as the Doctor has shown, killing a murderer or a traitor is of itself good and praiseworthy, because he is dangerous for the community...For although God never excepted this in the law, that is, although he did not say: "kill murderers and dangerous men," nevertheless, it would be evident to kill them, because by natural law it could be evident...(OH, 141)

Reason, thinks Benedict, cannot be adequately grasped independently of Christ. Thus, Fergus Kerr has documented the drive to a nuptial ontology in contemporary theology[10] and Matt Levering has drawn attention to the new centrality of a Christological treatment of human nature.[11] Prompting these trends is the famous paragraph 22 of *Gaudium et spes* that John Paul the Great was so fond of repeating: Christ fully reveals man to himself.

At the end of a recent article on natural law, Tracey Rowland asks: "Can indeed one have an account of natural law linked to the theological anthropology of *Gaudium et spes*, 22, without adopting at least some of the elements of de Lubac's criticisms of Baroque Thomism?"[12] Rowland does not develop her comment but its importance is clear. If the *duplex ordo* theory of the relationship between nature and grace is a falsification of Catholic tradition then the standing of natural law is presumably transformed. If human nature is never in principle isolated from the life of Christ then de Vitoria's handy separation of the norms of natural law from the norms of the New Law fails.[13] If Christ is constitutive of the meaning of human nature the norms of natural law must be *radicalized* in the life of Christ. If, as Thomas makes clear, the New Law knows no blood (ST II-II, q. 64, a. 4), then presumably no law knows blood. On the basis of this new Christocentric ontology, Aquinas's claim that natural law is a participation in the eternal law would not be the claim de Vitoria thought. Eternal law is not a rationally discernible normative order of prohibitions against the performance of intrinsically evil acts and therewith the permission to perform acts of justice to block such transgressive acts. A theory of war can be built on such an understanding of eternal law. It is hard to see how a theory of killing is possible if eternal law is modeled for us in the life of Christ. If, as Thomas says in his mature treatise on action and morals, his 1272 *De malo*, the precepts of the law follow the virtues, then the law is now radicalized in Christ's life of virtue.

The church's theory of homicide has hardly kept up with these theological developments but, surely, the implications for killing are profound. Perhaps now there is no Catholic natural law theory of war and the idea of holy war is a non-starter. Does the changed theological environment explain the sense of drift towards pacifism in recent papal pronouncements on world events?

A classic Thomistic gesture at this point would be to insist that since grace perfects nature then no matter de Lubac's claims about the right relationship between nature and grace the integrity of nature still stands. Of course, in the fourth chapter I offered an argument—that his position betrays equalitarianism—why we should be skeptical towards de Lubac's thesis. All the same, if Christ is not external to natural law, as my theory assumes, aren't the precepts now Christ's virtues? And if so, aren't contemporary theologians right to tolerate the collapse of the claims of nature?

How should we think of nature? This is, in fact, to ask about the metaphysics of the Incarnation. There is a tendency to think of the Incarnation as a simple triumph. It is a triumph, for sure, only not simple. A crucial insight is found in John Paul II. In a stunning formulation found in the *Theology of the Body*, John Paul II writes:

> The sacrament, as a visible sign, is constituted with man, inasmuch as he is a "body," through his "visible" masculinity and femininity. The body, in fact, and only the body, is capable of making visible what is invisible: the spiritual and the divine. It

has been created to transfer into the visible reality of the world the mystery hidden from eternity in God...[14]

Only the body makes visible the invisible but certainly, this is not to say the body is ontologically transparent. What makes our bodies sacramental is Christ's body, the body of He who is, as Balthasar puts it, "already always the one who has bled, 'the Lamb slain before the foundation of the world' (Apoc. 13, 8) in an 'eternal redemption' (Heb. 9, 12);"[15] the one whose body is marked by the wounds of love, about which Thomas and Bonaventure speak so eloquently.

Why is Christ sacrament? Not merely because He is love but because a body also. As John Paul II points out, "*sacramentum* originally meant the military oath taken by the Roman legionaries" (TB, 381, n. 98)—a pledging of the body to service. The body is mystery laden, not simply portending the full meaning of Christ's suffering but always already inclining mystery. The body is double in aspect, however, and inclining mystery must open as a wound. Totalitarian philosophies assume a solidarity rooted in identity but the body is always eccentric. Totalitarianism appeals—and in subtle ways as we saw in the fifth chapter when considering Singer's work—because the body has a propensity to identity. Simple identity, the will to justice that longs for purity and the cancellation of contingency, is a false account of the body. What is right here is no matter the mystery of the body, no matter its echo of love, the recalcitrance of the body to gratuity requires a new gratuity able to transform the body's vulnerability into the wound of love. Christ is this disclosure. Right solidarity though is already afoot in the inclination of the body. The *ovum* always inclines to the *novum*, fructified and ecstatic, solidarity deposes contingency even as it is deposed by it. Right solidarity is only possible through the wound. To think otherwise is the mistake of humanitarianism and to fail to see Easter as privilege the mistake of many theologians. Theologians enamoured of de Lubac's idea that human spirit is intrinsically ordered to God are too confident, in my opinion, in thinking there is an obvious distance between him and Rahner. As I showed in the fourth chapter, Rahner's notion of the supernatural existential makes Easter a required gift, it minimizes God's gratuity and thus God's privilege. The thesis of de Lubac fairs little better. To link God and human spirit so intimately suggests that human nature itself is a yonder beyond vulnerability. This is to minimize the raised position of the Cross in Easter. It precisely encourages what de Lubac hoped to avoid: Secularization. Humanitarianism is the belief that the wound is accidental to the body. Eliding the problematic status of the *ovum*, de Lubac encourages a secularization of the body and suffering. The body is always eucharistic, and natural law always sectarian, but it is the problematic status of the *ovum* that makes the Eucharist an accomplishment. Orthodox political theology is a politics of privilege because of the *ovum*.

Why? Benedict XVI, when Cardinal Ratzinger spoke of the victory of evolution and its evisceration of any traditional theory of nature able to support Catholic moral claims.[16] Perhaps Benedict is too quick.[17] Reminiscent of Carl Schmitt's friend-enemy distinction, biological phenomena, whether bacteria or apes, line up around in group/out group demarcations and war is shaped around this basic organizational principle.[18] Evolution assumes continuity amongst all species. If people like Besslar[19] and de Waal are right about the science then humanitarianism or an ethical cosmopolitanism has no foundation in nature: the behavior of bacteria and primates confirms the traditional social forms captured in the order of charity; first and foremost, biological forms look after those like themselves and close to themselves.

Can the turn to a new naturalism inside contemporary Anglo-American philosophy help think through the metaphysics of the Incarnation? De Waal's basic thesis is that humans have always been highly social creatures because descended from highly social creatures; our solidarity, like that of our ape forbearers,[20] is rooted in the emotions of reciprocity and reprisal (PP, 4; 57). Sketching his intellectual predecessors, de Waal sees a trajectory of thought stretching back from Westermarck, to Adam Smith, to Aquinas (PP, 18-19). De Waal puts these parts together: Aquinas emphasizes the role of deep-seated inclinations in the organization of human and animal life; Smith the centrality of emotion in social negotiations; and Westermarck a limited set of social emotions as the root of moral order, reciprocity, and reprisal. It follows from my second chapter that de Waal could rely on Aquinas for this last point, too.

Max Scheler's claim that all organisms are ecstatic[21]—social and in profound communication with the world about them—does appear to be right[22] and Aquinas's richer sense of the ecstatic also appears to be right. De Waal vigorously defends the position that apes are fundamentally empathetic, and to a remarkable degree. In one experiment, rhesus monkeys who had seen that if they took the offered food a companion received a shock were observed to go without food for between five and twelve days (PP, 29). De Waal is anxious to refute the basic assumption of liberal political theory that humans are fundamentally free and equal autonomous individuals who can choose their own social arrangements. Against the liberal political tradition, he writes:

> Hobbes and Rawls create the illusion of human society as a voluntary arrangement with self-imposed rules assented to by free and equal agents…free and equal people never existed. Humans started out—if a starting point is discernible at all—as interdependent, bonded, and unequal. We come from a long lineage of hierarchical animals for which life in groups is not an option but a survival strategy (PP, 4).

A political liberal, in fact, de Waal is nonetheless skeptical about humanitarianism since it downplays the passions, hierarchy, and privilege—all of which play a dominant role in biological life. If de Waal were an anthropologist he might also wonder about Thomas's claim that natural inclination beyond survival, reproduction, and sociality also seeks God. As pointed out in the Introduction, there is a notorious difficulty in natural law thinking: How does one move from the basic principles of natural law to specific legal arrangements? Thomas nowhere discusses a mechanism by which the derivations are made. Instructive here is de Vitoria who unashamedly runs together intuitional content, Roman law, history, ethnology, theology, and natural law reasoning to build a rich analysis of various problems facing the moral theologian. He relies heavily on custom, in other words. In my opinion, it is Carl Scmitt who has made this point most analytically.

In *The Nomos of the Earth*, Schmitt argues that law takes its initial character from the orientation of the land and land is first crafted religiously. Schmitt writes:

> "In the beginning was the fence. Fence, enclosure, and border are deeply interwoven in the world formed by men, determining its concepts. The enclosure gave birth to the shrine by removing it form the ordinary, placing it under its own laws, and entrusting it to the divine" (Jost Trier). The enclosing ring—the fence formed by men's bodies, the manring—is a primeval form of ritual, legal, and political cohabitation. In the further course of our investigation, it will prove quite fruitful to refer to this realization that law and peace originally rested on enclosures in the spatial sense. In particular, it was not the abolition of war, but rather its bracketing that has been the great, core problem of every legal order. (NE, 74)

Positive law made rich by land and religion completes the elementary legal norms of natural law and shapes a community. In consequence, within every legal order is also a preparedness for war as primatology and anthropology seemingly confirm. And because every political order is a sacred order,[23] some variant of, or analogue to, caesaro-papalism is inevitable. Political theology is then the clarification of which types of caesaro-papalism are orthodox and thus which wars are holy.[24] In the sixth chapter I argued against Schmitt's effort to separate theology from moral theology (CP 64-65) and sought to show against him how the classical accounts of just war killing remain valuable. I also argued there that the nation state is a privileged agency of war making and so agreed with Schmitt about the importance of the state. Theology, in other words, has a geography; in turn, this is another way of saying that nature has a value integrity of its own to which belongs the ever present possibility of killing.

Max Scheler is famous for the claim that the religious is inescapable and that one either loves God or some other god.[25] Who is the god of humanitarian democracy? Habermas helps here. Recall his statement that in the liberal tradition public law has neither a cosmological nor a soteriological nor a metaphysical origin; it is "self-referential." Aquinas explains that the basic attribute of the deadly sin of vanity is a fascination with novelty. The human crafted by humanitarianism is incessantly self-producing with the new, ever freeing the liberal self from theology, history, territory, and the enemy. This is not a variant on the Pauline *novitas mundi*, however, for the humanitarian, as Schmitt puts it, "there is no *ovum* in an old or renewable sense at all. There is only a *novum*."[26] In the late '40s, Kolnai spoke of totalitarianism incipient in liberal democracy and in 1995 John Paul II spoke of totalitarianism in the West systematically enabling the cancellation of the *ovum*. If liberal cosmopolitanism denies the enemy it does not follow there are no enemies at all and that formalized killing is at a stop (*EV*, para. 12-13 and 20).

Political theology can safely take as its starting point the place of the *ovum* at law. The arguments of the last few hundred pages show that this is not merely a claim about abortion but about the erosion of the privilege of the public authority to kill. Desire to destroy this privilege ultimately stems from a misunderstanding of the problem of vulnerability. Humanitarianism and even significant strains of contemporary theology, liberal and otherwise, elide the *ovum*: Both cancel the *ovum* albeit for very different reasons. Christ does not abandon man, the *novum* that is man redeemed is an adopted vulnerability bathed abundantly in the healing blood of love.

Notes

1. I. Kant, *Groundwork for the Metaphysics of Morals* (New Haven: Yale University Press, 2002), p. 43.
2. G. Sorel, *Reflections on Violence* (Cambridge: Cambridge University Press, 2004), p. 20.

3. P. Singer, *The President of Good and Evil: The Ethics of George W. Bush* (New York: Dutton, 2004), p. 99.
4. C. Schmitt, *The Crisis of Parliamentary Democracy* (Cambridge, MA: MIT, 1988).
5. P. Singer, *The President of Good and Evil: The Ethics of George W. Bush*, p. 103.
6. J. Habermas & J. Ratzinger, *The Dialectics of Secularization: On Reason and Religion* (San Francisco: Ignatius, 2006), pp. 27 and 24.
7. T. Rowland, "Natural Law: From Neo-Thomism to Nuptial Mysticism," *Communio* 35 (Fall 2008), p. 375.
8. M. Levering, "Natural Law and Natural Inclination: Rhonheimer, Pinckaers, McAleer," *The Thomist*, Vol. 70:2 (April 2006): 155-201; D. Crawford, "Natural Law and the Body: Between Deductivism and Parallelism," *Communio* 35 (Fall 2008), pp. 327-53. .
9. Benedict XVI, *Regensburg Address*, and previously stated in *The Dialectics of Secularization*.
10. F. Kerr, *Twentieth-Century Catholic Theologians: From Neoscholasticism to Nuptial Mysticism* (Oxford: Blackwell, 2007).
11. M. Levering, *Biblical Natural Law* (Oxford: OUP, 2008).
12. T. Rowland, "Natural Law: From Neo-Thomism to Nuptial Mysticism," p. 396.
13. In this light, see the reconsideration of the usury prohibition in C. Franks, *He Became Poor: The Poverty of Christ and Aquinas's Economic Teachings* (Grand Rapids, MI: Eerdmans, 2009).
14. As cited in Crawford, "Natural Law and the Body: Between Deductivism and Parallelism," p. 332.
15. Hans Urs von Balthasar, *Theological Anthropology* (New York: Sheed and Ward, 1967), p. 33.
16. J. Habermas & J. Ratzinger, *The Dialectics of Secularization: On Reason and Religion* (San Francisco: Ignatius, 2006), p. 69.
17. In his 2009 encyclical, *Charity in Truth*, Benedict is more skeptical about the basic correctness of evolutionary naturalism.
18. F. de Waal, *Primates and Philosophers* (Princeton, 2006), p. 54-5; hereafter, PP.
19. Gautam Naik, "Deep Inside Bacteria, a Germ of Human Personality," WSJ, September 8, 2009.
20. The exact linear relationship between humans and apes is now a rather open question with the discovery of the hominid fossil Ardi (Robert Lee Hotz, "Fossils Shed New Light on Human Past," WSJ, October 2, 2009).
21. M. Scheler, *The Human Place in the Cosmos* (Northwestern University Press, 2009).
22. See the work of Bonnie Bassler discussed in "Deep Inside Bacteria, a Germ of Human Personality."
23. See the remarkable essays by Bataille and Caillois et al. in *College of Sociology (1937-39)*, ed. Denis Hollier (Minneapolis, MN: University of Minnesota Press, 1988).
24. Is the myth of caesaro-papalism dead? Tolkien's LotR clearly plays on the theme. A basic storyline is the transformation of Gandalf the wizard from a St. Francis type figure to papal figure, complete with exorcisms of an Antichrist and a call to Caesar to wield the sword.
25. M. Scheler, *On the Eternal in Man* (Transaction, 2009).
26. C. Schmitt, *Political Theology II*, (Cambridge: Polity, 2008), pp. 128-9.

Appendix

THE "SUMMA THEOLOGICA" OF ST. THOMAS AQUINAS*
PART II. *(SECOND PART)*

QUESTION LXIV.

OF MURDER.

(In Eight Articles.)

IN due sequence we must consider the vices opposed to commutative justice. We must consider (1) those sins that are committed in relation to involuntary commutations: (2) those that are committed with regard to voluntary commutations. Sins are committed in relation to involuntary commutations by doing an injury to one's neighbour against his will: and this can be done in two ways, namely by deed or by word. By deed when one's neighbour is injured either in his own person, or in a person connected with him, or in his possessions.

We must therefore consider these points in due order, and in the first place we shall consider murder whereby a man inflicts the greatest injury on his neighbour. Under this head there are eight points of inquiry: (1) Whether it is a sin to kill dumb animals or even plants? (2)Whether it is lawful to kill a sinner? (3) Whether this is lawful to a private individual, or to a public person only? (4) Whether this is lawful to a cleric? (5) Whether it is lawful to kill oneself? (6) Whether it is lawful to kill a just

* Literally translated by Fathers of the English Dominican Province and Published by Burns Oates & Washbourne Ltd., Publishers to the Holy See, 1929.

man? (7) Whether it is lawful to kill a man in self-defence? (8) Whether accidental homicide is a mortal sin?

FIRST ARTICLE.

WHETHER IT IS UNLAWFUL TO KILL ANY LIVING THING?

We proceed thus to the First Article:—

Objection 1. It would seem unlawful to kill any living fling. For the Apostle says (Rom. xiii. 2): *They that resist the ordinance of God pur-chase to themselves damnation.** Now Divine providence has ordained that all living things should be preserved, according to Ps. cxlvi. 8, 9, *Who maketh grass to grow on the mountains . . ., Who giveth to beasts their food.* Therefore it seems unlawful to take the life of any living thing.

Obj. 2. Further, Murder is a sin because it deprives a man of life. Now life is common to all animals and plants. Hence for the same reason it is apparently a sin to slay dumb animals and plants.

Obj. 3. Further, In the Divine law a special punishment is not appointed save for a sin. Now a special punishment had to be inflicted, according to the Divine law, on one who killed another man's ox or sheep (Exod. xxii. 1). Therefore the slaying of dumb animals is a sin.

On the contrary, Augustine says (*De Civ. Dei* i. 20): *When we hear it said, ' Thou shalt not kill,' we do not take it as referring to trees, for they have no sense, nor to irrational animals, because they have no fel-lowship with us. Hence it follows that the words, ' Thou shalt not kill' refer to the killing of a man.*

I answer that, There is no sin in using a thing for the purpose for which it is. Now the order of things is such that the imperfect are for the perfect, even as in the process of generation nature proceeds from imperfection to perfection. Hence it is that just as in the generation of a man there is first a living thing, then an animal, and lastly a man, so too things, like the plants, which merely have life, are all alike for animals, and all animals are for man. Wherefore it is not unlawful if man use plants for the good of animals, and animals for the good of man, as the Philosopher states (*Polit.* i. 3).

---

* Vulg.,—*He that resisteth the power, resisteth the ordinance of God: and they that resist, purchase to themselves damnation.*

Now the most necessary use would seem to consist in the fact that animals use plants, and men use animals, for food, and this cannot be done unless these be deprived of life: wherefore it is lawful both to take life from plants for the use of animals, and from animals for the use of men. In fact this is in keeping with the commandment of God Himself: for it is written (Gen. i. 29, 30): *Behold I have given you every herb . . . and all trees . . . to be your meat, and to all beasts of the earth :* and again *(ibid.* ix. 3): *Everything that moveth and liveth shall be meat to you.*

Reply Obj. 1. According to the Divine ordinance the life of animals and plants is preserved not for themselves but for man. Hence, as Augustine says *(De Civ. Dei* i. 20), *by a most just ordinance of the Creator, both their life and their death are subject to our use.*

Reply Obj. 2. Dumb animals and plants are devoid of the life of reason whereby to set themselves in motion; they are moved, as it were by another, by a kind of natural impulse, a sign of which is that they are naturally enslaved and accommodated to the uses of others.

Reply Obj. 3. He that kills another's ox, sins, not through killing the ox, but through injuring another man in his property. Wherefore this is not a species of the sin of murder but of the sin of theft or robbery.

SECOND ARTICLE.

WHETHER IT IS LAWFUL TO KILL SINNERS ?

We proceed thus to the Second Article:—

Objection 1. It would seem unlawful to kill men who have sinned. For Our Lord in the parable (Matth. xiii.) forbade the uprooting of the cockle which denotes wicked men according to a gloss. Now whatever is forbidden by God is a sin. Therefore it is a sin to kill a sinner.

Obj. 2. Further, Human justice is conformed to Divine justice. Now according to Divine justice sinners are kept back for repentance, according to Ezech. xxxiii. n, / *desire not the death of the wicked, but that the wicked turn from his way and live.* Therefore it seems altogether unjust to kill sinners.

Obj. 3. Further, It is not lawful, for any good end whatever, to do that which is evil in itself, according to Augustine *(Contra Mendac.* vii.) and the Philosopher *(Ethic,* ii. 6). Now to kill a man is evil in itself, since we are bound to have charity towards all men, and *we- wish our friends to live and to exist,* according to *Ethic,* ix. 4. Therefore it is nowise lawful to kill a man who has sinned. *On the contrary,* It is written (Exod. xxii.

18): *Wizards thou shalt not suffer to live;* and (Ps. c. 8): *In the morning I put to death all the wicked of the land.*

I answer that, As stated above (A. 1), it is lawful to kill dumb animals, in so far as they are naturally directed to man's use, as the imperfect is directed to the perfect. Now every part is directed to the whole, as imperfect to perfect, wherefore every part is naturally for the sake of the whole. For this reason we observe that if the health of the whole body demands the excision of a member, through its being decayed or infectious to the other members, it will be both praiseworthy and advantageous to have it cut away. Now every individual person is compared to the whole community, as part to whole. Therefore if a man be dangerous and infectious to the community, on account of some sin, it is praiseworthy and advantageous that he be killed in order to safeguard the common good, since *a little leaven corrupteth the whole lump* (1 Cor. v. 6).

Reply Obj. 1. Our Lord commanded them to forbear from uprooting the cockle in order to spare the wheat, i.e. the good. This occurs when the wicked cannot be slain without the good being killed with them, either because the wicked lie hidden among the good, or because they have many followers, so that they cannot be killed without danger to the good, as Augustine says (*Contra Parmen.* iii. 2). Wherefore Our Lord teaches that we should rather allow the wicked to live, and that vengeance is to be delayed until the last judgment, rather than that the good be put to death together with the wicked. When, however, the good incur no danger, but rather are protected and saved by the slaying of the wicked, then the latter may be lawfully put to death.

Reply Obj. 2. According to the order of His wisdom, God sometimes slays sinners forthwith in order to deliver the good, whereas sometimes He allows them time to repent, according as He knows what is expedient for His elect. This also does human justice imitate according to its powers; for it puts to death those who are dangerous to others, while it allows time for repentance to those who sin without grievously harming others.

Reply Obj. 3. By sinning man departs from the order of reason, and consequently falls away from the dignity of his manhood, in so far as he is naturally free, and exists for himself, and he falls into the slavish state of the beasts, by being disposed of according as he is useful to others. This is expressed in Ps. xlviii. 21: *Man, when he was in honour, did not understand; he hath been compared to senseless beasts, and made like to them,* and Prov. xi. 29: *The fool shall serve the wise.* Hence, although it be evil in itself to kill a man so long as he preserve his dignity, yet it may be good to kill a man who has sinned, even as it is to kill a beast. For a bad man is worse than a beast, and is more harmful, as the Philosopher states (*Polit.* i. 1 and *Ethic,* vii. 6).

THIRD ARTICLE.

WHETHER IT IS LAWFUL FOR A PRIVATE INDIVIDUAL TO KILL A MAN WHO HAS SINNED?

We proceed thus to the Third Article:—

Objection 1. It would seem lawful for a private individual to kill a man who has sinned. For nothing unlawful is commanded in the Divine law. Yet, on account of the sin of the molten calf, Moses commanded (Exod. xxxii. 27): *Let every man kill his brother, and friend, and neighbour.* Therefore it is lawful for private individuals to kill a sinner.

Obj. 2. Further, As stated above (A. 2, *ad* 3), man, on account of sin, is compared to the beasts. Now it is lawful for any private individual to kill a wild beast, especially if it be harmful. Therefore for the same reason, it is lawful for any private individual to kill a man who has sinned.

Obj. 3. Further, A man, though, a private individual, deserves praise for doing what is useful for the common good. Now the slaying of evil-doers is useful for the common good, as stated above (A. 2). Therefore it is deserving of praise if even private individuals kill evildoers.

On the contrary, Augustine says (*De Civ. Dei* i.):* *A man who, without exercising public authority, kills an evildoer, shall be judged guilty of murder, and all the more, since he has dared to usurp a power which God has not given him.*

I answer that, As stated above (A. 2), it is lawful to kill an evildoer in so far as it is directed to the welfare of the whole community, so that it belongs to him alone who has charge of the community's welfare. Thus it belongs to a physician to cut off a decayed limb, when he has been entrusted with the care of the health of the whole body. Now the care of the common good is entrusted to persons of rank having public author-ity: wherefore they alone, and not private individuals, can lawfully put evildoers to death.

Reply Obj. 1. The person by whose authority a thing is done really does the thing, as Dionysius declares *(Cod. Hier.* iii.). Hence according to Augustine *(De Civ. Dei* i. 21), *He slays not who owes his service to*

* Can. *Quicumque penutit,* caus. xxiii., qu. 8.

one who commands him, even as a sword is merely the instrument to him that wields it. Wherefore those who, at the Lord's command, slew their neighbours and friends, would seem not to have done this themselves, but rather He by whose authority they acted thus: just as a soldier slays the foe by the authority of his sovereign, and the executioner slays the robber by the authority of the judge.

Reply Obj. 2. A beast is by nature distinct from man, wherefore in the case of a wild beast, there is no need for an authority to kill it; whereas, in the case of domestic animals, such authority is required, not for their sake, but on account of the owner's loss. On the other hand a man who has sinned is not by nature distinct from good men; hence a public authority is requisite in order to condemn him to death for the common good.

Reply Obj. 3. It is lawful for any private individual to do anything for the common good, provided it harm nobody: but if it be harmful to some other, it cannot be done, except by virtue of the judgment of the person to whom it pertains to decide what is to be taken from the parts for the welfare of the whole.

FOURTH ARTICLE.

WHETHER IT IS LAWFUL FOR CLERICS TO KILL EVILDOERS?

We proceed thus to the Fourth Article:—

Objection 1. It would seem lawful for clerics to kill evildoers. For clerics especially should fulfil the precept of the Apostle (1 Cor. iv. 16): *Be ye followers of me as I also am of Christ,* whereby we are called upon to imitate God and His saints. Now the very God Whom we worship puts evildoers to death, according to Ps. cxxxv. 10, *Who smote Egypt with their firstborn.* Again Moses made the Levites slay twenty-three thousand men on account of the worship of the calf (Exod. xxxii.), the priest Phinees slew the Israelite who went in to the woman of Madian (Num. xxv.), Samuel killed Agag king of Amalec (i Kings xv.), Elias slew the priests of Baal (3 Kings xviii.), Mathathias killed the man who went up to the altar to sacrifice (1 Mach. ii.); and, in the New Testament, Peter killed Ananias and Saphira (Acts v.). Therefore it seems that even clerics may kill evildoers.

Obj. 2. Further, Spiritual power is greater than the secular and is more united to God. Now the secular power as *God's minister* lawfully puts evildoers to death, according to Rom. xiii. 4. Much more therefore may clerics, who are God's ministers and have spiritual power, put evildoers to death.

Obj. 3. Further, Whosoever lawfully accepts an office, may lawfully exercise the functions of that office. Now it belongs to the princely office to slay evildoers, as stated above (A. 3). Therefore those clerics who are earthly princes may lawfully slay malefactors.

On the contrary, It is written (i Tim. iii. 2, 3): *It behoveth . . . a bishop to be without crime* * . . . *not given to wine, no striker.*

I answer that, It is unlawful for clerics to kill, for two reasons. First, because they are chosen for the ministry of the altar, whereon is represented the Passion of Christ slain *Who, when He was struck did not strike* ** (1 Pet. ii. 23). Therefore it becomes not clerics to strike or kill: for ministers should imitate their master, according to Ecclus. x. *2, As the judge of the people is himself, so also are his ministers.* The other reason is because clerics are entrusted with the ministry of the New Law, wherein no punishment of death or of bodily maiming is appointed: wherefore they should abstain from such things in order that they may be fitting ministers of the New Testament.

Reply Obj. 1. God works in all things without exception whatever is right, yet in each one according to its mode. Wherefore everyone should imitate God in that which is specially becoming to him. Hence, though God slays evildoers even corporally, it does not follow that all should imitate Him in this. As regards Peter, he did not put Ananias and Saphira to death by his own authority or with his own hand, but published their death sentence pronounced by God. The priests or Levites of the Old Testament were the ministers of the Old Law, which appointed corporal penalties, so that it was fitting for them to slay with their own hands.

Reply Obj. 2. The ministry of clerics is concerned with better things than corporal slayings, namely with things pertaining to spiritual welfare, and so it is not fitting for them to meddle with minor matters.

Reply Obj. 3. Ecclesiastical prelates accept the office of earthly princes, not that they may inflict capital punishment themselves, but that this may be carried into effect by others in virtue of their authority.

---

* Vulg.,—*Blameless. Without crime* is the reading in Tit. i. 7.
**Vulg.,—*When He suffered, He threatened not.*

FIFTH ARTICLE.

WHETHER IT IS LAWFUL TO KILL ONESELF?

We proceed thus to the Fifth Article:—

Objection 1. It would seem lawful for a man to kill himself. For murder is a sin in so far as it is contrary to justice. But no man can do an injustice to himself, as is proved in *Ethic.* v. ii. Therefore no man sins by killing himself.

Obj. 2. Further, It is lawful, for one who exercises public authority, to kill evildoers. Now he who exercises public authority is sometimes an evildoer. Therefore he may lawfully kill himself.

Obj. 3. Further, It is lawful for a man to suffer spontaneously a lesser danger that he may avoid a greater: thus it is lawful for a man to cut off a decayed limb even from himself, that he may save his whole body. Now sometimes a man, by killing himself, avoids a greater evil, for example an unhappy life, or the shame of sin. Therefore a man may kill himself.

Obj. 4. Further, Samson killed himself, as related in Judges xvi., and yet he is numbered among the saints (Heb. xi.). Therefore it is lawful for a man to kill himself.

Obj. 5. Further, It is related (2 Mach. xiv. 42) that a certain Razias killed himself, *choosing to die nobly rather than to fall into the hands of the wicked, and to suffer abuses unbecoming his noble birth.* Now nothing that is done nobly and bravely is unlawful. Therefore suicide is not unlawful.

On the contrary, Augustine says *(De Civ. Dei* i. 20): *Hence it follows that the words 'Thou shalt not kill' refer to the killing of a man;—not another man; therefore, not even thyself. For he who kills himself, kills nothing else than a man.*

I answer that, It is altogether unlawful to kill oneself, for three reasons. First, because everything naturally loves itself, the result being that everything naturally keeps itself in being, and resists corruptions so far as it can. Wherefore suicide is contrary to the inclination of nature, and to charity whereby every man should love himself. Hence suicide is always a mortal sin, as being contrary to the natural law and to charity.

Secondly, because every part, as such, belongs to the whole. Now every man is part of the community, and so, as such, he belongs to the community. Hence by killing himself he injures the community, as the Philosopher declares (*Ethic,* v. 11).

Thirdly, because life is God's gift to man, and is subject to His power, Who kills and makes to live. Hence whoever takes his own life, sins against God, even as he who kills another's slave, sins against that slave's master, and as he who usurps to himself judgment of a matter not entrusted to him. For it belongs to God alone to pronounce sentence of death and life, according to Deut. xxxii. 39, *I will kill and I will make to live.*

Reply Obj. 1. Murder is a sin, not only because it is contrary to justice, but also because it is opposed to charity which a man should have towards himself: in this respect suicide is a sin in relation to oneself. In relation to the community and to God, it is sinful, by reason also of its opposition to justice.

Reply Obj. 2. One who exercises public authority may lawfully put to death an evildoer, since he can pass judgment on him. But no man is judge of himself. Wherefore it is not lawful for one who exercises public authority to put himself to death for any sin whatever: although he may lawfully commit himself to the judgment of others.

Reply Obj. 3. Man is made master of himself through his free-will: wherefore he can lawfully dispose of himself as to those matters which pertain to this life which is ruled by man's free-will. But the passage from this life to another and happier one is subject not to man's free-will but to the power of God. Hence it is not lawful for man to take his own life that he may pass to a happier life, nor that he may escape any unhappiness whatsoever of the present life, because the ultimate and most fearsome evil of this life is death, as the Philosopher states *(Ethic,* iii. 6). Therefore to bring death upon oneself in order to escape the other afflictions of this life, is to adopt a greater evil in order to avoid a lesser. In like manner it is unlawful to take one's own life on account of one's having committed a sin, both because by so doing one does oneself a very great injury, by depriving oneself of the time needful for repentance, and because it is not lawful to slay an evildoer except by the sentence of the public authority. Again it is unlawful for a woman to kill herself lest she be violated, because she ought not to commit on herself the very great sin of suicide, to avoid the lesser sin of another. For she commits no sin in being violated by force, provided she does not consent, since *without consent of the mind there is no stain on the body,* as the Blessed Lucy declared. Now it is evident that fornication and adultery are less grievous sins than taking a man's, especially one's own, life: since the latter is most grievous, because one injures oneself, to whom one owes the greatest love. Moreover it is most dangerous since no time is left wherein to expiate it by repentance. Again it is not lawful for anyone to take his own life for fear he should consent to sin, because *evil must not be done that good may come* (Rom. iii. 8) or that evil may be avoided, especially if the evil be of small account and an uncertain event for it is uncertain whether one will at some future time consent to a sin, since God is able to deliver man from sin under any temptation whatever.

Reply Obj. 4. As Augustine says *(De Civ. Dei* i. 21), *not even Samson is to be excused that he crushed himself together with his enemies under the ruins of the house, except the Holy Ghost, Who had wrought many wonders through him, had secretly commanded him to do this.* He assigns the same reason in the case of certain holy women, who at the time of persecution took their own lives, and who are commemorated by the Church.

Reply Obj. 5. It belongs to fortitude that a man does not shrink from being slain by another, for the sake of the good of virtue, and that he may avoid sin. But that a man take stated him to be guilty. He that carries out the sentence of the judge who has condemned an innocent man, if the sentence contains an inexcusable error, he should not obey, else there would be an excuse for the executions of the martyrs: if however it contain no manifest injustice, he does not sin by carrying out the sentence, because he has no right to discuss the judgment of his superior; nor is it he who slays the innocent man, but the judge whose minister he is.

SEVENTH ARTICLE.

WHETHER IT IS LAWFUL TO KILL A MAN IN SELF-DEFENCE?

We proceed thus to the Seventh Article:—

Objection 1. It would seem that nobody may lawfully kill a man in self-defence. For Augustine says to Publicola *(Ep.* xlvii.): *I do not agree with the opinion that one may kill a man lest one be killed by him; unless one be a soldier, or exercise a public office, so that one does it not for oneself but for others, having the power to do so, provided it be in keeping with one's person.* Now he who kills a man in self-defence, kills him lest he be killed by him. Therefore this would seem to be unlawful.

Obj. 2. Further, He says *(De Lib. Arb.* i. 5): *How are they free from sin in sight of Divine providence, who are guilty of taking a man's life for the sake of these contemptible things?* Now among contemptible things he reckons *those which men may forfeit unwillingly,* as appears from the context (*ibid.*): and the chief of these is the life of the body. Therefore it is unlawful for any man to take another's life for the sake of the life of his own body.

Obj. 3. Further, Pope Nicolas* says in the Decretals: *Concerning the clerics about whom you have consulted Us, those, namely, who have killed a pagan in self-defence, as to whether, after making amends by repenting, they may return to their former state, or rise to a higher degree; know that in no case is it lawful for them to kill any man under any circumstances whatever.* Now clerics and laymen are alike bound to observe the moral precepts. Therefore neither is it lawful for laymen to kill anyone in self-defence.

Obj. 4. Further, Murder is a more grievous sin than fornication or adultery. Now nobody may lawfully commit simple fornication or adultery or any other mortal sin in order to save his own life; since the spiritual life is to be preferred to the life of the body. Therefore no man may lawfully take another's life in self-defence in order to save his own life.

Obj. 5. Further, If the tree be evil, so is the fruit, according to Matth. vii. 17. Now self-defence itself seems to be unlawful, according to Rom. xii. 19: *Not defending* (Douay,—*revenging) yourselves, my dearly beloved.* Therefore its result, which is the slaying of a man, is also unlawful.

On the contrary, It is written (Exod. xxii. 2): *If a thief be found breaking into a house or undermining it, and be wounded so as to die; he that slew him shall not be guilty of blood.* Now it is much more lawful to defend one's life than one's house. Therefore neither is a man guilty of murder if he kill another in defence of his own life.

I answer that, Nothing hinders one act from having two effects, only one of which is intended, while the other is beside the intention. Now moral acts take their species according to what is intended, and not according to what is beside the intention, since this is accidental as explained above *(Q. XLIIL, A. 3: I.-II, Q. LXXIL, A. 1).* Accordingly the act of self defence may have two effects, one is the saving of one's life, the other is the slaying of the aggressor. Therefore this act, since one's intention is to save one's own life, is not unlawful, seeing that it is natural to everything to keep itself in *being,* as far as possible. And yet, though proceeding from a good intention, an act may be tendered unlawful, if it be out of proportion to the end. Wherefore if a man, in self-defence, uses more than necessary violence, it will be unlawful: whereas if he repel force

* Nicolas I. Dist. 1., can. *De his clericis.*

with moderation his defence will be lawful, because according to the jurists,* *it is lawful to repel force by force, provided one does not exceed the limits of a blameless defence.* Nor is it necessary for salvation that a man omit the act of moderate self-defence in order to avoid killing the other man, since one is bound to take more care of one's own life than of another's. But as it is unlawful to take a man's life, except for the public authority acting for the common good, as stated above (A. 3), it is not lawful for a man to intend killing a man in self-defence, except for such as have public authority, who while intending to kill a man in self-defence, refer this to the public good, as in the case of a soldier fighting against the foe, and in the minister of the judge struggling with robbers, although even these sin if they be moved by private animosity.

Reply Obj. 1. The words quoted from Augustine refer to the case when one man intends to kill another to save himself from death. The passage quoted in the *Second Objection* is to be understood in the same sense. Hence he says pointedly, *for the sake of these things,* whereby he indicates the intention. This suffices for the *Reply* to the *Second Objection.*

Reply Obj. 3. Irregularity results from the act though sinless of taking a man's life, as appears in the case of a judge who justly condemns a man to death. For this reason a cleric, though he kill a man in self-defence, is irregular, albeit he intends not to kill him, but to defend himself.

Reply Obj. 4. The act of fornication or adultery is not necessarily directed to the preservation of one's own life, as is the act whence sometimes results the taking of a man's life.

Reply Obj. 5. The defence forbidden in this passage is that which comes from revengeful spite. Hence a gloss says: *Not defending your-selves,—that is, not striking your enemy back.*

EIGHTH ARTICLE.

WHETHER ONE IS GUILTY OF MURDER THROUGH KILLING SOMEONE BY CHANCE?

We proceed thus to the Eighth Article:—

Objection 1. It would seem that one is guilty of murder through killing someone by chance. For we read (Gen. iv. 23, 24) that Lamech slew a

---

* Cap. *Significasti, De Homicid. volunt. vel casual.* 11. ii. 2, 14.

man in mistake for a wild beast,* and that he was accounted guilty of murder. Therefore one incurs the guilt of murder through killing a man by chance.

Obj. 2. Further, It is written (Exod. xxi. 22): *If . . . one strike a woman with child, and she miscarry indeed . . ., if her death ensue thereupon, he shall render life for life.* Yet this may happen without any intention of causing her death. Therefore one is guilty of murder through killing someone by chance.

Obj. 3. Further, The Decretals** contain several canons prescribing penalties for unintentional homicide. Now penalty is not due save for guilt. Therefore he who kills a man by chance, incurs the guilt of murder.

On the contrary, Augustine says to Publicola *(Ep.* xlvii.): *When we do a thing for a good and lawful purpose, if thereby we unintentionally cause harm to anyone, it should by no means be imputed to us.* Now it sometimes happens by chance that a person is killed as a result of something done for a good purpose. Therefore the person who did it is not accounted guilty.

I answer that, According to the Philosopher *(Phys.* ii. 6) *chance is a cause that acts beside one's intention.* Hence chance happenings, strictly speaking, are neither intended nor voluntary. And since every sin is voluntary, according to Augustine *(De Vera Relig.* xiv.) it follows that chance happenings, as such, are not sins.

Nevertheless it happens that what is not actually and directly voluntary and intended, is voluntary and intended accidentally, according as that which removes an obstacle js called an accidental cause. Wherefore he who does not remove something whence homicide results whereas he ought to remove it, is in a sense guilty of voluntary homicide. This happens in two ways: first when a man causes another's death through occupying himself with unlawful things which he ought to avoid: secondly, when he does not take sufficient care. Hence, according to jurists, if a man pursue a lawful occupation and take due care, the result being that a person loses his life, he is not guilty of that person's death: whereas if he be occupied with something unlawful, or even with something lawful, but without due care, he does not escape being guilty of murder, if his action results in someone's death.

---

* The text of the Bible does not say so, but this was the Jewish traditional commentary on Gen. iv. 23.
** Dist. l.

Reply Obj. 1. Lamech did not take sufficient care to avoid taking a man's life: and so he was not excused from being guilty of homicide.

Reply Obj. 2. He that strikes a woman with child does something unlawful: wherefore if there results the death either of the woman or of the animated foetus, he will not be excused from homicide, especially seeing that death is the natural result of such a blow.

Reply Obj. 3. According to the canons a penalty is inflicted on those who cause death unintentionally, through doing something unlawful, or failing to take sufficient care.

Bibliography

Books

Anscombe, G.E.M. *The Collected Philosophical Papers of G.E.M. Anscombe, Vol. III: Ethics, Religion and Politics*. Minneapolis, MN: University of Minnesota Press, 1981.

Anscombe, G.E.M. *Ethics, Religion, and Politics*. Minneapolis, MN: University of Minnesota Press, 1981.

Aquinas, Thomas. *De Malo*. Oxford: Oxford University Press, 2001.

Arendt, Hannah. *Eichmann in Jerusalem*. London: Penguin, 1994.

Arkes, Hadley. *Natural Rights and the Right to Choose*. Cambridge: Cambridge University Press, 2002.

St. Augustine. *City of God*. London: Penguin, 1984.

St. Augustine. *Confessions*. London: Penguin, 1961.

Austin, John. *The Province of Jurisprudence Determined*. Cambridge: Cambridge University Press, 2001.

Bacevich, Andrew, and Eliot Cohen, eds. *War Over Kosovo*. New York: Columbia University Press, 2001.

Bakunin, Mikhail. *Statism and Anarchy*. Cambridge: Cambridge University Press, 2005.

Balazs, Zoltan and Dunlop, Francis. *Exploring the World of Human Practice: Readings in and about the Philosophy of Aurel Kolnai*. Budapest: Central European University Press, 2004.

von Balthasar, Hans Urs. *Dare We Hope "That All Men be Saved"?* San Francisco, CA: Ignatius Press, 1988.

Bañez, Dominicus. *Scholastica commentaria in primam partem angelici doctoris D. Thomae Aquinatis*. Venice: 1591.

Bendersky, Joseph. *Carl Schmitt: Theorist for the Reich*. Princeton, NJ: Princeton University Press, 1983.

Benedict XVI. *Deus Caritas Est*. December 25, 2005.

Bentham, Jeremy. *A Fragment on Government*. Cambridge: Cambridge University Press, 2001.

Berman, Harold. *Law and Revolution: The Formation of the Western Legal Tradition*. Cambridge, MA: Harvard University Press, 1983.

Berti, Giovanni. *De Theologicis Disciplinis*. Venice: Remondini, 1792.

Blackstone, William. *Commentaries on the Laws of England*. Philadelphia, PA: Rees Welsh & Company, 1902.

Bodin, Jean. *On Sovereignty*. Cambridge: Cambridge University Press, 2004.

St. Bonaventure. *The Journey of the Mind of God*. Indianapolis, IN: Hackett, 1993.

Braaten, Carl, and Christopher Seitz, eds. *I Am the Lord Your God: Christian Reflections on the Ten Commandments*. Grand Rapids, MI: Eerdmans, 2005.

Bryden, Alan, and Marina Caparini. *Private Actors and Security Governance*. Zurich: LIT, 2006.

Buckley, William J., ed. *Kosovo: Contending Voices on Balkan Interventions*. Grand Rapids, MI: Eerdmans, 2000.

Burke, Edmund. *Pre-Revolutionary Writings*. Cambridge: Cambridge University Press, 1993.

Calhoun, George. *The Growth of Criminal Law in Ancient Greece*. Westport, CT: Greenwood Press, 1973.

Camus, Albert. *The Rebel*. New York: Vintage, 1991.

Camus, Albert. *Resistance, Rebellion, and Death*. New York: Alfred A. Knopf, 1961.

Capreolus, John. *On Virtue*. Washington, DC: The Catholic University of America Press, 2001.

Charles, Daryl. *Retrieving the Natural Law*. Grand Rapids, MI: Eerdmans, 2008.

Churchill, Winston. *A Roving Commission*. New York, NY: Charles Scribner's Sons, 1930.

Cicero. *Murder Trials*. London: Penguin, 1990.

Cohen, Edward. *Ancient Athenian Maritime Courts*. Princeton, NJ: Princeton University Press, 1973.

Cohen, Gerry. *If You're So Egalitarian, How Come You're So Rich?* Cambridge, MA: Harvard University Press, 2000.

Congregation for the Doctrine of the Faith. *Dominus Iesus*. Boston, MA: Pauline Books and Media, 2002.

Coleman, Jules and Scott Shapiro, eds. *The Oxford Handbook of Jurisprudence and Philosophy of Law*. Oxford: Oxford University Press, 2004.

Cordesman, Anthony. *The Lessons and Non-Lessons of the Air and Missile Campaign in Kosovo*. Wesport, CT: Praeger, 2001.

Cuneo, Terence, and René van Woudenberg, eds. *The Cambridge Companion to Thomas Reid*. Cambridge: Cambridge University Press, 2004.

Curran, Charles. *The Moral Theology of Pope Paul II*. Washington, DC: Georgetown University Press, 2005.

Dellapenna, Joseph W. *Dispelling the Myths of Abortion History*. Durham, NC: Carolina Academic Press, 2006.

Delsol, Chantal. *Icarus Fallen*. Wilmington, DE: Intercollegiate Studies Institute, 2003.

Donaldson, Thomas and Thomas Dunfee. *The Ties That Bind*. Cambridge, MA: Harvard Business School Press, 1999.

Dulles, Avery. *The Splendor of Faith*. New York, N.Y.: Crossroads, 1999.

Duphinais, Michael and Matthew Levering, eds. *John Paul II & St. Thomas Aquinas*. Ann Arbor, MI: Sapientia Press, 2006.

Dworkin, Ronald. *A Matter of Principle*. Oxford: Oxford University Press, 1986.

Fassard, Gaston. *Par-delà le fascisme et le communisme*. Paris: FNAC, 1945.

Ferguson, Niall. *Colossus: The Rise and Fall of the American Empire*. London: Penguin, 2005.

Finnis, John. *Aquinas: Moral, Political and Legal Theory*. Oxford: Oxford University Press, 1998.

Finnis, John. *Moral Absolutes*. Washington, DC: The Catholic University Press of America, 1991.

Finnis, John. *Natural Law and Natural Rights*. Oxford: Oxford University Press, 1980.

Friedman, M. *Double Jeopardy*. Oxford: Oxford University Press, 1969.

Frings, Manfred. *The Mind of Max Scheler*. Milwaukee, WI: Marquette University Press, 1997.

Gagarin, Michael. *Drakon and Early Athenian Homicide Law*. New Haven, CT: Yale University Press, 1981.

Giles of Rome. *On Ecclesiastical Power*. In *Medieval Political Philosophy*, edited by Ralph Lerner and Muhsin Mahdi, 391-401. Ithaca, NY: Cornell University Press, 1983.

Glover, Johnathan. *Humanity: A Moral History of the Twentieth Century*. New Haven, CT: Yale University Press, 2000.

Gratian. *The Treatise on Laws*. Washington, DC: The Catholic University of America Press, 1993.

Griswold, Charles. "Imagination: Morals, Science, and Arts." In *The Cambridge Companion to Adam Smith* edited by Knud Haakonssen. Cambridge: Cambridge University Press, 2006.

Haakonssen, Knud. *The Science of a Legislator*. Cambridge: Cambridge University Press, 1989.

Harro, Höpfl. *Jesuit Political Thought*. Cambridge: Cambridge University Press, 2004.

Herodotus. *The History*. Chicago, IL: The University of Chicago Press, 1987.

Hibbs, Thomas. *Aquinas, Ethics, and Philosophy of Religion: Metaphysics and Practice*. Bloomington, IN: Indiana University Press, 2007.

Hittinger, Russell. *The First Grace: Rediscovering the Natural Law in a Post-Christian World*. Wilmington, DE: Intercollegiate Studies Institute, 2003.

Hösle, Vittorio. *Morals and Politics*. Notre Dame, IN: University of Notre Dame Press, 2004.

Hösle, Vittorio. *Objective Idealism, Ethics, and Politics*. South Bend, IN: St. Augustine's Press, 1998.

Huizinga, John. *The Waning of the Middle Ages*. New York: Dover Publications, 1999.

Ignatieff, Michael. *Virtual War: Kosovo and Beyond*. London: Chatto & Windus, 2000.

The Independent International Commission on Kosovo. *The Kosovo Report*. Oxford: Oxford University Press, 2000.

King James I/VI. *Political Writings*. Cambridge: Cambridge University Press, 1994.

John Paul II. *Dives in misericordia*. November 30, 1980.

John Paul II. *Reconciliatio et Paenitentia*. December 2, 1984.

John Paul II. *Evangelium Vitae*. March 25, 1995.

John Paul II. *Fides et Ratio*. September 14, 1998.

John Paul II. *Man and Woman He Created Them: A Theology of the Body*. Boston, MA: Pauline Books & Media, 2006.

Jeffreys, Derek. *Defending Human Dignity: John Paul II and Political Realism*. Grand Rapids, MI: Brazos Press, 2004.

Journet, Charles. *The Meaning of Evil*. New York, NY: P.J. Kennedy & Sons, 1963.

Kagan, Robert. *Imperial Grunts*. New York, NY: Random House, 2005.

Kant, Immanuel. *Lectures on Ethics*. Indianapolis, IN: Hackett, 1963.

Kaplan, Robert. *The Coming Anarchy*. New York, NY: Vintage, 2001.

Keegan, John. *The Illustrated Face of Battle*. New York, NY: Viking, 1989.

Kerr, Fergus. *Twentieth-Century Catholic Theologians*. Oxford: Blackwell, 2007.

Kladstrup, Donald & Petie. *Wine and War*. New York, NY: Broadway, 2002.

Kolnai, Aurel. *Disgust*. Chicago, I.L.: Open Court, 2004.

Kolnai, Aurel, *Early Ethical Writings of Aurel Kolnai*. Aldershot: Ashgate, 2002.

Kolnai, Aurel. *Ethics, Value, and Reality*. New Brunswick, NJ: Transaction Publishers, 2008.

Kraynak, Robert. *Christian Faith and Modern Democracy*. Notre Dame, IN: University of Notre Dame, 2001.

Lefort, Claude. *The Political Forms of Modern Society*. Cambridge, MA: The MIT Press, 1986.

Levering, Matt. *Biblical Natural Law*. Oxford: Oxford University Press, 2008.

Levering, Matthew. *Christ's Fulfillment of Torah and Temple*. Notre Dame, IN: University of Notre Dame Press, 2002.

Levi, Anthony. *Cardinal Richelieu and the Making of France*. New York, NY: Carroll & Graf, 2000.

de Lubac, Henri. *The Drama of Atheistic Humanism*. London: Sheed & Ward, 1949.

MacIntyre, Alasdair. *After Virtue*. Nortre Dame, IN: University of Notre Dame, 1981.

MacIntyre, Alasdair. *Dependent Rational Animals*. Chicago, IL: Open Court, 1999.

Malthus, Thomas. *An Essay on the Principle of Population*. Cambridge: Cambridge University Press, 1992.

Manent, Pierre. *A World beyond Politics?* Princeton, NJ: Princeton University Press, 2006.

Manent, Pierre. *The City of Man*. Princeton, NJ: Princeton University Press, 1997.

Marcin, Raymond. *In Search of Schopenhauer's Cat: Arthur Schopenhauer's Quantum-Mystical Theory of Justice*. Washington, DC: The Catholic University of America Press, 2006.

Maritain, Jacques. *Man and the State*. Washington DC: The Catholic University of America Press, 1998.

McAleer, Graham J. *Ecstatic Morality and Sexual Politics: A Catholic and Antitotalitarian Theory of the Body*. New York, NY: Fordham University Press, 2005.

Milbank, John. *Truth in Aquinas*. London: Routledge, 2001.

Miller, William. *Eye for an Eye*. Cambridge: Cambridge University Press, 2005.

Moore, Michael S. *Act and Crime: The Theory of Action and Its Implications for Criminal Law*. Oxford: Oxford University Press, 1993.

Moore, Michael S. *Educating Oneself in Public: Critical Essays in Jurisprudence*. Oxford: Oxford University Press, 2000.

Moore, Michael S. "Good without God," in *Natural Law, Liberalism, and Morality*, edited by Robert George, 251-259. Oxford: Oxford University Press, 1996.

Moore, Michael S. *Placing Blame: A General Theory of Criminal Law*. Oxford: Oxford University Press, 1998.

Nemo, Philippe. *What is the West?* Pittsburgh, PA: Duquesne University Press, 2006.

Neuhaus, Richard John. *End of Democracy?* Dallas, TX: Spence Publishing Company, 1997.

Neuhaus, Richard John. *The Naked Public Square: Religion and Democracy in America*. Grand Rapids, MI: Eerdmans, 1984.

Nietzsche, Friedrich. *Genealogy of Morals*. Oxford: Oxford University Press, 1996.

Nota S.J., John. *Max Scheler: The Man and His Work*. Chicago, IL: Franciscan Herald Press, 1983.

O'Donovan, Oliver. *The Just War Revisited*. Cambridge: Cambridge University Press, 2003.

Pinckaers, Servais. *The Sources of Christian Ethics*. Washington, DC: The Catholic University of America Press, 1995.

Plotinus. *The Enneads*. London: Penguin, 1991.

Proudhon, Pierre-Joseph. *What is Property?* Cambridge: Cambridge University Press, 2007.

Rager, John. *Bellarmine and Democracy*. Shelbyville, IN: Qualityprint, 1926.

Rahner, Karl. *Theological Investigations* vol. 1. Baltimore, MD: Helicon Books, 1965.

Ratzinger, Joseph. *Values in a Time of Upheaval*. San Francisco, CA: Ignatius, 2006.

Ricoeur, Paul and Rico, Paul. *Figuring the Sacred*. Minneapolis, MN: Fortress Press, 1995.

Rowland, Tracey. *Culture and the Thomist Tradition: After Vatican II*. London: Routledge, 2003.

Salmond, John. *Jurisprudence*. 12th ed. London: Sweet & Maxwell, 1966.

Scheler, Max. *On the Eternal in Man*. New Brunswick, NJ: Transaction Publishers, 2010.

Scheler, Max. *Nature of Sympathy*. New Brunswick, NJ: Transaction Publishers, 2007.

Scheler, Max. *Ressentiment*. Milwaukee, WI: Marquette University Press, 2003.

Scheuerman, William. *Carl Schmitt: The End of Law*. Lanham, MD: Rowan & Littlefield, 1999.

Schmitt, Carl. *The Theory of the Partisan: A Commentary/Remark on the Concept of the Political*. East Lansing, MI: Michigan State University Press. http://www.msupress.msu.edu/journals/cr/schmitt.

Schmitt, Carl. *The Concept of the Political*. Chicago, IL: The University of Chicago Press, 1996.

Schmitt, Carl. *Four Articles*. Washington, DC: Plutarch Press, 1999.

Schmitt, Carl. *Land and Sea*. Washington, DC: Plutarch Press, 1997.

Schmitt, Carl. *The Leviathan in the State Theory of Thomas Hobbes: Meaning and Failure of a Political Symbol*. Westport, CT: Greenwood Press, 1996.

Schmitt, Carl. *Three Types of Juristic Thought*. Westport, CT: Praeger, 2004.

Schmitt, Carl. *The Tyranny of Values*. Corvallis, OR: Plutarch Press, 1996.

Schmitt, Carl. *War/Non-War?* Corvallis, OR: Plutarch Press, 2004.

Schnabel, Albrecht and Ramesh Thakur, eds. *Kosovo and the Challenge of Humanitarian Intervention*. Tokyo: United Nations University Press, 2000.

Schulz, Fritz. *History of Roman Legal Science*. Oxford: Oxford University Press, 1946.

Scott, Peter and William Cavanaugh, eds. *Blackwell Companion to Political Theology*.

Scruton, Roger. *The Meaning of Conservatism*. South Bend, IN: St. Augustine's Press, 2002.

Scruton, Roger. *The West and the Rest*. Wilmington, DE: ISI, 2002.

Simpson, A.W. Brian. *Cannibalism and the Common Law*. Chicago, IL: The University of Chicago Press, 1984.

Singer, Peter. *Animal Liberation*. New York: HarperCollins, 1975.

Singer, Peter. *A Darwinian Left: Politics, Evolution and Cooperation*. New Haven, CT: Yale University Press, 1999.

Singer, Peter. *Rethinking Life and Death: The Collapse of Our Traditional Ethics*. New York, NY: St. Martin's Press, 1994.

Smith, Adam. *Lectures on Jurisprudence*. Indianapolis, IN: Liberty Fund, 1982.

Smith, Wesley. *The Culture of Death*. San Fransisco, CA: Encounter Books, 2000.

Smith, Wesley. *Forced Exit*. New York, NY: Random House, 1997.

Sokolowski, Robert. *Moral Action: A Phenomenological Study*. Bloomington, IN: Indiana University Press, 1985.

Spencer, Herbert. *The Principles of Ethics*. New York, N.: D. Appleton & Co., 1910.

St. Anthony of Florence. *Summae Sacrae Theologiae, iuris pontificii et Caesarei*. Venice, 1571.

Staude, John. *Max Scheler: And Intellectual Portrait*. New York, NY: The Free Press, 1967.

Steyn, Mark. *America Alone: The End of the World as We Know It*. New York, NY: Regnery, 2006.

Stirner, Max. *The Ego and Its Own*. Cambridge: Cambridge University Press, 2005.

de la Taille, Maurice. *The Hypostatic Union and Created Actuation by Uncreated Act*. West Baden Springs, IN: Wed Baden College, 1952.

Talmon, Jacob. *The Origins of Totalitarian Democracy*. New York, NY: W.W. Norton & Co., 1970.

Thomas, George. *Double Jeopardy: The History, the Law*. New York, NY: New York University Press, 1998.

Todd, Olivier. *Albert Camus: A Life*. New York, NY: Alfred A. Knopf, 1997.

Tolkien, J.R.R. *The Fellowship of the Ring*. Boston, MA: Houghton Mifflin Company, 1994.

Uniacke, Suzanne. *Permissible Killing: The Self-Defence Justification of Homicide*. Cambridge: Cambridge University Press, 1994.

Waldon, Jeremy. *God, Locke, and Equality*. Cambridge: Cambridge University Press, 2002.

Weigel, George. *A Witness to Hope*. New York, NY: Cliff Street Books, 1999.

Wiggins, David. *Needs, Values, Truth*. Oxford: Oxford University Press, 1998.

Yoo, John. *The Powers of War and Peace: The Constitution and Foreign Affairs after 9/11*. Chicago, IL: The University of Chicago Press, 2005.

Yoo, John. *War by Other Means*. New York, NY: Atlantic Monthly Press, 2006.

Articles

Akinrinade, Babafemi. "International Humanitarian Law and the Conflict in Sierra Leone." *Notre Dame Journal of Law, Ethics & Public Policy* 15, no. 2 (2001), 391-454.

Annas, George. "Conjoined Twins—The Limits of Law at the Limits of Life." *New England Journal of Medicine* 344: no. 14 (2001): 1104-1108.

Annas, George. "Siamese Twins: Killing One to Save the Other." *Hastings Center Report* 27, no. 2 (1987): 27-29.

Arkes, Hadley. "Letter to the Editor." *The Wall Street Journal*, May 17, 2007, sec. A.

Banat, Amanda Bryant. "Solving the Problem of Conflict Diamonds in Sierra Leone: Proposed Market Theories and International Legal Requirements for Certification of Origin." *Arizona Journal of International and Comparative Law* 19, no. 3 (2002): 939-974.

Barilan, Michael. "One or Two: An Examination of the Recent Case of the Conjoined Twins from Malta." *Journal of Medicine and Philosophy* 28, no. 11 (2003): 27-44.

Benedict XVI. *Homily at the Mass for the Election of the Supreme Pontiff*. April 2005.

Benedict XVI. *University of Regensburg Address*. September 12, 2006.

Bonino, Serge-Thomas. "Nature and Grace in *Deus Caritas Est*." *Nova et Vetera: The English Edition of the International Theological Journal* 5, no. 2 (2007): 231-248.

Bottum, Joseph. "Christians and the Death Penalty." *First Things* (August/September, 2005).

Bottum, Joseph. "The New Fusionism." *First Things*, June/July 2005: 32-6.

Bowring, Philip. "The West Ignores Low Birthrates at Its Peril." *International Herald Tribune*. October 23, 2004.

Chua Soo Meng, Jude. "Garrigou-Lagrange on Aristotle and Aquinas." *Modern Schoolman* 78, (2000): 71-87.

Congregation for the Doctrine of the Faith. "Worthiness to Receive Holy Communion: General Principles." June 2004.

Cook, Martin. "'Immaculate War': Constraints on Humanitarian Intervention." *Ethics and International Affairs* 14, no. 1 (2000): 55-66.

Cook, Martin. "Moral Foundations of Military Service." *Parameters: US Army War College* 30, (Spring 2000): 117-130.

Dunlop, Francis. "Scheler's Theory of Punishment." *Journal of the British Society for Phenomenology* 9, (1978): 167-174.

Epstein, Richard. "Trust Busters on the Supreme Court." *The Wall Street Journal*. July 12, 2006.

Fonte, John. "Liberal Democracy vs. Transnational Progressivism: The Future of the Ideological Civil War within the West." *Hudson Institute* Orbis, (Summer 2002).

Glendinning, Lee. "Diamonds Whose Price is Measured in Blood." *Guardian*, October 18, 2004.

Gormally, Luke. "The Maltese Conjoined Twins." *Second Opinion* 8, (October 2001): 36-52.

Granchi, Jennifer. "The Wrongful Birth Tort: A Policy Analysis and the Right to Sure for an Inconvenient Child." *South Texas Law Review*. Fall, 2002: 1261-1287.

Grant, K. "False Tears of the Doctors who Dealt Sentence of Death." *The Scotsman*. November 12, 2000.

Hackett, Kristin. "The Fragile X Men: Scientific Advances Compel a Legislative Treatment for Wrongful Life and Wrongful Birth." *Journal of Law and Technology*. Fall, 1987: 249-272.

Hewitt, Hugh. "Death by Committee: What the Groningen Protocol Says about Our World, and Where It Might Lead Next." *The Weekly Standard*, December 2, 2004.

Hittinger, Russell. "Abortion Before Rose." *First Things* (October 1994), 14-16.

Hodge, C. Cavanaugh. "Casual War: NATO's Intervention in Kosovo." *Ethics and International Affairs* 14, (2000): 39-54.

James, Annabelle, Nick Taylor, and Clive Walker. "The Reform of Double Jeopardy." *Web Journal of Current Legal Issues* 5, (2000), http://webjcli.ncl.ac.uk/2000/issue5/james5.html.

Jensen, S.J. "The Trouble with *Secunda Secundae* 64:, 7: Self-Defence." *The Modern Schoolman* 83 (2006): 143-162.

John Paul II. *Address of John Paul II on the Occasion of the Commemoration of the Fiftieth Anniversary of the European Convention on Human Rights*. November 3, 2000.

John Paul II. *Address to the United Nations General Assembly*. United Nations. October 5, 1995.

John Paul II. *Message of Pope John Paul II for the Celebration of the World Day of Peace*. January 1, 2000.

Kaveny, M. Cathleen. "The Case of Conjoined Twins: Embodiment, Individuality, and Dependence." *Theological Studies* 6, no. 4 (2001): 752-86.

Kaveny, M. Cathleen. "Conjoined Twins and Catholic Moral Analysis: Extraordinary Means and Casuistical Controversy." *Kennedy Institute of Ethics Journal* 12, no. 2 (2002): 115-140.

Knowles, Lori. "Hubris in the Court." *Hastings Center Report* 31, (January/February 2001).

"Kofi and U.N. Ideals." *The Wall Street Journal*. December 14, 2006.

Kolnai, "Dignity." *Philosophy* 51, (1976): 251-271.

Kolnai, Aurel. "The Humanitarian versus the Religious Attitude." *The Thomist* 7, no. 4 (1944): 429-57.

Kugler, Itzhak. "Necessity as a Justification in Re A (Children)." *Journal of Criminal Law* 68, no 5. (2004): 440-450.

Landler, Mark. "Empty Maternity Wards Imperil a Dwindling Germany." *The New York Times*. November 18, 2004.

Lazarus, Simon and Ian Millhiser. "Re-balancing the Scales of Justice." *Guardian Unlimited*. November 22, 2002.

Levering, Matt. "Natural Law and Natural Inclinations: Rhonheimer, Pinckaers, McAleer." *The Thomist* 70, no. 2 (2006): 155-201.

Linton, Martin. "Second Time Unlucky?" *Guardian Unlimited*. July 17, 2001.

London, Alex John. "The Maltese Conjoined Twins." *The Hastings Center Report* 31, no. 1 (January/February 2001): 48-50.

Lysaught, M.T. "Is it Killing? Jodie, Mary, and God." *Commonweal*. October 20, 2000.

Malcom, J.L. "Mad Dogs and Englishmen." *The Wall Street Journal*. June 17-18, 2006.

May, William. "Jodie and Mary: Separating the Maltese Twins." *National Catholic Bioethics Quarterly* 1, no. 3 (2001): 407-16.

McAleer, Graham J. "Business Ethics and Catholic Social Thought." *Nov et Vetera: The English Edition of the International Theological Journal* 4, no. 1 (2006): 17-27.

McAleer, Graham J. "The Conservative Moral Philosophy of Max Scheler and Aurel Kolnai." *Modern Age* (Summer 2006): 217-225.

McAleer, Graham J. and Becker, Jamey. "Contemporary Jesuits! You Have But Two Choices: The Politics of John Paul II or Ultramontanism." *Budhi: A Journal of Ideas and Culture* 4, (2000): 283-297.

McAleer, Graham J. "Pleasure: A Reflection on Benedict XVI's *Deus Est*." *Nova et Vetera: The English Edition of the International Theological Journal* 5, no. 2 (2007): 315-324.

McAleer, Graham J. "Rebels and Christian Princes: Politics and Violence in Camus and Augustine." *Revista Filosófica de Coimbria* 16, (1999): 253-267.

McAleer, Graham J. "Two Case Studies in Schelerian Moral Theology: The Vatican's 2005 'Instruction' and Gay Marriage." *Nova et Vetera: The*

English Edition of the International Theological Journal 6, no. 1 (2008): 205-218.

Moore, Michael S. "Moral Reality." *Wisconsin Law Review.* 1980, 1062-1156.

Moore, Michael S. "Moral Reality Revisited." *Michigan Law Review.* 1992, 2425-2533.

Moore, Michael S. "Torture and the Balance of Evils." *Israel Law Review* 23, (1989): 280-344.

Neuhaus, Richard John. "A Curious Encounter with A Philosopher from Nowhere." *First Things* 120, February 2002: 77-96.

Plattner, Marc. "Sovereignty and Democracy." *Policy Review* 122, (December 2003).

Posner, Richard. "Blackstone and Bentham." *Journal of Law and Economics* 19, no. 3 (1975): 569-606.

Ramos-Horta, Ramón. "War and Peace." *The Wall Street Journal*, May 13, 2004.

Ramsay, S. "Landmark Ruling on Siamese Twins in U.K." *The Lancet.* September 2, 2000.

Reno, R.R. "Theology's Continental Captivity." *First Things* 162, (April 2006): 26-33.

Rhinehart, Kelly. "The Debate over Wrongful Birth and Wrongful Life." *Law and Psychology Review.* Spring, 2002: 141-157.

Roberts, Melinda. "Can it Ever Be Better Never to Have Existed? Person-Based Consequentialism and a New Repugnant Conclusion." *Journal of Applied Philosophy* 20, no. 2 (2003): 159-185.

Rosenthal, Alexander. "The Problem of the *Desiderium Naturale* in the Thomistic Tradition." *Verbum Analecta NeoLatina* 6, (2004): 335-344.

Rooney, Ben. "The PlayStation Theory of War." Review of *Virtual War: Kosovo and Beyond*, by Michael Ignatieff. *The Daily Telegraph*, February 19, 2001.

"Land Warfare." *The Economist.* November 18, 2000: 29-33.

Ryan, Peter. "Must the Acting Person Have a Single Ultimate End." *Gergorianum* 82, (2001), 325-335.

Saunders, Lucinda. "Rich and Rare Are the Gems They Wear: Holding De Beers Accountable for Trading Conflict Diamonds." *Fordham International Law Journal* 24, no. 4 (20010, 1402-1476.

Schaub, Diana. "How to Think about Bioethics and the Constitution." AEI Bradley Lecture. June 7, 2004.

Scruton, Roger. "The Dangers of Internationalism." *The Intercollegiate Review*, (Fall/Winter 2005): 29-35.

Stone, Martin. "Making Sense of the Natural Desire to See God," in *Platonic Ideas and Concept Formation in Ancient and Medieval Thought.* 211-232. Leuven: Leuven University Press, 2004.

Strauss, Leo. "German Nihilism." *Interpretation* 26, no. 3 (1999): 353-78.

Sulmasy, Daniel. "Heart and Soul: The Case of the Conjoined Twins," *America.* December 2, 2000.

Swancara, Frank. "Medieval Theology in Modern Criminal Law." *Journal of the American Institute of Criminal Law and Criminology* 20, no. 4 (1930): 489-499.

Thomasma, David. "The Ethics of Caring for Conjoined Twins: The Lakeberg Twins." *Hastings Center Report* 26, no. 4 (1999): 4-12.

Thorp, Arabella, and Sally Broadbridge. "The *Criminal Justice Bill*." *House of Commons Research Paper* 02/74, (2002).

United States Catholic Conference. *Responsibility, Rehabilitation, and Restoration: A Statement of the Catholic Bishops of the United States*. Washington, D.C.: 2000.

Wasserman, David. "Killing Mary to Save Jodie: Conjoined Twins and Individual Rights." *Philosophy and Public Policy Quarterly* 21, no. 1 (2001): 9-14.

Weigel, George. "Europe's Problem – and Ours." *First Things* 140, (February 2004): 18-25.

Weigel, George. "Moral Clarity in a Time of War." *First Things* 129, (January 2003): 20-27.

Weigel, George. "Papacy and Power." *First Things* 110, (February 2001): 18-25.

Weigel, George. "World Order: What Catholics Forgot." *First Things* 143, (May 2004): 31-38.

Weigel, George, and Rowan Williams. "War and Statecraft: An Exchange." *First Things* 141, (March 2004): 14-21.

Westen, Peter. "The Three Faces of Double Jeopardy: Reflections of Government Appeals of Criminal Sentences." *Michigan Law Review*. 1980

Wilcoxon, Kimberly. "Statutory Remedies for Judicial Torts: The Need for Wrongful Birth Legislation." *University of Cincinnati Law Review*. Spring, 2001: 1023-1053.

Wojtyla, Karol. "Act and Experience." *Analecta Husserliana* 5. (1976): 269-280.

Films

The Fellowship of the Ring. DVD. Directed by Peter Jackson, 2001; New Line Platinum Series, 2002.

I Am Legend. DVD. Directed by Francis Lawrence, 2007; Warner Home Video–DVD, 2008.

Lord of War. DVD. Directed by Andrew Nicol. 2005; Lions Gate, 2006.

Index